Simple Minds

Simple Minds

Dan Lloyd

A Bradford Book
The MIT Press
Cambridge, Massachusetts
London, England

153
L79s

Library of Congress Cataloging-in-Publication Data

Lloyd, Dan Edward, 1953–
  Simple minds / Dan Lloyd.

  p.   cm.
  "A Bradford book."
  Bibliography: p.
  Includes index.
  ISBN 0-262-12140-9
  1. Cognition. 2. Human information processing.
3. Neuropsychology. I. Title.
BF311.L59   1989   88-26808
153—dc19   CIP

For my parents

Contents

Preface

Of what are minds made? Lately, this question has invited two answers, both convincing, but not easy to reconcile. First, minds are made of thoughts or "mental representations," dynamic internal states with content, or in other words states that are *about* or refer to things outside of themselves. Minds teem with *beliefs* about kangaroos or jackhammers, *desires* for peace or pancakes, *feelings* about songs or siblings, *ideas* about xenophobia or zithers, and a miscellany of queries, hopes, fears, inklings, dreams, urges, and pangs. Second, minds are made of matter, specifically, a dense tangle of billions of nerve cells, designed through long evolution for self-maintenance and coordinated interactions with the world and other minds. That is, minds are made of brains.

Thought and matter: To many, these have seemed to be two fundamentally distinct substances. Descartes gave this metaphysical dualism its classic expression and also saw its deepest problem: How do the two distinct realms of thought and matter interact? The rise of science and its growing hegemony have encouraged the rejection of dualism and the emergence of a different view of the relation of thought and matter. The more recent view is monistic—positing one basic stuff of the universe—and materialistic—that stuff is matter. Thought is part of the natural material world, subject to the evolutionary pressures that constrain all life. According to this naturalism, thinking is a natural process of brains and other highly organized complex dynamic systems. There is no separate mind or soul, and so there is no problem concerning the interaction of mind and matter.

Though the naturalism just described escapes the problem of interaction, in many ways it remains an article of faith more than fact. Naturalism supposes that the human brain, and the brains of some animals, are organs of thought or representation—but what is it about those brains that makes them thoughtful? In the most general terms, what sorts of physical systems are sufficient to embody the representations typical of thinking? Do animals have mental

representations? Could a nonbiological system—a computer perhaps—think?

The basic hypothesis of naturalism leaves these fundamental questions unanswered. These questions express the new problem of mind
and body, the question of how the mind comprises the brain. This is a
fundamental question of cognitive science, the science of dynamic
representing systems, and also the central question addressed in *Simple Minds*. My aim is to outline a theory of representing systems, a
central component of a naturalistic science of mind. Through argument and thought experiment I hope to delineate the physically
sufficient conditions for representing, describing representing systems in terms concrete enough to guide the empirical study of minds.
I also hope to elaborate the central theory beyond its basic statement,
indicating how it might be harnessed in explanations of further aspects of thought and cognition.

In the three chapters of part I, I approach a theory of representation
from three distinct directions. Chapter 1 describes the work a theory
of representation should do, the questions it should answer. The
point of such a theory is to reconcile matter and thought, to explain
how to build representations from purely physical parts. A theory of
material representation also needs to explain the properties of representation. It must account for familiar aspects of representation in
general, such as the fact that representations can be accurate or inaccurate, that their content is specific but limited by the perspective or
"point of view" of the representation, and so forth.

Chapter 2 surveys two widely discussed approaches to representation. The first holds that representation can be ascribed to a system
whose internal interactions follow patterns of logic. The second holds
that representation is simply another word for correlation between
events inside the head and events in the surrounding environment. I
detail problems with both views, but from these problems extract two
further guides toward a theory: Since innards alone are not enough,
representation must be built from a dependent relation between the
inner and outer worlds. But since simple correlation is also insufficient for representation, the relation between the inner and the
outer must be mediated by more complex intervening states. Representations, in short, arise in certain types of information processing
networks.

Having set aside two main contemporary contenders for a theory of
representation, it remains for chapter 3 to build a positive theory of
representation that can meet the various standards outlined in chapter 1. I approach the theory through a sequence of thought experiments, each describing a simple information processing network and

analyzing its features. This imaginary "evolution" leads to a surprisingly simple device that meets, although minimally, the goals of chapter 1. I call the resulting theory the "dialectical theory of representation." It describes how a device which integrates inputs from multiple channels can come to be a representing device.

I think the theory developed in part I is sufficient as a theory of a type of representation, but this would be merely academic if no living or artificial brain worked that way. Accordingly, in part II I try out a few applications of the theory. Real and simulated neural networks are the theme of a vast and fast-moving body of research—any book on the topic is likely to be rapidly superseded. Instead of attempting a survey, chapters 4 and 5 offer an introductory sampling of the field. Chapter 4 tours the explosive revival of connectionism, or parallel distributed processing. Chapter 5 surveys neural networks in two animal brains. Uncovering representations in complex systems is not always easy, but they are there and playing a role in cognition. The two chapters exemplify the potential application of a theory of representation as a tool of analysis and interpretation and outline some serious unanswered questions for the empirical study of more sophisticated representing systems.

Part III extends the theory of representation toward other aspects of "higher" cognition. In various ways, the dialectical theory of representation fits smoothly with plausible theories of aspects of language use, consciousness, and reasoning. Each of the three chapters in part III could be a separate book (and may be, in the end), but they are included here to provide, if not the big picture of mind, at least the big snapshot.

Chapter 6 explores the processes of "metarepresentation," in which representations in the brain inherit the content of public representations. I suggest that a sophisticated dialectical representing system can thereby emulate conventional representational systems, especially human language, and thus acquire nearly unlimited representational power.

Chapter 7 takes on the quandaries of consciousness. I argue that several types of conscious experience are matched by aspects of representation and suggest that to be conscious of something is to represent it in a certain way. The content of the representation employed determines whether the conscious state is one of perceptual awareness, reflection, or introspection. Another type of conscious state, however, does not seem to be representational. This is sensation, and I suggest that it is subrepresentational information that brains use but cannot represent.

Finally, chapter 8 describes a basic pattern in human cognition.

Despite the ideals of logic, human reasoning follows patterns which look more like narrative, inner stories which link events in a temporal order without the explicit guidance of logic or scientific law. Narrative thinking arises naturally in the hardware of complex dialectical representing systems. Thus, the stories we tell may reflect the biological organization of our brains more deeply than we might have suspected. The book closes with a discussion of the mind studying itself. Perhaps the complexities of the brain will motivate a narrative study of the mind. Compared to a study of mind modeled after a science like physics, the narrative approach may be better suited to human understanding.

Simple Minds, in sum, is a preliminary study of the mind in nature. It is preliminary because we are near the beginning of our scientific understanding of both cognition and the brain, and thus near the beginning of the effort to bridge mind and matter. This is a time of competing "isms," of fancy terminology for obscure or vague processes, of rampant black boxes, of hand waving. This is also an exciting time of suggestive fragments, bold proposals, and free speculation. As I have joined in the brainstorm, I have struggled to keep my explanations, arguments, and speculations concrete and straightforward. I've tried to keep *Simple Minds* simple not only to avoid needless obscurity but also to include readers who are not (yet) professionally obsessed with cognitive science. I hope I can convey both the deep problems that cognitive science faces and its exciting promise of a grand synthesis of brain and mind.

Far from being definitive, this book should be a starting point for critical discussion among both students and scholars in the several disciplines of cognitive science. I hope that the book's shortcomings catalyze the next phase of theory, serving as an invitation to readers not merely to vivisect *Simple Minds* but to risk a contribution to the creation of a subsequent positive theory of the mind.

Acknowledgments

I think of scholarship as an ongoing conversation, both spoken and written. *Simple Minds* is one statement in a philosophical and scientific discussion to which I have been listening, with an occasional contribution, for several years. This book is not the last word in that conversation, certainly not in the community of cognitive science nor in my own conversations on mind and brain. Neither is it the first word; many friends and colleagues have contributed both thoughtful and material support.

During the summers of 1984 through 1986, I did much of the preliminary work at the Marine Biological Laboratory in Woods Hole, Massachusetts. In that ideal environment I met several neuroscientists who guided the first steps of the project. Dan Alkon, Izja Lederhendler, Shawn Lockery, and Jill London have all been generous with their time, thought, and reprints. In 1986, the population of philosophers at the MBL doubled with the arrival of Kathleen Akins, who was then and remains a source of welcome insight. Those Woods Hole encounters led to two early papers on the topics in this book (Lloyd 1986, 1987). Outside of Woods Hole, the conversation expanded to include Jane Abrams, Jonathan Bennett, Susan Brison, Arthur Danto, Daniel Dennett, Jay Garfield, George Graham, Paul Smolensky, and Betty Stanton.

I wrote the first draft during 1986–87 as a Mellon Faculty Fellow in the Humanities at Harvard University. The fellowship provided not only the time and resources for writing but further opportunities for fruitful discussion, this time with Bill de Vries, James Deutsch, John Dowling, Alison MacIntyre, Randy O'Reilly, Hilary Putnam, and Jay Ruckl. Emily Backus, Shawn Lockery, Terry Sejnowski, and George Wittenberg all read sections of early drafts and made many helpful comments. The first full draft was a third longer than the final draft, so I am particularly grateful to those who worked through the whole manuscript: Daniel Dennett, Bill de Vries, and Jay Garfield.

In 1987, draft in hand, I joined the faculty at Trinity College. My six philosophical colleagues, Miller Brown, Howard DeLong, Drew Hyland, Helen Lang, Richard Lee, and Maurice Wade, have exemplified the ideals of collegiality, and the friendly and energetic Trinity faculty have provided a community in which scholarship and teaching can both flourish. Several colleagues have helped with both major and minor revisions. Dina Anselmi, Laura Foley, and Richard Lee have been particularly helpful with comments on large portions of the manuscript. Trinity is not too far from the headquarters of the Propositional Attitude Task Force, the site of many fruitful discussions of topics in this book. Lee Bowie, Jay Garfield, Murray Kitely, Meredith Michaels, and Ken Taylor were regular participants.

Three people deserve special mention. The indefatigable Jay Garfield has blended helpful criticism with steadfast support dating back to our days as philosophy majors at Oberlin College. His comments have improved this book in many places. Mark Rollins and I have been talking about everything for twelve years. Many of the ideas of the book first surfaced in these free-wheeling discussions, and (perhaps as a result) both our careers and our interests have progressed in parallel. Finally, Cheryl Greenberg has enlivened the final months of revision. She has been my last editor, and the most thorough. But in addition to being the muse of common sense and clear language, she has been a constant and loving companion. To her, and to all these colleagues and friends, I extend warm thanks.

PART I

Representation from the Bottom Up

Chapter 1
Of Minds and Brains

The road up and the road down are one and the same road.
—Heraclitus, Fragment 60

1.1 Behavioral Explanation from the Top Down and the Bottom Up

The New Problem of Mind and Body

Submitted for your consideration: a thought experiment concerning the explanation of behavior (adapted from Dewdney 1987). Imagine a black sphere, about five inches in diameter, with the following "behavioral" repertoire: It rolls slowly and steadily in a straight line on any flat surface until it hits an obstacle. Then, sometimes after bumping the obstacle several times, it suddenly rolls off in a new direction, apparently selected at random. The bump-and-turn tactic gets the black sphere out of dead ends and eventually out any open door. There is no visible force pushing or pulling the sphere. How does it work?

Here's a first guess: Behind each of the modest "behavioral dispositions" of the sphere lies a specialized internal mechanism whose functioning explains the disposition. For example, since the sphere is sensitive to obstacles, its innards might include an "obstacle detector." We can worry later about how the obstacle detector works; for now, all we care about is what it does, how it contributes to the function of the sphere as a whole. The input to the detector, then, is some information about the motion, or lack of it, of the sphere (we suppose it to be a crude detector, for the sphere responds to all obstacles in the same way). The detector must send its output to some sort of steering mechanism, which in turn affects a motor in contact with the inside surface of the sphere. Since this hypothesis decomposes the sphere into a system of interacting functional modules, we might call it the modular hypothesis. (For more on this style of explanation, see Haugeland 1978, 1985; Cummins 1983.) The modular hypothesis provides an explanation, however crude and incomplete, of the behavior of the sphere.

But it is not the only possible explanation. An alternative hypothesis might explain all of the observed dispositions with one internal mechanism, a toy automobile that runs freely on the smooth inside surface of the sphere. The wheels of the internal car could be greater in diameter than the height of the chassis, so that the car can move whether right side up or upside down. When the sphere is unencumbered, the car motors up the inside surface, causing the sphere to roll in the direction the inner car is pointing. If the sphere hits an obstacle, the car climbs the inside surface of the sphere and flips over, repeating the climb and flip routine until the car chances to land facing away from the obstacle, at which time the sphere rolls in that new direction. We might call this model of the mysterious sphere the inner vehicle hypothesis, after the hypothesized toy car.

How could we determine which hypothesis is true? There are two general approaches. First, we might continue to study the behavior of the sphere, with particular attention to details which might reflect the operations of one internal mechanism rather than another. For example, if the inner vehicle hypothesis is correct, we would expect that when the sphere hits an obstacle, a moment will pass before the inner car climbs the wall far enough to flip over and land facing a new direction. Since the speed of the unencumbered sphere is also the speed of the inner toy car, we can compute how long this hesitation, the "flip latency," should be. Then we test whether the sphere behaves accordingly, nudging obstacles long enough for the inner car to flip over (or to flip several times, hesitating for some whole multiple of the flip latency). If so, then we have some confirmation of the inner vehicle model. (The modular model might also conform to the flip latency, but if so, it conforms by coincidence, since there is no particular reason why the sequence from obstacle detection to turning should take exactly the same time as the flip latency.) Further behavioral experiments could add support to one model or the other.

These tests are "top down" approaches to discovering the internal structure of the sphere. We examine it as a whole and from the outside, treating the black sphere as a black box. After enough experimentation, we may feel that we have eliminated all the rival hypotheses. Then we will be justified in believing the remaining hypothesis, whatever it turns out to be.

There is, however, a second method for determining the internal structure and function of the sphere: to open it up. We can understand it thereby "from the bottom up," examining its separate components on the inside, their interaction, and their connections to the surface of the sphere. The bottom up approach is direct and decisive—as long as we know what we're looking for. If we find a little car inside, or the interconnected modules of the modular hypothesis, fine. But if we find a shifting mass of magnetized thumbtacks, we may not know just what has been confirmed. Does some part of the mass function as an obstacle detector and some as a steering mechanism? These questions can lead to another cycle of top down hypothesizing and bottom up examination, now directed at the components of the sphere. Finally, however, our top down hypotheses and bottom up observations should converge on a single explanation. This is how the sphere works and why it moves the way it does.

Simple as the black sphere is, its study anticipates two approaches to the explanation of behavior by many complex creatures, including human beings. Like the sphere, the workings of a complex animal can be independently probed from either the top or the bottom. But, unlike the elementary sphere, complex animals exhibit a wide range of complex behavioral capacities employed to further the general goals of survival and reproduction. These capacities include the following: (1) response to distal stimuli—the ability to tailor responses to conditions at a spatial or temporal distance (toads, for example, coordinate the tips of their tongues with the position of nearby bugs, while rats remember the mazes of yesterday); (2) problem solving— the ability to spontaneously produce a novel response to a novel set of environmental conditions (a dog running toward a narrow gap in a picket fence with a long stick in its mouth turns its head sideways to fit the stick through); (3) communication—behavior whose main effect is to influence the behavior of conspecifics and other interested parties (squid produce complex and largely undeciphered displays of coloring on their bodies as part of courtship, aggression, or predator deception (Moynihan 1985)). Each of these capacities falls on a continuum reaching from relatively simple creatures to the likes of us.

What is going on inside these creatures that might explain these behavioral capacities? At least one hypothesis has a long history: Creatures like the above have *minds*. Some of them have rudimentary minds; others, humans, have full-fledged minds, minds in the proper sense of the term. But what, apart from possessing a complex generator of behavior, does it mean to have a mind? To this question there are two answers, one originating in tradition and common sense, the other in science. The first, subject to a little straightening from philosophers, is the conception of mind found in "folk psychology." In this view, the mind is principally made of two basic states—*beliefs* and *desires*—which interact, subject to the transformations of *perception* and *reason*, and ultimately bring about *action*. We folk readily apply our everyday expertise in cases like this: Why does A reach for a hanging banana with a stick? Because she desires to eat the banana, believes that prodding it with the stick will bring it within reach, and acts accordingly. Though folk psychology usually concerns folk like us, its application to animals is straightforward. Agent A above might well be an ape, and belief-desire explanations settle smoothly on some of nature's dumbest: The fly buzzes against the window, for example, because it wants to be where the light is brighter and believes (wrongly) that there is an unobstructed path through the window frame. Even if talk of insect belief and desire is metaphorical, it is an easy and obvious metaphor. As a result, the lower boundary of the minded is fuzzy in the view of folk psychology.

A second category of mind model is of more recent vintage: *Cognitive psychology* has emerged as the discipline committed to the scientific study of the mechanisms of mind. The model preferred by this discipline substitutes for belief and desire the more general notion of *representation;* for the processes of reasoning (and to a lesser extent, perception), it substitutes *cognition*. Unlike folk psychology, cognitive psychology proposes specific hypotheses and subjects them to laboratory tests. The result, accordingly, comes much closer to being a scientific theory than the comfortable but rumpled posits of folk psychology. But in other respects, the two approaches are similar: Both are top down in that, like the first look at the black sphere, they study their subjects whole and from the outside, treating them as black boxes. The cognitive psychologist proposes that certain mechanisms exist inside her subjects and that these explain a particular observed behavior. But only the behavior, not the mechanism, is observed. Although it may be well confirmed, knowledge of the innards is indirectly inferred.

Just as there were two ways to study the black sphere, however, there are two ways to approach more complex behaving systems. The second route works from the bottom up. Distinct from both folk psychology and cognitive psychology, the neurosciences, particularly behavioral neurobiology and neurophysiology, study behavior as the ultimate manifestation of the function of nervous systems. In current practice, many neuroscientific hypotheses are indirectly supported, but ideally the neurosciences afford direct observations of the structure and function of individual nerve cells and from that bottom can work up toward an understanding of larger parts of nervous systems. In some future age, the neurosciences promise a complete understanding of the brain, and with that our descendants will be able to explain the behavior of living creatures in detail.

In the golden age of science, we may hope to test the hypothesis of mind against the details of the brain. Perhaps then we will succeed in "reading" the brain, directly observing inner representations in their physical form. If so, the mind hypothesis will be confirmed, and minds will be securely placed among the natural phenomena of our world. In other words, the convergence of top down and bottom up approaches will vindicate a naturalism about the mind. Mental states—the representations posited by cognitive psychologists or the beliefs and desires alluded to in folk psychology—will turn out to be real, physical entities in the natural world. Golden age neuroscience would then turn out to include psychology, thereby showing how to make minds out of brains.

But this is not the only possible golden age. It may also be that the terms and categories of future neuroscience will not match any of the terms and categories of either cognitive or folk psychology. If so, then we have at least three options. First, we may choose to continue using psychological and mental description and explanation, but with the reservation that their terms do not refer to real entities. That is, we will regard our mind-talk as *instrumentalistic,* useful for prediction but not literally descriptive of the brain (Dennett 1978a, 1987a). Second, we may regard mind-talk as a quaint anachronism reminiscent of phlogiston-talk and weather-god-talk. Then, except in poetry, we will eliminate the mental from both our conception of the world and our language, replacing it with the language and concepts of the brain science of that far-off future (P. M. Churchland 1979, 1981; P. S. Churchland 1986). Finally, we may simply succumb to the mystery of it all and declare that there is an unknown separate substance, a mind-stuff outside of nature.

The ultimate choice among naturalism, instrumentalism, eliminativism, and dualism waits at the end of a long research program. The hard problems lying between our present questions and their distant answers set a long-range agenda for cognitive science. What do we need to know in order to align the mind and brain? First, of course, we need to know more about both brain and mind. Our brains contain somewhere around 10^{11} neurons, and each of them can be connected to up to several thousand other cells, sometimes at distances up to several feet. Using a combination of noninvasive recording and imaging techniques and inferring from the indirect evidence of lesions and other neurological impairments, science has made extraordinary progress toward understanding the function of different parts of the human brain. But the study of brain operation at the neural level is in its infancy. Neurons have been typed and studied, some circuits traced through the tangled neuropil, and several functional modules of the brain have been extensively explored, especially in animal brains, but the detailed function of the human brain remains subject to speculation.

Similarly, cognitive psychology has examined human cognitive performance in myriad experimental settings and proposed theories of many aspects of cognition. The time for "unified theories of cognition" (Newell 1987) is ripe, but it may be a long time before any one theory wins a consensus. Meanwhile, the "microtheories" suffice. As in brain science, understanding the parts precedes understanding the whole.

Each science thus has both progress to report and a full agenda ahead. The reconciliation of mind and brain waits on their successes—but not only on their separate progress. There is a third issue, independent of the flourishing research in either field: How will these two fields, with their separate terms, laws, and theories, speak to each other? We will ultimately need bridging hypotheses to link the psychological and the neural, theories which specify the potential physiology of psychological processes. We need, that is, a *reductive* theory of the central aspects of mind, a theory that explains how the mental (cognitive) is built out of nonmental (physiological) parts. Such a theory need not insist that the mind be made of a particular substance nor need it specify every aspect of the physical construction of minds. But it does need to define its central mental terms in a nonmental vocabulary. Only with such a theory in hand will the brain science of the future recognize its encounter with the mind—if there is such an encounter. This is the new problem of mind and body, the problem of bridging the sciences of the mind and the sciences of the brain; it is also the central problem addressed in this book. It encompasses the following questions (among others): What sort of physical system is sufficient to be minded? We suppose that the human brain is an organ of thought or representation, but what is it about the brain that makes it a representing system? Do some animals have minds? Could another sort of system altogether also be a mind?

Simple Minds
Because the bridging theory will link the complexities of cognitive psychology (and folk psychology) on the one side with the even greater complexities of brain science on the other, it too will be complex in its final form. Making progress now, in the Bronze Age of Cognitive Science, requires some radical simplification of the central issues. I propose to concentrate, accordingly, on one central aspect of the concept of mind, namely, *representation*. A *non*reductive account of representation would run like this: A representation is an entity

with content or meaning; in other words, a representation is *about* or *of* something outside of itself. These statements are true to the concept of representation, but they explain it by importing other representational terms. Content, meaning, "aboutness," and "ofness" are all *semantic* terms, different ways of characterizing the relationship of a symbol and what it stands for. They are, in short, synonyms for "representation." My aim is to explain what all these representational terms have in common, that is, to explain representation without appeal to other semantic terms. Instead, I hope to characterize representation in terms of nonrepresentational and nonsemantic aspects of the functions of systems and the probabilistic dependencies among events. This reductive inquiry will occupy part I of *Simple Minds*.

Representation is an apt theme for several reasons. First, representation, as noted, is central to cognitive psychology and several nearby fields (including linguistics and artificial intelligence). Indeed, the "cognitive" in cognitive science might be glossed as "representational." Second, representationality is a basic feature of the beliefs and desires central to folk psychology and its rational reconstructions: We have, for example, beliefs *about* stars and bagels, desires for romance or a cup of coffee. Whether conscious or unconscious, beliefs and desires all seem to have the common property of representationality, so the account of representation is ipso facto a component of a reductive account of folk psychology.[1] Third, unlike beliefs and desires, which flourish entirely in private, representations have public exemplars (for example, a photograph, a line drawing, a sentence, or a program in LISP). Like their elusive psychological kin, these are also exemplary bearers of content. This kinship suggests that there is a genus, representation-in-general, of which the varieties of inner and outer representations are species. Our familiarity with public representations can thus assist us in describing representation-in-general, an important component of the analysis of representation in psychology. Section 1.2 codifies the central intuitions about representation-in-general and outlines the differentia of representation in psychology. This discussion, however, is not yet a theory of representation but rather a list of the features of representation for which a finished theory must account.

There are many theories that are about representations (indeed, any theory in cognitive psychology will be about them). These talk about the interaction of representations or distinct representational systems, or the links among representations and perception or behavior, or the construction of complex representations out of more basic representations. There are somewhat fewer theories that are reductive in the sense outlined above, theories that describe what representations are without recourse to other representational concepts. The main contenders are discussed in chapter 2. My own contribution to the theory of representation appears in chapter 3. There, following strategies suggested by Jonathan Bennett (1964), Daniel Dennett (1978b), and Valentino Braitenberg (1984), I will undertake a bit of "synthetic psychology." The synthetic approach begins by imagining artificial "animals" with simple mechanical brains and deducing the behavior of these *gedanken*-beasts. In the inquiry into representation, we will start at the bottom by imagining the behavior of some simple synthetic organisms and extend and elaborate them through a sequence of thought experiments until one becomes complex enough to be a plausible representing system. To the extent that representation is central to the mind, the philosophical analysis of representation together with a raft of exercises in thought engineering will give us a theory of mind "from the bottom up."

In sum, the project is to imagine simple minds. A simple mind lies just over the line of mindedness with a bare toehold on the categories we want to understand. As such, it won't seem like much of a mind at all—intuition may demand more to found a mind than the synthetic devices that will appear in these pages. But a simple mind, I hope, compensates for its simplicity by clearly displaying the grounds for whatever mindedness it possesses. Simple minds are obvious minds. The toehold will also be sufficient, I hope, as a platform from which to build toward more complex minds. As synthesis gathers momentum, in parts II and III, a picture of minds like ours will emerge. In those chapters, I look at neural networks in theory and practice, at the relation of thought and language, at consciousness, and at the basic patterns of cognition. The continuum and systematic connections of simple to complex is reinforcing at both poles: Building a complex mind out of simple components vindicates the simple starting point while explaining the emerging complexity. Simple minds, it is hoped, yield understanding of all minds.

Simple minds embodied in simple physical systems provide basic bridges between the mind and brain, the top down and the bottom up. Thus, we will need to attend to both of the sciences that need to be bridged. From the cognitive side, I will lean most heavily on representation and later on consciousness and other cognitive concepts. From the neural side, I will incorporate functional properties of neurons and brains as needed. Moreover, empirical research will provide opportunities for application and confirmation of the hypotheses proposed here. If this essay contains a viable theory, then we will all want to know if the theory is realized in various natural systems. In other words, the synthetic theory of mind is also an analytical tool to be applied to real systems. Since our understanding of those real systems is limited, we will encounter simple minds in another aspect: as simple brains, and as the simpler subsystems of complex brains. These relatively simpler systems afford somewhat easier analysis. In them we may find the precursors of cognitive states of more complex minds.

All in all, the aim of *Simple Minds* is to lay the foundations of a natural philosophy of mind. Building as it does on natural science, and asking questions very like those of science, a developed natural philosophy of mind will be partly contingent. The traditional philosophical ideal of discovering logically necessary and sufficient conditions for the concepts of mind will not be appropriate here. Success, instead, means sufficiency within the frameworks of science and philosophy. The approach to certainty is asymptotic at best: Communal efforts weed out rival theories until, finally, either we have the truth—or we don't know what else to say. That these aspirations fall short of Olympian certainty is no occasion for shame, since they meet the ideals of science exactly, and the track record of science is not bad. A theory that meets all these standards may not be inevitable, but it will be empirically and conceptually apt. (Exemplary works in the new natural philosophy include Dennett 1983, 1984a,b, discussing cognitive ethology and artificial intelligence; Fodor 1975, 1983, with its links to linguistics and cognitive psychology; and P. S. Churchland 1980, 1986 and P. M. Churchland 1986, addressing neuroscience.) In short, the hypotheses proposed will, I hope, enjoy a good fit with a medley of constraints including empirical findings and philosophical intuition. The proposed theories succeed or fail according to the work they do: Can they clean up existing quandaries, unify disparate phenomena, and guide future research, all without doing violence to other, nonnegotiable intuitions? To this task we now turn.

1.2 Representation: The Metatheory

So far, representation has been introduced as the common vehicle of content in two familiar versions of the "mind hypothesis," the appeal to belief in folk psychology and the appeal to mental or cognitive representation in cognitive science. We ultimately seek a reductive theory of representation, a theory that explains how representations are made out of nonrepresentational parts. Only with such a theory, I suggest, will we be able to solve the problem of mind and brain and the open question of the convergence of psychology and neuroscience.

But how will we find such a theory? The purpose of this section is to expose some guiding intuitions. These take two forms. First, there are familiar features of both outer and inner representations that a theory of representation must preserve and explain. Second, there are special conditions placed on a theory of representation for it to find a place in psychology and to serve as the bridge between mind and brain.

Thus intuition guides the hand toward a sketch of a "metatheory" of representation—a theory that outlines the work a theory of representation must do and the problems it must solve. The conceptual features made explicit in the metatheory, then, provide an ongoing test for various candidate theories. Some very elegant theories may fail to fit the metatheory—at best these will be theories of something other than representation. Or, one hopes, one theory may mesh neatly with the pretheoretical measurements of representation, thus winning the strongest philosophical support.

From there, we may embark on a long empirical quest for such representations in actual systems. However, the quest may fail. We may not find representations in any systems of interest to us. The result is still progress: then we will know just what representations are—and that in the systems under consideration they don't exist.

What follows, then, is a primer of representation, comprising both the features of representation in general and the differentia of representation in psychology. The common pretheoretical understanding of representation cues the first four headings. Three final constraints follow broad theoretical glances at psychology, evolution, and nature. Each constraint following is a capacity of representation, a feature which a representation must be able to manifest, even though in some circumstances a representation will not manifest the capacity. As I will point out repeatedly, an adequate theory of representation must permit the capacity to be unrealized in specific cases. Definition by capacity is a familiar style of characterization in biology and mechanics. Spleens, for example, are characterized by their functional capacity to make and store red blood cells. But a spleen that is not actually making or storing blood at a particular time is nonetheless still a spleen at that time. The capacity that makes an organ a spleen need not be continuously realized, but spleens nonetheless possess that capacity continuously. So also, as we shall see, with representation.

Constraint 1: Representation and Accuracy
Representations, both inner and outer, have the preeminent capacity to capture and convey the way things are. A successful theory of representation, then, must explain how representations can accu-

rately represent their objects. But the capacity of accuracy is not always realized: Representations can represent the way things are, but just as readily can misrepresent their world. Just as we acknowledge the hardy truth-bearers on which we rely, we feel the sting of familiar forms of error: misses, those representations which omit something we wish had been represented, and false alarms, those representations which signal the presence of something which is not in fact present.

A line drawing of you might illustrate these capacities. It could accurately represent the way you wear your hair, but totally omit another feature—an ear, for example (a miss). And that depicted sixth finger on your left hand—another mistake, one presumes, in this case a pictorial false alarm. Our inner representations, of course, can be right or wrong in just these same ways.

Let us bundle these observations under the heading of the capacity for informativeness. (Information, we shall see, has a technical use, but that is not presupposed here.) Since representations can, but need not, be vehicles of truth, it is a capacity with a dual face: a capacity for accuracy, tempered by the possibility of error. A theory of representation must explain both accuracy and error. Accordingly, if a theory of representation entails that representations are always accurate, then it is a theory in trouble.

Constraint 2:   Representation and Focus
Imagine a language with one noun, "stuff"; one verb, "to do"; and one adverbial and adjectival construction, "like, you know." Discourse in that language is limited to questions and assertions about whether stuff, like, you know, does stuff. Even a language restricted to "slab," "board," "brick," and similar concrete nouns comes closer to the power of actual representational systems. Compared to stuff-speak, actual representational systems have a capacity for specificity. Representations can pick out specific objects (events, individuals, or situations). The line drawing alluded to above is a positive example: It is a picture of you (vs. stuff) and depicts your posture, overall shape, and a good number of other specific details about you. If we are personally acquainted, ideas I have about you also seem to display this specificity, though I will mentally represent details other than those in the line drawing.

Now compare yourself to the sketch of yourself. In the comparison, we note that the specificity of representation goes only so far. Another line drawing might represent aspects of you which this omits (a back view, for instance). And there are many facts about you which no line drawing can capture (your hair color, voice, weight, or smell).

We might say that the representation is limited by its perspective. Perspective, in turn, has two aspects. Some perspectival limits are due to limitations of the representational system overall; call these the limits of sensitivity. Other limits depend on the limiting circumstances of particular representations; call these the limits of point of view. Inner representations, if there be such, also exhibit these limits of perspective. A visual image of you will not represent the sound of your voice and will be indefinite about many of your visible features.

These two capacities, specificity and perspective, might be paired under the broader intuitive head of focus. Focusing on something is a way of picking it out, isolating it from its background and context. At the same time, in picking out a focal object or properties, we exclude other objects or properties from representation.

The ambivalent force of focus, selection constrained by perspective, is reflected in the ascription of content to representations. Though the following phenomena are elusive, they are real enough to demand acknowledgment in a theory of representation. Imagine a painting of William Shakespeare. Shall we say that the painting depicts the man, born in Stratford, who authored *Hamlet* and dozens of other plays? If the picture represents Shakespeare and these descriptions are true of him, then it represents him under those and any other true descriptions. Yet the painting does not represent Shakespeare *as* the author of *Hamlet*. The fact of authorship is not represented, or to put it another way, the painting does not show Shakespeare's authorship of any particular play. In that light, the picture seems not to represent a man who is the author of *Hamlet*, since it does not represent anything about *Hamlet* at all.

The example suggests that our intuitive ideas about the content of representations are ambiguous. We might distinguish two kinds of content that could be ascribed to a representation: First, a representation's *explicit content* is the information the representation itself conveys, independent of any fact about the real object or situation represented (if any). Second, a representation's *extensional content* is the actual object(s) or event(s), under any description, which the representation denotes—its extension, in short. The extensional content of the Shakespeare painting is indeed the author of *Hamlet*; any description of Shakespeare will also serve as a description of the work's extensional content. In contrast, the explicit content is limited to what the painting depicts, namely, a person with various facial and bodily features. That's all the drawing literally shows.

The distinction between explicit and extensional content is plainest, perhaps, in cases of fictive representation. A picture of a unicorn, for example, represents a horse-like animal with a horn on its head—that much is explicit in the picture. But in another sense, the picture represents nothing, since no unicorns exist for it to depict—it is a representation without extensional content.

The distinction between explicit and extensional content is not always easy to draw, and so our intuitions about the nature of these two aspects of content are not easy to specify. Thus, on this issue a theory of representation should legislate and clarify the distinction for us. For now, we need merely observe the relationship between the two kinds of content, extensional and explicit, and the two aspects of focus, specificity and perspective. Specificity refers to the capacity of a representation to pick out specific objects as its content, applying to some and sailing past others. It reflects the assignment of specific extensions to representations. But the powers of specificity are circumscribed by the limits of perspective. Representations only explicitly represent some aspects of their extensions; what they capture (or omit) reflects the limits of perspective.

Internal representations exhibit this ambivalence in content as well (as Fodor notes (1981:235)). In a sense, Gertrude does believe that the murderer of old Hamlet is a fit husband, since after all she believes that Claudius is a fit husband, and Claudius is that same murderer. But her inner representations don't represent Claudius as the murderer of her first husband—heaven forbid! From her perspective, Claudius is the man who was so flattering during the funeral, and so forth. She represents him within the perspective of the explicit content of her representations, though he is, extensionally, much more than she takes him to be. As are we all.

Constraint 3: Representation and Articulation
Suppose our familiar language of (spoken and written) sentences were replaced by a system of grunts and blots, where each grunt or blot uniquely stood for what individual sentences in our present language stand for. Suppose, further, that the grunt/blots are inarticulate in the sense that we cannot interpret them by examining their parts—blot/grunts are simply assigned randomly to sentences, and thus the relation of shape to meaning is arbitrary. Every sentence in the language would have to be learned somewhat as we originally learned the vocabulary of our native language. Just as there are, in general, no rules for interpreting word meanings on the basis of meaningful subwords, so there would be no way to compute blot meaning on the basis of meaningful subblots. Clearly such a language would be a disaster, practically impossible to learn, absurdly unwieldy, and singularly inept for describing and communicating novel facts about the world (Davidson 1965).

The extremity of blotese spotlights another familiar feature of representational systems, a capacity for articulation. Real representational systems compose meaningful representations out of independently meaningful parts. Thus, articulate (or composite) representations can be interpreted through decomposition into meaningful subunits. The immediate example is the sentence, comprising meaningful words in a specific order. But nonlinguistic media also include articulate representations. The line drawing again: interpretable drawing parts (sketches of your head, torso, limbs, etc.) are juxtaposed in a composite representation with an overall interpretation—it represents you.

The line drawing example reminds us to be sparing in our reliance on language in the exploration of representation. Representations are languagelike in the general feature of articulation but should not be tethered to subject-predicate structures. Donald Davidson (1986) has drawn attention to the distinction between representing that a spot is green and representing a green spot. Only one of these representations is expressed in subject-predicate form. Perhaps the other (and all representations) are covertly in subject-predicate form—but this possibility should not be assumed at the outset. (On these issues, see chapters 5 and 6.)

Do our intuitions about mental representations fit the capacity for articulation? Perhaps it is not immediately obvious that they do, but indirect considerations suggest that if there are inner representations at all, then they exhibit articulation and compositionality (Fodor 1986, 1987: Appendix; Block 1986). If our inner representations were inarticulate, we would in effect be thinking in blotese, with unique and original representations for each thought. Further, we would be unable to combine the inner grunts into composite representations. Among other problems, this would obscure our ability to understand composite representational systems, like languages and pictorial systems.

This capacity for articulation, however, has its limit. As we analyze the line drawing into meaningful parts we ultimately reach minimal or basic representational components. For example, we could play a game where we take turns erasing part of the drawing, with the rule that whatever remains must still be interpretable. After a few rounds, the representation depicts your face only, and shortly after that, your Cheshire-cat grin. But this is a finite game. Finally, representationality collapses and only marks remain. The moral of this game is that articulation ultimately bottoms out with atomic representations, representations whose parts are not representational in themselves.

In sum, atomicity and articulation interlace; representational systems are chunky, with minimal chunks that can be linked to form bigger chunks.

Constraint 4:   Representation and Asymmetry
A fourth constraint is familiar (e.g., from Goodman 1968) but bears repeating: Representation is an asymmetrical relation. A line drawing may represent you, but you do not, by that token, represent the drawing. Similarly, our idea of the sundae just ordered represents a sundae, but the sundae doesn't represent the idea.

The four capacities above reflect features common to representational systems in general. Our target here is more specific. We seek the content-bearers that will figure in psychology, and we assume that these will be distinct from public representational systems in at least two respects. First, these inner representations will be exempt from the formative influences of convention, since convention requires the coordinated deployment of arbitrary tokens. This deployment in turn requires that users are able to compare their own uses of tokens with those of others—but the inner representations belonging to others are always out of sight. Second, the resources for inner representation were not the products of special acts of creation; they emerged, instead, through evolutionary adaptation of internal structures that once had another use. The category of representation we seek is that of natural representation. These assumptions suggest two other guideposts; the metatheoretical differentia of the species of natural psychological representations, the content bearers that figure particularly in the mind. Representations should play a role in the explanation of cognition, and the capacity for representation should be a capacity that could have arisen through natural selection.

Constraint 5:   Representation and Cognitive Role
Steven Kosslyn (1980) has suggested that our capacity for mental imagery could be metaphorically analyzed as a system involving an image display device analogous to a cathode ray tube—the mind's CRT. Suppose, briefly, that, contrary to Kosslyn's hedging about the reality of the inner CRT, this were to be literally true: On some fold of cerebral cortex the passing show replays in technicolor, as much like inner TV as one would like. By this astounding discovery, would we have settled the issue of inner representations in psychology? Daniel Dennett (1982a) has pointed out that we would not, because it may turn out that although the mind's TV is tuned in, no one is watching. That is, the apparent representations might be mere artifacts, causal dead ends that flicker across the brain without any further effects of

their own. Being causally inert, these hypothetical images could play no role in producing other mental states or, ultimately, behavior. We could therefore ignore them completely in building our psychology. Thus, in psychology, representations must be put to work. They must play a role in the explanation of behavior, or there will be no psychological function for them. We might say that a system in which representations play a cognitive role is a *content-driven* system (also see Dennett 1982b; Fodor 1987:12).

But the requirement that representations have a cognitive role in the systems which contain them is also a capacity that may go unrealized in specific cases. Particular representations may evaporate without a trace. What is necessary, however, is that the system in which they occurred was one in which they could have made a difference, either to other representations or to behavior.

How sophisticated or complex are the effects of representations? We should guard against importing overly sophisticated processes of uptake. For example, suppose we require of a representation that its bearer be conscious of it. Such a requirement leads to a regress, since to be aware of something involves representing it. So, to be aware of a representation involves forming a representation of the representation. But if all representations must be the objects of consciousness, then we will face a regress of secondary states of consciousness, each required to boost its object into the representational realm. We will return to this point in chapters 3 and 7. For now, let us watch out for theories of representation that come with cognition built in.

Constraint 6:   Representation and Evolution
Constraints 1 through 4 describe features common to all representations, from cuneiform inscriptions to the idea of blue. The fifth constraint, concerning cognitive role, applies only to those representations at play in psychology. The sixth constraint rests on a more general hypothesis, that representation is a part of the natural world, and hence that our target is a species of natural representation which may be distinct from the guiding exemplars of public representation.

Many representational systems were coined in the agora of human civilization, but the humans who coined them got *their* internal representational capacities by other means—the patient and intricate tinkering of natural selection. The evolutionary ancestors of representing systems were systems doing other things, and the former begat the latter by lucky stumbling among the available resources more than by any inspired leap to new orders of complexity. Thus one question a theory of representation should answer concerns the evolution of representation: How did representational systems emerge from simpler nonrepresentational systems? We hope that our theory of representation is consistent with at least one likely evolutionary history of representation. We might call this the constraint of evolutionary plausibility.

In one sense, however, this is a weak constraint. Brains don't fossilize, so the best we can do is to tell plausible tales, just-so stories that display how certain systems might have got to their present state. If the claim being supported is merely that a given system could have evolved and not that the system evolved through just these stages, then the just-so story seems innocent enough, an incremental addition to the plausibility of the system being described. (Accordingly, the inability to guess at how natural selection got from A to B barely undermines the reality of B.)

Even if the evolutionary history of representation is uncertain, the processes of selection cast a useful organizing net over our enterprise. Consider the birth-to-death quandary of competing life—especially ambulatory life. For a particular animal interacting with other animals in a particular environment, certain behaviors will be rewarded with a full stomach, cozy shelter, gratified lust, or some other renewal of life's lease. But for each of these fortunate acts, myriad others, barely different, are dead wrong. Motile organisms, accordingly, need whatever capacities they can muster for guidance. Their guiding faculties need to inform them with respect to distal objects and situations. They need to keep those objects and situations straight, and they need to successfully confront and sometimes anticipate novel situations, and they need to coordinate the details of situations with the details of behavior. The needed faculty, thus, had better be *accurate, specific, articulate* (in at least a limited sense), and subtly *efficacious*. There's the metatheory once again. Mothered by necessity, something with the features of representation might well exist in nature. But what sort of system could have these features? This is our question.

Constraint 7:   Representation and Reduction
A final constraint repeats a central theme of section 1.1. Our goal is a reductive theory of representation. Candidate theories should account for representationality without themselves appealing to unanalyzed bearers of content (a sense of reductive also used in Block 1986). To paraphrase Fodor, if representationality is real, then it must really be something else (1987:98). But this is not to suggest that developing a reductive theory of representation means that we should eliminate all talk of representation. Cell biology can be

reduced to biochemistry, but it would be a mistake to stop talking about cells. Representations may be at least as robust and useful to psychology as cells are to biology—we shall see. (Also see P. S. Churchland 1986:296.)

The motivation for this final constraint was discussed in the previous section. We seek to find the mind in the brain, or more specifically, to find inner, natural representation in the material world. To do so, we need a theory that analyzes representation into nonrepresentational components or capacities.

Because we will be trying to build representations out of other stuff, we might save trouble later by a quick look at that stuff now. Unlike the innocent and nontendentious metatheory of representation, the ontology about to be assumed has doubters as well as friends. Some stones are best left unturned—I will stipulate a few relations among a few basic entities. Simplicity is the aim (and for the next few paragraphs philosophers are the audience).

Basically, there are events. Events will be understood here in Kim's (1969, 1973) sense: An event is the instantiation of a property at a time. That sense of event is quite general. For example, objects might exemplify the property of "erupting," "erupting in 1884," "erupting continuously from 1884 to 1886," "being a volcano," "being a photograph of a volcano," "being near a volcano." Accordingly, events need not be instantaneous—event-talk can subsume talk of states and processes. (Events can have temporal and spatial parts.) Thus, we can talk of representations as events interchangeably with talking of them as objects with certain properties. And we can talk of the objects of representations as events as well. In most contexts, convenience of usage will dictate the choice between object-talk and event-talk. Generally, in the following chapters objects will be abbreviated with capital letters (and subscripts, as needed) and events with lowercase letters (and subscripts).

We will also assume that the stew of events is organized in standard ways. Events can be related by being *members* of various sets of events, or by being *parts* of composite events. Individual events can be tokens of event types, members of hierarchically arranged superordinate categories. The eruption of Krakatoa is an element of the set of volcanic eruptions, in turn a subset of the set of natural cataclysms. The initial explosion and subsequent lava flow, in contrast, are both parts of the larger event of the eruption of Krakatoa. (And so also with objects.)

Further, may we adopt for the time being a modest realism? We will assume, first, that individual events (and objects) are real, and second, that some orderings of events—some conceptual schemes—

are better than others in that they more accurately reflect an underlying structure of the world. In our set-theoretical carving, then, we embrace the idea of natural kinds, distinct in reality from arbitrary and accidental assemblies. Similarly, some concatenations of events manifest nomic regularities, as opposed to mere correlation.

With respect to parts and wholes of events and objects—the mereology of our conceptual scheme—some unities are real and true. This last, mereological, plank of modest realism is particularly important, since it underlies the others. Before events can be netted in sets or lumped in composites, they must be individuated. The assumption that there is a reality underlying the mereology amounts to the assertion that events and objects fall under natural kind categories—call them "natural events" and "natural objects," individuals that enjoy the pride of place of natural kinds in our conceptual scheme.

The idea of a natural event contrasts with the treatment of events in general in probability theory. Probability theory conceives events as sets of "sample points" or "outcomes" drawn from a space of possibilities. Events can be combined by both disjunction and conjunction: One composite event might be the union of two (sets of) sample points, while another composite event might be their intersection. There are no restrictions on which events can be combined with others by the successive applications of disjunction and conjunction. The basic mereology of a conceptual scheme, in contrast, suggests a distinction between two classes of possible concatenations of events, partitioning the natural from the artificial events. Fertilization, gestation, and giving birth are parts of a composite event, reproduction. Giving birth and withdrawing $10,000 from a bank account is, prima facie, an artificial event. In the first case, we see the two component events as parts of a larger whole; in the latter, we do not. Human inquiry is, in part, the effort to distinguish natural from artificial events. The natural events exhibit a unity and robustness unlike the artificial; the robustness is discovered, not posited. In short, modest realism asserts that it is not ad hoc to dismiss the ad hoc from the catalogues of reality.

What makes the realism modest is that it takes no stand on the one true conceptual scheme. It is not, for example, a scientific realism, since it allows for extrascientific facts. But given the elusiveness of our target, we will welcome any scientific facts we have and appeal to them with the same emphasis as do card-carrying scientific realists. Is scientific realism ultimately true? In this essay I will regard the question of the ultimate conceptual scheme as what Douglas Adams (1985) calls an SEP—Someone Else's Problem.

Though fiercely contentious in the world at large (see especially

Putnam 1981, 1986), within the confines of the search for representation and consciousness, the assumption of modest realism should not betray us. We assume that there are facts about events and objects. We need only be warned against individuating those events and objects by their role in semantic or representational relations, and then appealing to them in the explication of representation, thereby begging the question. With that caveat, we may turn from metatheory to theory, the work at hand.[2]

Chapter 2
What Natural Representation Is Not

It sounds like magic: signifying something by multiplying sound and fury. Unless you put cream in you won't get ice cream out no matter how fast you turn the crank or how sophisticated the "processing." The cream, in the case of a cognitive system, is the representational *role of those elements over which the computations are performed. And the representational role of a structure is, I submit, a matter of how the elements of a system are related, not to one another, but to the external situations they "express."*
—Fred Dretske (1983)

Chapter 1 introduced the topic of representation and outlined the questions a respectable theory of representation should answer. In this chapter, we begin the central task of theory construction. Following chapter 1, we can describe the inquiry as a quest for a special category of events. We seek to describe under what conditions an event can have content, where the content can be accurate (or not), specific (to a point), and articulated (in many cases). These content-bearing events should have a role to play in psychology and should be plausible products of natural selection. Finally, the events need to be characterized without any circular appeal to semantic or representational terminology. In the end, we hope for a theory that not only satisfies these conceptual requirements but is concrete enough to inform some hypotheses in the empirical sciences of the mind.

This chapter tours two main approaches to naturalized representation. Both characterize representations relationally: Events become representations when they enter into certain relations with other events. The first approach, "internalism," defines representation in terms of relations among events internal to the organism or representing system. The second approach, which I will call "externalism," defines representation as a relation of probabilistic dependency between a representing event and the event it represents, where that event is frequently external to the organism or representing system. I will argue that although both of these approaches are suggestive, neither fully succeeds. In response, chapter 3 suggests and defends an alternative.

2.1 Internalism

Representation and Relations among Internal Events

Suppose you are visiting a distant country where English is spoken, and amid some ordinary sentences you hear an unfamiliar sound, approximately described as [aham]. Two possibilities occur to you: Perhaps [aham] is a mere sound, an indigenous throat-clearing, with no meaning or grammatical role in the language; or perhaps [aham] is a word, "aham," and thus the language of this land is a dialect of English slightly distinct from your mother tongue. You can settle the issue with some careful listening. It should quickly become obvious whether [aham] occupies a regular grammatical role, and if it does, from the contexts of its occurrence you will be able to narrow down the meaning of "aham" far enough to be able to use "aham" correctly in sentences of your own, and ultimately to utter truths including "aham." You might accomplish all this without ostension, that is, without the pointing out of any ahams (if the word is a noun) or explicit display of ahaming (if it is a verb).[1] Instead, you can determine the meaning of the sound strictly from the contexts of its utterance. You will have expanded your vocabulary on the strength of the network of connections between "aham" and the known representational vehicles with which it interacts. The fable narrates a particular case of a classic view of word meaning: [Aham] is a word in the language if it occupies a functional role in the language appropriate to meaningful words. Its precise meaning can be determined by the details of the functional role "aham" turns out to occupy. (The *locus classicus* of this view of meaning is Wittgenstein 1953.)

The case of "aham" suggests a continuum of similar experiments, each involving travel further from home to language communities with increasingly unfamiliar linguistic practices. We imagine, in incremental steps, encountering increasingly unknown languages. In each case one can learn new terms without ostension as long as there is an overlap between the familiar and the new language. But as we leap further from our native tongue, we eventually approach a point where this strategy of learning meaning through use begins to break down. Too many sentences contain too many unknown words, and our hypotheses about individual word meanings can no longer be confirmed by fitting our guesses into familiar sentential contexts. And by extension we expect that encountering a wholly unfamiliar (and untranslated) language would leave us wholly clueless about word meaning (and hence sentence meaning) unless we are helped by matching words and sentences with what they represent. Only when speakers of the new language are able to point to denotations in our presence will we be able to learn the language.

These tales have lessons for the inquiry into representation. The experiments describe learning that something is a representation, and learning the meaning of a representation, just by examining its interactions with other representations (whose content is already known to us). A model of inner representation might follow similar lines: Perhaps an inner token becomes a representation when it interacts in the right ways with other representations. The analogy leads to the further suggestion that the content of the inner representations depends solely on their inner context, and one need not look outside the brain in order to determine the content of an inner representation. The suggestion is that inner representations acquire their meaning by the functional roles they occupy in a network of interacting inner representations.

The story had a negative moral as well, and this too can be brought over to the analogous account of inner representation. You could only learn a new language without recourse to the links between the language and the world if that language overlapped with a language you already knew. There appeared to be a critical mass of preestablished representations which had to be present in order to get the candidate representations off the ground. Similarly, the analogy suggests that the "innards only" idea of representationality presupposes a kernel of preestablished internal representations. If these represent, then other representations can be described through relations with the kernel. The problem, of course, is explaining the representationality of the kernel. The fable of language learning suggested the need for ultimate contact with the world of denotations. By analogy, the suggestion is that some kernel of inner representations must get its representationality from some link to the outer world.

One theory of inner representation, however, tries to draw the positive moral without the negative. This theory holds that every inner representation derives its representationality from its relations to other inner events, and that at no point must one appeal to the world outside the representing system. Following Jonathan Bennett ("Belief and Behavior," lecture notes, Syracuse University, 1983), I will call this theory by the suggestive title of *internalism*. Internalism is the view that representationality depends on dynamic relations between events internal to a representing system. We will have more to say about those dynamic relations shortly; first, however, note that internalism excludes relations with the external world from its account of inner representation. In contrast to behaviorist methodology, which recommends that organisms be regarded as black boxes nested in a world of observable stimuli and responses, the internalist recommends that organisms be regarded as glass boxes nested in a black world (attributed to Keith Gunderson in Dennett 1981). Accordingly, internalism is also known as *methodological solipsism*. (The phrase originates with Putnam 1975, but the dominant version is Fodor 1980 (and appended commentaries). Also see Fodor 1987; Garfield 1988.) The solipsism of the approach lowers the curtain on the outside world, the natural context inhabited by the system under study. It contrasts with metaphysical solipsism, the extreme position that the outside world doesn't exist. Methodological solipsism is the weaker suggestion that with respect to psychology one should proceed *as if* the outside world did not exist.

"Functional Role Semantics" for Inner Representations
Internalism holds that an internal event is a representation if it interacts in the right way with other inner events. What is the nature of that interaction, and what sorts of events are involved? In the tale of [aham], a sound became a representation by interacting with other (preestablished) representations. Internalism cannot follow this suggestion, however. If we appeal to preestablished representations, then we have merely put off the main question of the nature of representation itself, for we will want to know why the preestablished kernel is itself representational. Rather than enter this short and unsatisfying regress, the internalist imagines a network of interacting events, none of which would be a representation in isolation but which together exhibit some sort of dynamism or structure that warrants calling the whole system a representing system. Thus, interpretation begins with the whole system, and only secondarily assigns meaning to separate representations. The meaning of a particular representation in the whole system, on this theory, is the functional role the event plays with respect to the rest of the system. The theory, accordingly, is called *functional role semantics* (FRS). (See Block 1986 for review and references.) Figure 2.1 is a programmatic sketch of the FRS view.

Here we behold a nest of representations, specific events r_i through r_m. None are representations in isolation, but their proximity to each other prompts a semantic chain reaction. The whole moves at once; each event is a representation because a critical mass of its neighbors are.

But what exactly are the dynamic relations that boost mere interactions into the realm of representation? We can answer this through a

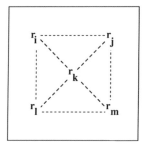

Figure 2.1
Interanimated networks of representations, pulling together.

nice example due to John Haugeland, who poses an interpretation
task in cryptarithmetic, part of which I will recount here (1985:102).
Suppose we are looking at a dynamic system and have analyzed its
operation as a flow of uninterpreted symbols, each of which is initially as obscure as [aham]. In one respect, our task here resembles
the encounter with [aham] in that we will base our interpretation of
any one symbol on its context. But in another respect, the two interpretation tasks differ. In the present case, unlike the case of [aham],
we cannot rely on any preestablished representations. We begin our
interpretation totally in the dark. As we look inside, we watch the
uninterpreted symbol strings change from one to another. Here are a
few of the observations:

(1) OEO changes into N

(2) NIBM becomes G

(3) HCHCH becomes KON

Guessing that we're watching some sort of calculation, we might try
various translations of letters into numbers and arithmetic operators.
One of Haugeland's translations yields:

(1) $=5=$ becomes /

(2) /92× becomes 7

(3) 83838 becomes $+ =/$

Not very promising. But ultimately, one translation yields:

(1) $1 + 1$ becomes 2

(2) 27/3 becomes 9

(3) $8 \times 8 \times 8$ becomes 512

Our hunch is confirmed; apparently the system under consideration is a simple calculator. The interpretation that turns letter transformations into the above numerical calculations strikes us as the best
because it is the one interpretation that makes the three statements
true. In order to extend the interpretation beyond the three statements, we need only assume that the translations of the letters will
remain consistent and that the dynamic rules that the system follows
are truth-preserving. The rules, in short, are rules of inference, and so
the dynamism of a representing system is the dynamism of logic.
Systems that meet these standards, according to functional role semantics, are entitled to representationality. Haugeland's motto: "If
you take care of the syntax, the semantics will take care of itself."

We are thus invited to view the brain as an inferential system,
wherein representations occupy inferential roles. Given truths at the
start, this system generates new truths while maintaining the old.
The proposal resembles the story of "aham," save for its demand that
some kernel of the system win representationality by other means. By
FRS, the whole moves at once, each part sustaining the other. Even if
we were disconnected brains, floating in vats of Gatorade, we would
be representational systems as long as our cryptic neural dynamics
could be interpreted.

Problems for Functional Role Semantics
What works for a pocket calculator may not work so well for you and
me, however. We turn first to what might be called the problem of
idiosyncrasy (also known as the "collateral information" problem
in Block 1986). The calculator interpretation succeeded because each
symbol string was a deductive (arithmetic) consequence of its prede-
cessors. Natural thought patterns are not nearly so rigid. Suppose
you, our friend Edgar, and I are walking by the park in spring, and at
the same moment we happen to think, "There's the park." What
thought comes next to each of us? I may think that daffodils are nice,
while you reflect that April is the cruellest month, and Edgar mur-
murs, "Ah, bear in mind this garden was enchanted." "There's the
park" seems to be the same thought (or representation) in each of
us—we have that much in common at least. But in light of our next
association, "There's the park" occupies three very different functional roles, varying with the divergent psychological states springing
from our common initial thought. If (as FRS asserts) meaning is func-
tonal role, then we are not thinking the same or even similar thoughts
after all. FRS seems to expand the denotation of a thought to include
its connotation. (A similar problem with FRS is discussed in Fodor
1985.)

Defenders of FRS may simply accept the conclusion that we are each radically idiosyncratic representational systems. Such acceptance comes at a price: Communication becomes a mystery, since similar expressions (like "There's the park") reflect different thoughts, and psychology becomes a practical impossibility, since assigning content to inner representations involves tracing a complex and idiosyncratic network of interacting representations. A more moderate response is to impose an idealization on FRS, as follows: Only some functional interactions among internal states are "meaning-fixing"; the rest are irrelevant. In other words, thoughts have a core inferential role, which is relatively constant among thinkers, and a surrounding haze, a peripheral associative role, which can vary. With respect to the core inferential role of our thoughts, we are not so different from calculators or from each other. We suppose that you, Edgar, and I will overlap in at least some of the logical consequences we deduce from "There's the park." A less idiosyncratic FRS could base the meaning of the inner representation on those core inferences.

FRS, in the above example, is troubled by thoughts sharing the same content but with different causal roles from person to person. Fodor (1985) has also discovered a related problem, which we might call the problem of logical interchangeability: thoughts with the same inferential role but different contents. Any thought P is inferentially equivalent to its combination with any other thought Q in the form "P and (Q and not-Q)." For example, anything that entails or can be deduced from "There's the park" can equally entail or be deduced from "There's the park, and either I'm human or not." But those two thoughts certainly have different contents. The friend of FRS might once again invoke a distinction between the core and the peripheral functional role as an escape from the problem. In this case, core inferential role is the same for the two propositions. But the peripheral causal roles might be quite different—one might often come to think "There's the park" but rarely hit upon the insight, "There's the park, and either I'm human or I'm not," even though the latter is logically warranted in exactly the same contexts as the former. That difference in functional role, perhaps, accounts for the difference in content between the two propositions. This time meaning is fixed through the peripheral functional role, not the core inferential role.

Thus we face two initial problems with the FRS proposal: Similar thoughts with diverging peripheral associations were assigned diverging contents, and different thoughts with similar inferential roles were assigned similar content. Neither result accords with our intuitions about the content of inner representations. Both of these objections invited a fix through a distinction between core and peripheral causal roles. Distinguishing the core and the periphery will be a tricky matter, but that doesn't matter, because the cure is worse than the disease. In each case, the distinction was applied to a different end. To answer the problem of idiosyncrasy, we excluded peripheral content in order to save the commonality of thought among different thinkers. But in response to the problem of logical interchangeability, we included that same periphery in order to capture the content differences among logically equivalent propositions. We can't have it both ways, but saving one intuition scuttles the other. The two problems thus lead directly to a dilemma for functional role semantics.

This dilemma is not the sole trouble for FRS. The optimistic example from Haugeland with which we opened finesses an important further question, which we might call the glop problem. In Haugeland's cryptarithmetic we confronted a series of letters, tokens from an alphabet we already knew. (Most examples used to illustrate FRS begin with letters or words, making the glop problem harder to appreciate.) The brain's alphabet, in contrast, will not be so conveniently spelled out, ripe for interpretation (a problem mentioned in Cummins 1983:38; Dennett 1981: note 9; and discussed at length in Dennett 1982b). Interpretation, in other words, begins with inarticulate glop and requires two separate stages: First the glop gets articulated into uninterpreted symbols; then the uninterpreted symbols are interpreted as representations. Let's consider the first stage. By what rules does one map glop onto uninterpreted symbol strings?

One guiding principle seems obvious enough: Be consistent. That is, when one object or event is assigned to a symbol type, succeeding similar objects or events should be assigned to the same symbol type. (And so [aham] is always interpreted as "aham.") But here, and everywhere, trouble follows the word "similar." Which properties should cosymbolic tokens share? If they must share every property, then we simply assign every object its own symbol and then ponder the project of interpreting a symbol string in which every symbol is unique and nonrepeating. So we instead declare that some subset of properties of the glop is relevant to symbol assignment. Since we have in mind that the symbols we seek have a dynamic cognitive role, the properties can be quickly narrowed down to causal properties. But this is not enough, since every object has its private infinity of causal properties as well. Every object will resemble another with respect to some of these properties, and each will differ from another with respect to others. Our task here is complicated by the fact the glop-to-symbol relationship is many-one. That is, many different arrangements of uninterpreted matter can be one symbol: a, A, **A**, *a*.

Our best hope might seem to lie in the Haugeland strategy: Try out various interpretations, and when the shoe fits, wear it. In the original cryptarithmetic example, we were helped by what Dennett (1987a:136) calls the "cryptographer's constraint": the larger the text or system to be decoded, the fewer the sensible interpretive options (also see Haugeland 1984: chapter 3). Even the three coded computations of Haugeland's example constrained the possible interpretations enough to provide a unique solution. But the cryptographer's constraint will not help us at the glop level. The translation from glop to uninterpreted symbols lacks the guiding lights of truth and reason that illuminated the translation from uninterpreted symbols to interpreted representations. The taxonomy of symbols needn't make sense. Thus, with enough ingenuity, we can always figure out a scheme of interpretation that carves our glop into symbols that then can be interpreted as nice syllogisms. For example, earlier we borrowed Haugeland's uninterpreted calculator:

(1) OEO becomes N

(2) NIBM becomes G

(3) HCHCH becomes KON

Here's an alternative interpretation scheme:

Initial O = "all" (here understood as an uninterpreted letter string)

Noninitial O = mere noise, not part of any symbol

E = "men"

Terminal N = "mortal"

Nonterminal N = noise

IBM or HCHCH = "Socrates"

G = "man"

K = noise

And so, the calculator is really spinning out syllogisms. You say, "Surely this is a cheat!" Indeed, it is contrary to convention to lump letters together as I did in order to produce this interpretation. But that is just the problem of glop, especially glop in the head: There are no conventions to get us started. Conventional signs need to be public signs; for a convention to work, all the users must have public access to the representation, so that the otherwise arbitrary relation between the representation and what it represents can be stabilized among users. Inner representations, of course, are not public in this required sense. Though neuroscience may point to the tokens of a particular inner representation, we don't in ordinary life wear our brains on our sleeves. We can't start decoding the brain's writing, not only because we don't know the code, but because we don't even recognize the symbols to be decoded.

Returning to the example, we can't rule out that HCHCH is one complicated letter, cosymbolic with IBM. Offering more glop doesn't help, since one can always introduce more context into the interpretation, railroading the glop into any uninterpreted symbol scheme one chooses. Any complex system could be assigned an interpretation, whether it is genuinely representational or not. A theory of representation, it seems, should preserve the distinction between representational and nonrepresentational systems and should make that distinction a matter of fact to be discovered about various systems rather than something to be created by clever interpreters (Garfield 1988:68, 93). And this, it seems, FRS lacks the resources to accomplish.

Functional role semantics faces another problem as well. This problem could be called that of the unanswered question, and to develop it, we begin by reconsidering the central tenet of FRS: Events become representations because of their interactions with other events. Recall that the representationality of one event cannot be based on the representationality of another, on pain of a regress. Rather, the whole moves at once. The whole system has that special something, dynamic inferential structure, and that makes representing systems distinct. But why should that dynamism create representationality? What is it about dynamic inferential structure that makes it sufficient for representation? The friends of FRS assume, of course, that if a system has a unique interpretation, then for that system the question just raised has been answered. Once again, if the shoe fits, wear it. But if we examine why FRS seems intuitively "right," I think we find that its appeal traces to certain implicit assumptions that motivate the theory. These assumptions, in turn, harbor an alternative view of representation.

To spell this out, we need only press one question: Why? Why is an individual event a representation (in the FRS view)? Because of its place in a network of representations—this answer is explicit. But we are after a bigger question: Why does the whole system represent? Here we cannot talk about the interaction of the system with other representations. We have expanded the question to the system boundaries, and internalism declares we need look no further. Yet, somehow, events in the system represent events in the great wide world. Why? On this question, FRS has nothing to say. FRS, I am suggesting, does not answer the central question of representation: Why are certain physical systems representing systems and others not?

This is an important question, so I will ask it again, in a slightly different form. Version two: Presumably big inferential engines like ourselves could lose significant chunks and still fall under the interpretation rules of FRS and thereby continue to represent. We imagine, accordingly, a continuum of "meaning lesions," paring a rich mind down to something inferentially very lean. At some undetermined and probably fuzzy point, we encounter a minimal interpretable system, something that has just barely enough inferential structure to get off the ground as a representational system. We needn't describe that system, since, once again, I am merely concerned to point out that we can next ask: By virtue of what does the minimal kernel represent? We've stripped it of its external representational neighborhood, so we must appeal to something else. But what?

At this point, any friend of functional role semantics will feel some exasperation. I have, in both formulations of the central question, missed the point. FRS, says its defender, has resources to link representational systems to the worlds they represent, and the ultimate questions I have pressed can be readily answered. But as we canvass the possibilities, we will find that each turns FRS into a covert instance of another type of theory.

One possibility can be found in Leibniz (1677, translated in Weiner 1951:10), in a discussion of the representationality of symbols ("characters" in his terms):

> Characters must show, when they are used in demonstrations, some kind of connection, grouping, and order which are also found in the objects, and . . . this is required, if not in single words, . . . then at least in their union and connection.

Dynamic inferential structures represent the world by virtue of corcorresponding to it. They are, in other words, isomorphic with the world they represent. (For a similar proposal in recent cognitive science, see Shepard and Cooper 1982:185.) It may be that dynamic inferential structure, similar to the dynamic world, looks so obviously representational because of a strong intuition that isomorphism is the root of representation. Isomorphism, however, is a bad foundation for representation, for three reasons. First, to conclude that two structures are isomorphic depends on comparing their parts and internal relations, and this in turn rests on an interpretation of what is salient on both sides of the comparison. This is already difficult in cases where the isomorphs are public and familiar as, for example, in mimetic theories of art and pictorial representation (Goodman 1968, Heil 1981, Lloyd 1982). The problem only worsens when one isomorph is in the head. There again we face the glop problem, the problem of what configurations are even candidates for being compared to external circumstances. So the problems of interpretation just canvassed reappear when we attempt the special, isomorphic interpretation.

Second, if we decide that inner states mean what they most resemble, then we will have trouble allowing for the possibility of error. An erroneous representation ought to be isomorphic with nothing (otherwise it would be correct); but then, if it has no isomorph, why would it be a representation at all? If we say that it would represent what it would be isomorphic to, if its isomorph existed, then we have wildly extended the class of representations to include everything, since anything in the world might have an isomorph, with the result that we are surrounded by representations we never suspected—they just happen to be errors, one and all. This problem deepens the first, since some interpretation schemes will make some of their purported representations accurate and others inaccurate. The possibility of inaccuracy introduces another source of slack in any interpretation scheme.

Third (and last), even if we meet the first problems, it may happen by chance that one representation is isomorphic with two distinct situations. Which one is the privileged content of the representation? I may have a distinct mental image of mint growing in our backyard. Suppose that, unbeknownst to me, somewhere in the universe there is another backyard with mint identical to that at home. To the extent that my image and mint-linked psychology is isomorphic to the local mint and its context, so is it isomorphic also to the cosmic mint far away. (Readers will recognize this as a Twin Earth case, similar to that in Putnam 1975.) If isomorphism is the determiner of representationality, then when I think about local mint, I am to exactly the same extent thinking about the corresponding mint in the parallel world. This seems counterintuitive.

Why do dynamic inferential systems seem to represent? Isomorphism is an obvious, though flawed, answer. But the why questions are not over: Why does isomorphism suggest representationality? Another piece of philosophical fantasy suggests an answer: Imagine two visually identical canvasses, A and B. A is James Whistler's *Arrangement in Gray and Black* (the famous portrait of his mother). B is indistinguishable from A, but it is not a portrait. Instead, B is the fortuitous product of a boiler explosion in the basement of the Van

Meegeren and Sons Art Restoration Company. The shock wave of the blast splattered half a warehouse of paint across several hundred stretched canvasses, and one of them dried to an astonishing likeness of the Whistler portrait. (Puzzle cases like this are frequently employed, with entertaining and enlightening consequences, in the aesthetic works of Arthur Danto (1981, 1986).) Is B a representation? I would argue that it is not, since its resemblance to A (the genuine portrait) is purely accidental. That is, the particular pattern of pigment on the surface of B is no more or less likely to occur than the patterns on any of the other splattered canvasses. These other canvasses are mere smears, not representations; B has no special claim to representationality, in spite of its similarity to a genuine representation.

Yet intuitions diverge on this puzzle case, and I think it is revealing to consider why B might seem to be a representation. First, note that if we came upon B without knowing its fortuitous genesis, we would certainly suppose it to be a representation. But why? The answer, I think, is that randomly splattered paints are highly unlikely to fall in a pattern that looks so much like a portrait, let alone a portrait of Whistler's mother. Thus, if we see such a pattern, we may safely conclude that it is in fact a portrait. But in that surmise we suppose that B is the product of a causal process typical of portraiture, and it is this supposition, not merely B's pattern, upon which B's apparent representationality rests. I am suggesting, in sum, that the foundation of representation lies not in what B and A have in common, a certain isomorphic pattern of colors on their surfaces, but rather in what distinguishes them: A is the product of specific causal processes that trace ultimately to the sitter for Whistler's portrait, whereas the accidental B is not.

The general moral of the tale is that beneath isomorphism is another foundation for representation, and it is one that links representing systems to the situations in the outside world that they represent. Linking inner representations with the outer world denies the fundamental principle of internalism, but to good effect: We escape the problems of idiosyncrasy. The thoughts that occur to you, Edgar, and me in the park can be similar in content because they all arise from a relation between each of us and the park itself, and this similarity can be preserved despite many other idiosyncrasies in association and inference. Further, we are better off with respect to the glop problem, since we can look for events in the brain that are correlated with environmental stimuli and use these correlations to begin interpreting. Finally, in breaking out of the internalist box we can explain why dynamic inferential structure seems to provide the key to representation. The dynamism of inference is isomorphic with the dynamism of the world, but that is an unsatisfactory answer until we know why the isomorphism holds. The answer to this, I have suggested, is that the inner dynamism depends on the outer (see also Devitt and Sterelny 1987:102). But this is no longer internalism, the view that representation can be explained by considering the innards alone.

2.2   Dependency and Representation

Now we cast our net still wider, locating the alleged representing event in a network of relations that reaches beyond the boundaries of the representing system. Figure 2.2 sketches a network of potentially relevant events in r's neighborhood, events related to r in (so far) unspecified ways, occurring both inside and outside of the system that includes r. For the sake of clarity, assume that the diagram reflects the temporal order of occurrence of the events depicted. Some of them are prior to r (and lie to its left), while others are subsequent to r (and fall on the right). We can carve the schematic system in several ways. First, we can refer to events upstream from r, i_1 through i_n and u_1 through u_n. Call these r's *afferents*. These are distinguished from events "downstream" from r, d_{1-n} and o_{1-n}, the *efferents*. In addition, we can refer to events that are inside the R-system, *inner events* (u_{1-n}, r, and d_{1-n}) and distinguish them from *outer events* (i_{1-n} and o_{1-n}). The innards thus include afferent and efferent inner events, and the outer events ("outards"?) likewise include outer afferent events, inputs and outputs to the system. With this sketch in hand, we can lay out theoretical options for theories of representation.

The preceding section considered representation as a property of complex dynamic systems. Internalism held that the relevant relata comprised other internal events (u_i and d_i) exclusively, but I reviewed several problems with that position. If representation depends on

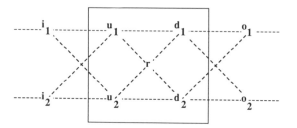

Figure 2.2
Part of a complex network of events.

relational properties, then some of the relata, at least, must be found outside of the representational system. Not internalism but rather some version of externalism will be true. This is progress, but the result seems to leave us as far as ever from a theory of representation answering to the constraints outlined in chapter 1. Among the events in figure 2.2 are one or more that are singled out as what is represented, what r is about. What facts about the network of r's afferents and efferents will enable us to specify r's content uniquely? We will narrow the options in two ways: by specifying the nature of the relations relevant to representation, and by exploring the effects of structured complexes of events—representational networks.

Representation and Causality
What kind of relation links a representation and what it represents? Internalism considered the mind in isolation from its surroundings and thereby left the question of representation hanging. To close this gap, we might turn naturally to causality to link the inner and the outer, holding (to a first approximation) that representations represent their causes. A causal theory of representation immediately prunes the event net by narrowing the class of relevant relations to those holding between events and their causal antecedents. That specification also promises to explain the capacity for accurate representation. If the correlation of representations and subjects is a general feature of representations, occurring at frequencies greater than chance, then we will need an explanation for its routine occurrence. Causal connections might provide that account.

However, three commonplace features of causality make trouble for its employment in the service of representation. First, the cause of an actual event must be another actual event. This generates the problem of error. If every effect represents its cause, then there can be no representations without actual events for their content, so every event becomes an accurate representation of its cause. Yet the possibility of error is basic to representation (a fact flagged in section 1.2); simple causality cannot account for representation. (Cf. Dretske and Enc 1984.)

Second, a causal antecedent either precedes its consequent in time, or is simultaneous with it. Thus, if effects are representations, they can represent events only in the past or immediate present, relative to the representation. But the theory of representation should allow for representations of future events (since desires, intentions, hopes, and fears are all representational states "directed at" the future). Furthermore, representations, especially linguistic representations, can have content that could not obviously enter into causal relations with the representation. One can think about the number 11, or the class of all amphibians, or astronomical events transpiring right now at a distance of 10,000 light years, but it is difficult to see how these contents —unlike the mint along the walk—could cause the thoughts I'm having about them here and now.

Third, it is reasonable to suppose that every event has myriad contributing causal ancestors. But, to repeat another point from section 1.2, representation is more specific. Only some of those ancestors count as the represented events. Furthermore, the represented event is often not the immediate antecedent of the representation: Between the mint plants and my perception lie many causal intermediaries, including rays of light, retinal images, and neural events. One hopes that in this straightforward case the theory of representation will pick out the mint, not the intermediaries. Causality alone seems unable to do so.

Each of these problems will loom large in discussions to follow (error returns in this chapter and the next, future and general contents in the next chapter and chapter 6, and specificity in all three chapters just mentioned). For the moment the three problems suggest that causality, in the commonsense version employed here, cannot be the relation we seek. Replacing causality with another relation will offer the first step toward meeting the problems.

The positive appeal of causality lay in its prima facie ability to explain the accuracy of representations (when they are accurate). Causality explained the regular correlation of representations and represented events. It explained the correlation by straightforwardly explaining how the occurrence of representations could depend on the occurrence of the events they represent. It is the last relation, dependency, upon which I hope to build.

Let us define dependent and independent events in terms of probability. One event is independent of another when its occurrence (or nonoccurrence) has no effect on the likelihood of the other. This is just the sense of independence employed in probability theory, understandable in terms of conditional probability. $Pr(a|b)$ states the conditional probability that a will occur, on the assumption that b occurs; $Pr(a)$ is the probability of a's occurrence, independent of b. When $Pr(a|b) = Pr(a)$, a and b are said to be independent events; otherwise, they are dependent.

What is the connection between statistical, or probabilistic, dependency and causality? It may turn out that the best analysis of causality will be in terms of dependency, as some philosophers (e.g., Suppes 1984, Dupré 1984) have suggested. I propose to take a less tendentious route, and simply flag those probabilistic relations with their own terms. Such mutually influencing events will be called *dependent* events, and their relations will be relations of dependency.

The shift to dependency affords some room to move on two of the three problems facing causal theories of representation. First, regarding error: It may be true of a particular event that given the occurrence of the event a particular antecedent has a very high probability. And yet, despite the high probability, the antecedent may not have occurred. While this is not yet an account of error, it breaks the iron bonds between antecedents and consequents. But it nonetheless permits us to pick out the most probable event among all the possible antecedents of a given actual event—a discrimination that we will find handy.

At the same time, however, dependency relations preserve the virtues of causality by reflecting the regular correlation of representations and features of the world. When we seek to explain how representations are accurate, when they are in fact accurate, we can use dependency in the same role as causality. Accurate representations are not generally accidents. They arise, instead, in systems that have evolved to exploit correlations between inner and outer events (Dennett 1978a, Stampe 1979). It seems plausible, then, that representation can be assembled out of the high conditional probabilities that make specific representations effective in the lives of organisms.

And in the philosophical arena, dependency has a heartening earthly tug: It may be that some of my thoughts about the mint in my backyard also happen to be true of another patch of mint, some light years distant. But the remote plants, unlike those at hand, are independent of my thoughts. Dependency plausibly explains why my thoughts are about these plants and not their distant doubles.

Dependency also provides a first step around the problems of representing the future. A dependency relation between two events is asymmetric in the sense that, except in special cases, $Pr(a|b) \neq Pr(b|a)$. This enables us to speak of the direction of dependency: When the conditional probability of event a, given b, is greater than the conditional probability of b given a, then the direction of dependency is from a to b. Henceforth, solid arrows will indicate the direction of dependency between diagramed events, as in figure 2.3. Note that saying that dependency is directed from a to b does not entail that dependency is somehow one way, that one event can be dependent

a ————————▶ b

Figure 2.3
Direction of dependency when $Pr(a|b) > Pr(b|a)$.

on another, but not vice versa. Rather, direction simply marks a comparative value of two conditional probabilities. Furthermore, since $Pr(a|b)/Pr(b|a) = Pr(a)/Pr(b)$, direction of dependency is equally a function of the independent probabilities of a and b. Where $Pr(a)$ is greater than $Pr(b)$ (and a and b are dependent), then the direction of dependency is from a to b. But the numerical values of those two independent probabilities are not tied to temporal order. Thus dependency can extend from future events to present and past events.

Dependency thus offers some leverage on representationality. Some, but not enough: We still wonder how an event could be dependent on an abstraction or a universally quantified class. In these respects, dependency does not offer enough to be a theory of representation. But in another respect, dependency offers far too much. Every event is dependent on each of an unlimited number of other events. Representation, in distinction, is not nearly so gregarious.

2.3 Representation and the Flow of Information

Appealing to relations of dependency in the search for representation has circumvented some problems at the cost of exacerbating others. Specificity has been a salient casualty, and this section concerns a sustained attempt to meet this problem. Accordingly, the focus is on focus. Representations select one or a small handful of events as what they represent. But every event enters into relations of mutual dependency with myriad other possible events.

Consider, for example, the many events upon which a photograph depends. The properties of a photograph depend not only on the properties of its object, but on (among others) the integrity of the camera, the potency of developer and fixer, the sobriety of the photographer in the darkroom, and so forth. But among these dependencies only one is the proper object of the photograph. (In English, strange to say, we refer equally to the proper object as the subject of the photograph.) Such narrow selectivity is an expected feature of evolved representational systems as well. An inner representation is like a photograph in at least one respect: Its occurrence is not only dependent on, say, the tiger that has fixed its gaze on the bearer of the representation. It is likewise dependent on, and carries information about, the felicity and smooth metabolic functioning of retina, nerve, and brain, and indeed on the sobriety of the organism. But, likewise, the response of the system had better respect the selectivity of the representation and respond appropriately to the tiger, disregarding all the other dependencies.

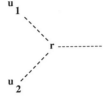

Figure 2.4
Lateral alternatives.

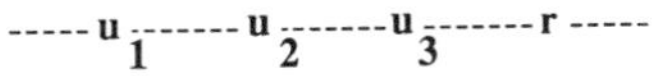

----- u -------- u --------u --------r -----
    1   2   3

Figure 2.5
Linear dependencies.

In order to simplify the discussion, we will attend for now to the (inner and outer) afferents to the representation. The upstream sprawl has two distinct dimensions. First, for any representation we face the problems of alternative lateral dependencies (or what Stampe (1979) calls "synchronic selectivity"). Figure 2.4 isolates two of the lateral alternatives. Event r depends on each of two events, so r's occurrence indicates that the probability of both u_1 and u_2 is increased. If r is the fixing of a photograph, then events at r are dependent on the reflectance properties of the subject and on the presence of film in the camera. (Of course, there are many such dependent events.) Representations selectively represent particular objects among this lateral sprawl.

Representations are also selective of their objects along a linear (Stampe: diachronic) dimension. That is, they select among the chain of preceding dependent events leading up to the representation. Figure 2.5 smooths out one of the dependency chains leading up to r, illustrating linear specificity. Consider again an ordinary photograph. Between the sitter and the resulting glossy eight-by-ten, many intermediate causes intervene, including the photographic negative. But the photograph is neither a picture of its negative nor of the other intermediate causes. Internal representations likewise point to specific objects and situations among the linear series of events. Perceiving a tiger is like taking a picture. Between the inner representation and the charging beast lie many dependent events, including the retinal image of the tiger. Our theory of representation needs to explain how the tiger, and not the retinal image, comes to be the object of representation. It must account for linear selectivity.

The appeal to dependency among events will thus need to be augmented or modified to capture these two dimensions of selectivity.

Two routes are open: First, further conditions can be imposed on the dependency relation between pairs of events. In other words, we can demand further restrictions on the nature of the representing relation. Or we can back up the relation of representation and object with further, auxiliary relations. In effect, we embed the representation and object in a dependency network involving other dependent events beside the pair of representation and proper object. Of course, whatever representations are, we expect them to fit into networks, but this route turns some sort of network embedding into a requirement for a sufficient theory of representation. The success of such a theory, accordingly, lies in the details of the required network. Since both sorts of ideas have been explored in a ground-breaking work by Fred Dretske, *Knowledge and the Flow of Information* (1981), his thought will be our point of departure.

Strict Channels
The title of Dretske's book suggests an important connection that I have yet to make explicit: the link of cognition with information. Information is generally conceived of as flowing along causal paths. An information source is the antecedent of two causally linked (and thereby dependent) events; the receiver is the consequent. But any relation of dependency is sufficient for information transmission in its original technical sense (first elucidated, though not in these terms, in Shannon and Weaver 1949). When two events are dependent, an information channel is said to connect them. The conditional probabilities may differ only slightly from the independent probabilities, indicating poor information transmission; but as long as there is some dependency, some information will get through. We can think of any event, then, as occurring within a network of dependent events, with information channels of varying degrees of effectiveness as links.

These few comments barely touch the content of information theory (for instance, I've said nothing about the computation of amounts of information generated or transmitted), but these brief allusions will be sufficient here. Indeed, some writers have questioned the extent to which Dretske himself actually leans on the mathematical theory of information (e.g., Foley 1987; nonetheless, part I of Dretske's book is an excellent introduction to both "regular" information theory and Dretske's customized changes). Instead, we turn directly to the problems we would like Dretske's theory to solve.

The problem of alternate dependencies, the lateral sprawl, is met by Dretske's important modification of information theory, a modification that yields not only a theory of representation but an approach to belief, perception, cognition, concept formation, and knowledge. So far, I have been speaking of information transmitted between events whenever the events are dependent on each other (that is, whenever their conditional probabilities differ from their independent probabilities). Dretske turns dependency in just this sense into a theory of "informational content" simply by requiring that for a representation r to carry the informational content that an event x has occurred, the conditional probability of x given r ($Pr(x|r)$) must be 1 (1981:65). The definition carries an additional condition, a relativization to background knowledge of the receivers of the signal (representation). Nothing in the discussion here turns on that qualification, however; events linked by such a channel exhibit complete dependency in one direction, at least. We might call a channel that meets this condition a perfect or strict channel. Representational dependencies, in other words, are not matters merely of likelihood, but of certainty. I will call the information transmitted over a strict channel "information$_c$" to flag this certainty condition.

The high standards of information$_c$ are primarily motivated by Dretske's epistemological aspirations. The motivation for the strict channel requirement traces, I believe, to a principle concerning the transitivity of information transmission. Dretske aptly calls this the "Xerox principle":

> If A carries the information that B, and B carries the information that C, then A carries the information that C. (1981:57)

As he observes, something like the Xerox principle must be true, given that any channel between two dependent events can be subdivided into a sequence of dependent events—as I also noted in introducing the problem of linear specificity. But Dretske introduces the Xerox principle not in terms of events but rather in terms of propositions ("that A," etc.). On the Xerox principle, he comments (ibid.),

> I take this to be a regulative principle, something inherent in and essential to the ordinary idea of information, something that any theory of information should preserve. For if one can learn from A that B, and one can learn from B that C, then one should be *able* to learn from A that C.

Again, information is characterized in terms of communicated propositions rather than relations between events. The effect of this is to introduce distinct epistemic standards under the heading of the "ordinary idea of information." The phrase "learns that p," along with "sees that p," "discovers that p," and similar phrases, are factive— when sentences including these phrases are true, then p in the "that" clause is also true. Their use is of a piece with "knows that p" in that they all presuppose that p is true. And in contexts abounding in these factive phrases, the phrases "carry the message that p" and "carry the information that p" likewise seem to imply that p is true. The inference to p is deductive: If A carries the information that p, that doesn't mean that p is merely probable. Dretske drives this home in his discussion of the Xerox principle, where he imagines the cumulative effect of chaining less-than-certain messages. Even small probabilities of falsehood accumulate to lead to paradox—signals that convey the information that p when p has a low probability of being true. These paradoxes can be avoided only by positing strict channels at every step in the flow of information.

It may be that Dretske's reasoning is true to the ordinary concept of information. And it is quite likely that something like information$_c$ will be appropriate to an information-based theory of knowledge, but we can question its application in an inquiry into representation. (The problems I find with Dretske's theory as a theory of representation, accordingly, should not be taken as criticism of his epistemology. Rather, they suggest that the theory of representation and the theory of knowledge should be detached from each other. One definition won't serve both.)

Unlike the various epistemic verbs, to represent that p in no way entails that p is true. Nor is there an obvious analog to the Xerox principle with respect to representation. Even in cases where we do observe some transitivity of representation (e.g., pictures of pictures), the chaining seems finite and doesn't require perfect transmission. If this is contrary to the commonsense meaning of information (and I'm not sure it is), then so much the worse for information as the root of representationality. Our descriptions of dependencies among events (and channels understood as the links between dependent events) shall serve us without smuggling unwanted epistemic baggage.

But the details of Dretske's motivation need not detain us further. Instead, let us take up one application of Dretske's information$_c$, its role in a theory of representation. It does seem to help us with one flank of the problem of specificity, namely the sprawl of lateral alternatives. Returning to figure 2.4, if u_1 is the only event with a conditional probability of 1, given r, then u_1 is the object of representation. If u_1 and u_2 both have conditional probabilities of 1 (given r), then the representation represents their conjunction.

Although the narrowing of representation-relations to information-bearing relations subject to Dretske's certainty constraint seems to help with the lateral problem, it leaves the linear problem unresolved. Figure 2.5 still schematizes a dimension along which representations will be indeterminate even after dependency relations are stripped down to certainty relations. Between a photogenic sitter and the final print are several information-bearing intermediaries which determine the final print just as surely as the properties of the sitter. If the print bears information$_c$ about the sitter, then it bears information$_c$ about these intermediaries. But it doesn't represent anything but the sitter. Thus, strict channels provide for lateral specificity but not for linear specificity. We will thus follow Dretske's next move, toward specifying representational networks.

Information$_c$ in Disjunctive Networks

Dretske pursues the issue of linear specificity in his discussion of perception (1981: chapter 6) and proposes an information theoretic solution. Figure 2.6 schematizes the circumstances that, according to Dretske, afford a principled account of selectivity. In this case, r carries information$_c$ about o, that is, r occurs only as an eventual consequence of o. But o can exert its inevitable influence on r through either of two routes, c_1 or c_2. In the example, c_1 causes r, but r does not carry the information$_c$ that c_1 is its cause, because r might have resulted equally from c_2. But the causal regularities are so arranged that either c_1 or c_2 carries the information$_c$ that o occurred, and so r also carries that information, through what we might call *transparent intermediaries*. Because r carries the information$_c$ that o occurred, but not the information that any particular intermediary occurred, in contexts like that of figure 2.6, information-bearing states bear information$_c$ about selected antecedents.

Dretske applies this feature of information transmission to the problem of proper objects in perception and finds a nice fit. Perception provides perceivers with stable percepts reflecting the stable distal objects in the environment. Yet the specific intermediaries between objects and percepts can vary widely—consider, for example, the dancing retinal image. Our perceptual world inherits none of the sweeps and jiggles of saccadic motion; we see through them and form no percepts of our own retina at all. It's plausible, then, that

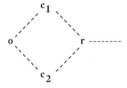

Figure 2.6
Alternative intermediate channels.

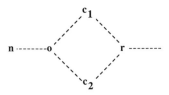

Figure 2.7
Antecedent causes to the object of perception.

percepts selectively encode information at the right selective distance due to the transparency of intermediate channel conditions.

The problem is slightly more complex than illustrated in figure 2.6, since a distal object of perception may also carry information about its antecedents (figure 2.7). While information passes through c_1 and c_2 transparently, r still carries information about both n and o. But, as ever, only one of those is the proper object of perception. (Dretske's example: the ringing of the doorbell and the button that causes it. We hear the bell, not the button being pushed, though the sensory states of hearing carry information that the bell is ringing and that the button is being pushed.) To solve this aspect of the problem of selectivity, Dretske departs from pure information theory to offer a definition of "primary representation" (1981:160; I've changed the letters to match the figures here):

> R gives primary representation to property O (relative to property N) = R's representation of something's being N depends on the informational relationship between O and N but not vice versa.

Primary representation is a relative term, so r might give primary representation to n relative to some precursor m. Thus, the proper object of perception pops out as the object whose properties r gives last (or most) primary representation to. There is, in other words, no state between the proper object o and r which r also carries information$_c$ about. Thus, three gears turn in the Dretskean representation machine to provide an account of linear specificity: information$_c$ transmitted over channels meeting two network conditions— transparent intermediaries and primary representation. Each gear requires the other two to get the whole account moving. But all three are in trouble.

Can the combined resources of transparent intermediaries and primary representation solve the problem of the proper objects of representation? I would argue that they cannot. First, returning to figure 2.6, note that r does carry information$_c$ about the states intermediate

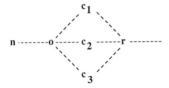

Figure 2.8
A third transparent intermediary joins the team.

to o and r itself. Namely, it carries the information that the disjunction, c_1 or c_2, occurred. And since r carries information about o by virtue of the information link between o and c_1 or c_2, then r gives primary representation to the disjunction. That may seem a bit unfair to the elegance of Dretske's solution, but the theory provides no obvious escape. One cannot, for example, rule out the idea of representations of disjunctions, since obviously sentences represent disjunctive situations. Perception can be disjunctive too: We may perceive that something is an A or a B, but we don't know which. (Similar objections were raised by Ginet 1983 and Loewer 1987.)

Dretske is aware of this problem and addresses it in a recent paper (1986). He asks us to imagine a system that varies in its informational structure over time. Suppose figure 2.7 sketches a given network at time t_1. Then we imagine the network adds a new transparent intermediary, c_3 (as shown in figure 2.8). Networks of this type might be said to have *variable intermediaries.*

The mechanism mediating this change is easy enough: Associative conditioning creates the new channel by a training course during which c_3 is paired with c_1 or c_2. Now Dretske asks for a time-invariant characterization of the disjunctive antecedents. At t_1, r indicates the occurrence of c_1 or c_2. At t_2, r indicates a different disjunction, c_1 or c_2 or c_3. However, throughout the period in question r indicates the occurrence of o. That difference, apparently, is the difference on which to hang the selectivity of representation. The proper object of a representation will be the time-invariant event toward which r gives primary representation.

The solution has a nice resonance, being the temporal analogue of the original proposal of transparent intermediaries. But despite that, it strikes me as ad hoc. The trouble for both transparent and variable intermediaries might be summed up in a phrase: the possibility of fixity. We simply imagine complex systems that don't change over time. These fixed systems don't acquire new possible intermediaries and so possess time-invariant disjunctive intermediaries (imagine them as in either figure 2.7 or 2.8—the important point is that these systems don't change). For example, various input modules in human perception (see Fodor 1983, Garfield 1987) might be fixed in informational structure. But these same systems might nonetheless be in the business of producing and exporting representations. There is, in short, no conceptual barrier between fixity and sophisticated cognition. It may be true in general that systems that represent can also learn, but if so, it is a contingent, empirical fact, not one to be settled by fiat in order to fix a technical difficulty in the theory of representation. (I return to this issue—as an empirical question—in chapter 5.)

The possibility of fixity undermines not only the proposal of variability over time, but also the original proposal of transparent intermediaries. For example, I expect that it is likely that the pathways between touch receptors on my skin and the location of the tactile representation in the brain are relatively fixed (though probably multiple)—the intermediaries are not informationally$_c$ transparent. Yet tactile representations are no less selective of proper objects than visual representations: I perceive a pressure on my skin and not an impulse in my spinal cord. Even if the actual physiology turns out Dretske's way, the possibility of fixed intermediaries nonetheless stands as a counterexample to the proposed account, if it is proposed as an analysis of representation.

But in the end the discussion of intermediaries may be needless, for the device of transparent intermediaries works only in tandem with the certainty condition on information. But information$_c$ is jeopardized by the problem of error, exactly as the basic causal theory of representation was. Since information$_c$ is tied to conditional certainty, there is no way for a representation to misrepresent. On Dretske's theory, the occurrence of a representing event guarantees (by definition) the occurrence of the event represented. Thus, all our representations must be true, despite our supposed capacity for error. Would that it were so!

Several writers have questioned Dretske on this issue (see especially Fodor 1984, 1987, Dennett 1987b). We can safely skirt the fray because any next move grants the point against information$_c$. That is, any theory binding representation to certainty cannot allow for misrepresentation—and thus, I suggest, fails as a theory of representation. And conversely, any theory that allows for the possibility of misrepresentation cannot be a theory based on information$_c$. Information$_c$ must go, and from this negative moral we chart a course.[2]

Recall that with information$_c$, Dretske introduced a special constraint on the information channel between representations and what they represent. Given the troubles (and their epicyclic repairs) that followed the proposal of strict channels, we might do well to back up and begin again with the unvarnished concept of dependency among events. But we may take one powerful general suggestion away from Dretske's important book: Networks display emergent properties beyond the properties of the single channels that comprise them. We are searching for a theory that meets the intuitive standards of representation set out in chapter 1. To networks we turn, for further tinkering.[3]

Chapter 3
Toward a New Theory of
Natural Representation

If the point is to uncover very general, very abstract principles [of] cognitive organization. . . , why not make up a whole cognitive creature, a Martian three-wheeled iguana, say, and an environmental niche for it to cope with? I think such a project could teach us a great deal about the deep principles of human cognitive psychology. . . .
—Daniel Dennett (1978b)

3.1 Synthesizing a Simple Representing System

When Vehicles Ruled the Earth
The previous chapter reviewed two plausible approaches to inner representation. The first, functional role semantics, would call an internal state a representation only if it played a functional role in a complex interpreted network of internal states. I argued first, that finding an interpretation that fits any natural network will be extremely difficult, and second, that even if we interpret a whole system, we could still ask why we should regard the interpreted system as a representation or assemblage of representations. Both of these problems led naturally to the suggestion that representation depends on relations involving the world outside the representing system. Events inside a representing system represent events in the outside world not because the inner resembles the outer, nor because we have been clever enough to interpret the one as a map of the other, but rather because the internal events depend on the external. Following Dretske (1981), I expressed the relation of dependency of the inner on the outer as one of information transmission. Though information is a powerful and suggestive concept here, I argued that we need more: Chapter 2 suggested that, in contrast to representation, information is both too strict (since there is no room for error) and too lax (since any information bearer carries information about myriad other events). Without some further constraint, information provides a bad fit with the metatheory of representation set out in chapter 1.

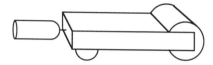

Figure 3.1
A simple Braitenbergian vehicle.

A new approach to the problem is in order, and we may well find one in an imaginary prehistory created by Valentino Braitenberg (1984). We are to imagine a flat, smooth plain populated by wheeled, self-powered "vehicles." Figure 3.1 depicts a simple example. This specimen is a relative of Braitenberg's premier species. A simple photocell at the left mediates the vehicle's myopic contact with the world. The photocell is connected to a motor that drives a single fat wheel at the right, driving the vehicle in whatever direction it happens to be facing. It whirrs in light, rests in darkness. Let us nickname this vehicle "Squint."

What can a vehicle like Squint teach us about representation? Squint will be the starting point for an exercise in "synthetic psychology." We will design a fleet of vehicles, simple motile information processors, and deduce their behavior. The vehicles we study in the exercise can be easily understood because we created them; being synthetic, their simple innards hide no covert or mysterious works. We can use them to build from the bottom up, from the creature spotted in figure 3.1 toward creatures with more complex behavioral capacities. As we imagine this emerging complexity, we can also observe the properties of the internal systems, the brains behind the operation. Ultimately, some internal states of these systems begin to exhibit the capacities we associate with representation. We will consider these suggestive examples at length as they emerge.

If we succeed in building from the primeval Squint to a more cognitive creature, we may also reap a second benefit. One of the pretheoretical constraints on representation was evolutionary plausibility. The capacity for representation in living things emerged from simpler prerepresentational capacities, so theories of representation are aided by accounts of how that evolution might have occurred. Ideally, we would like to trace the actual evolution of representation, but this record may be lost. We must settle instead for a "just-so" story, one inspired (as is Braitenberg's) by biological examples (the theme of chapter 5 of this book). In embarking on a journey of synthetic evolution, we must remember that evolution is blind, and that any complexity must develop incrementally from simpler beginnings and must serve the basic aim of continuing survival

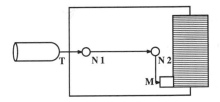

Figure 3.2
The flow of information through a simple vehicle.

for a species. Squint, our vehicle, offers an illustrative starting point. We will follow Braitenberg in supposing that our synthetic vehicles are subject to selective pressures analogous to those facing living things. We assume, then, that Squint must tailor its responses to features of the world, and we will also assume that in the land of vehicles, as in the actual world, light is an important bearer of environmental information. Let's evaluate Squint's prospects in its imaginary world and set out from there to generate some adaptive variations on a vehicular theme.

Figure 3.2 schematizes the innards of Squint. We discover that the connection between the transducer (T) and the motor (M) is straightforward, passing through two identifiable nodes, N_1 and N_2. N_1 and N_2 simply conduct the energy they receive (we will imagine more sophisticated nodes in a moment). Suppose, however, that we also discover that the circuit is unreliable; instead of being of steadfast copper, the wiring is of some other material that conducts rather poorly and is imperfectly insulated from the surroundings— somewhat like the axons that mediate information transmission in living things. Events other than the activity of T can cause response in N_1, N_2, and M. The extraneous events include spontaneous activity in the circuit, or other forms of stimulation, like a sudden shock.

As a result of these potential intrusions, Squint faces a problem of false alarms. We find that Squint will zing along not only in response to light detected at the transducer T but also in response to the errant afferent events just described. The alternative upstream possibilities undermine the reliability of Squint as a light-lover. If Squint's survival were dependent on successful detection of light and jeopardized by false alarms, then Squint's prospects dim.

False alarms, of course, are not Squint's only risk. It is equally prey to misses, or false nonalarms—lapses in the circuitry that allow light to go undetected. If Squint were a member of a reproducing species, subject to the demolition derby of natural selection and able to mutate over the long haul, we might expect it to develop safeguards against both false alarms and misses. Here, however, we will concentrate primarily on the problem of false alarms and consider what we might do to protect Squint from the intrusion of wild or random energy fluctuations. There is a background reason for considering Squint's problems with accuracy: accuracy is a capacity of representation. As Squint gets better at detecting stimuli, we will find that it also begins to exhibit the properties described in the metatheory of representation in 1.2.

In the pursuit of reliability, we might upgrade the basic material of Squint's circuits. Suppose, however, we are stuck with something like the raw neural material that was Squint's original endowment. A possible improvement, retaining the unimproved wiring material, is sketched in figure 3.3. C denotes an auxiliary information channel connecting nodes N_1 and N_2. Because the auxiliary channel is made of the same dubious stuff as the original channel, we can doubt its independent reliability—stray energy might provoke it to signal when no light is present, as with the original channel. But the alternative causes of events along line C are different alternative causes from those that undermine the uniqueness of the other channel. Because events at C are dependent on (among others) events at N_1, N_2 can use C as a "checking channel." When N_2 receives input over its regular (unreliable) channel, and its (also unreliable) checking channel, it nonetheless enjoys somewhat higher confirmation of activity in N_1. Of course, if C's activity alone were enough to prompt N_2, then with C's own inherent unreliability we would merely add another source of false alarms. But we avoid that outcome by replacing N_2 with another sort of node, A. Suppose that A requires more than one active input line in order to send its signal to the motor. We imagine A, in other words, as a threshold device (a term from Braitenberg 1984), with a threshold that cannot be exceeded by either channel alone. In this context, A is an and-gate, changing state (and activating the motor) only when inputs arrive over both of its input channels. Multiple channels also help with the problem of misses. In this case, we exploit their redundancy by having them feed a node that is active when any input channel is active—an or-gate, in short. (Channel

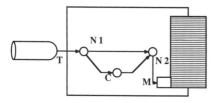

Figure 3.3
An auxiliary information channel.

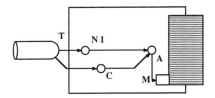

Figure 3.4
A longer-distance checking channel.

multiplication and redundant signalling are standard features of digital computers.)

Squint's chances of escape from false alarms thus improve by the addition of a second channel and attendant and-gate. We might win further improvements with further channels, up to a limit beyond which the increment of improvement is no longer worth our (evolutionary) effort. But even as we appreciate the increased reliability of the communication between N_1 and A, we note that we have not removed the source of unreliability at N_1. False alarms that trigger N_1 can still throw Squint off its simple track. Let us, then, simply extend the upstream reach of the auxiliary channel, as in figure 3.4. The side channel now receives its primary input from the phototransducer, finessing more of the sources of uncertainty in the basic Squint. Like the earlier channel-checking mechanism, the function of C in this context is to disambiguate, but now it is not events at N_1 that are confirmed at a higher probability but events at T, the transducer. Again, C itself can be shaky, but if its alternative causes differ from those for N_1, then the overall probability of getting things right is increased. The mechanism at C, as it were, looks beyond N_1 to T. The mechanism at A that exploits the channel confirmation is the same, however: It is a threshold device functioning as an and-gate. It requires input on both channels. When those dual inputs are there, A's accuracy (its correlation with events at T) is improved.

But transducers are fallible as well. Our policy of security through redundancy (up to a limiting point of least return) dictates the obvious next step—we will give Squint two "eyes" (figure 3.5). Now, if T_1 sparks a wild signal, A will remain quiescent until the signal from T_1 is joined by one from T_2. Only then will A activate the motor. One lesson of this workbench evolution, so far: The case of Squint suggests that one simple route to the important basic goal of reliability lies in multiple channels. If we want to be sure that the signal received really comes from a particular source—not as a "side affect"—then a simple guarantor is the apparatus of multiple channels terminating at a threshold device working as an and-gate.

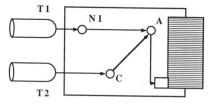

Figure 3.5
Extra transducers further increase reliability.

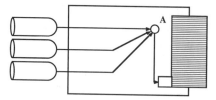

Figure 3.6
Majority rule in a simple vehicle.

Of course, the two-channel case is the simplest, and iterating the auxiliary channels can win further security from false alarms. Such systems will be fail-safe, unlikely to act when stimuli are not present. But our efforts to increase the reliability of these simple systems are paradoxically self-defeating. While false alarms decrease in a multiple channel system, the possibility of "false nonalarms" or misses increases. Now if even one channel is interrupted, the whole system freezes.

Thus, our efforts to make Squint reliably insensitive to wild inputs must be tempered with an effort to make it reliably sensitive to the right stimuli. How are we to do this? One solution takes advantage of the hardware already before us—multiple channels and threshold devices. Suppose now that Squint is equipped with three transducers and three input channels, but as before, these feed one threshold device, as in figure 3.6. In this case, the threshold device requires input from any two of its three input channels. Now if one channel is interrupted, the other two pick up the slack, so the system overcomes a miss on any one channel. But at the same time, if one channel is perturbed by a wild signal, it alone is not enough to trigger a false alarm. Two channels are still required to motivate the vehicle. Thus, majority rule in the threshold device affords a balance between the avoidance of two different kinds of error.

In living systems, just as in simple vehicles, there will be a complex balancing between oversensitivity and insensitivity to various stimulus energies. It would be an excellent exercise in synthetic psy-

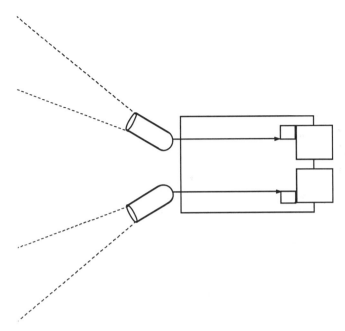

Figure 3.7
Pivoted transducers for directional sensitivity.

chology to work out the alternatives for striking that balance. Here, however, that exercise would be a complicating digression. Vehicles like that in figure 3.6 thus indicate the start of a road not taken. The vehicles to come could be similarly elaborated to allow for majority rule, thereby avoiding potential misses, but I will continue to explore the simplest vehicles with two channels and a threshold device acting as an and-gate. They will provide plenty of opportunities for synthetic psychology.

Squint has two photoreceptors, used for just one purpose. Yet their sheer location necessitates that their inputs are different; hence each bears slightly different information about the environment. Thus, we might want to exploit the differences in input. Among many possibilities, we start, following Braitenberg's second vehicle, with a wide-eyed Squint (figure 3.7).

The modifications of Squint, from left to right: First, we exploit the different positions of the transducers by pivoting them outward. This exaggerates their functional differences; now they are responsive to light sources in different directions. This change would be relatively minor in the old Squint, but here it is harnessed to create a new breed of vehicle: The two transducers separately drive two wheels, causing the vehicle to veer away from any light source not directly in its path.

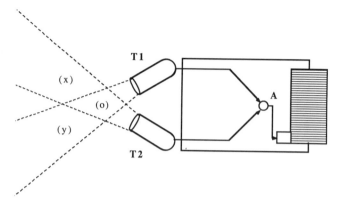

Figure 3.8
Transducers with overlapping receptive fields.

(If the connections crossed from the left transducer to the right wheel, and from the right transducer to the left wheel, it would careen toward any light source. Braitenberg suggests that observers of the resulting behaviors of these two vehicles would see "aggression" and "fear.") In its metamorphosis, however, the wide-eyed Squint no longer exhibits the reliability of its ancestor. We might expect, then, confirmatory channels along each sensory-motor pathway, ultimately leading to a redoubling of the receptors and so on in a recapitulation of the evolution of the original dual-channel Squint. The drive for reliability, then, fuels an evolutionary arms race, multiplying transducers and effectors through the generations.

Turning wide-eyed afforded Squint the opportunities for more discriminating responses to its environment. But there could be other simple but fruitful changes in the sensory apparatus. Figure 3.8 depicts a cross-eyed Squint. The original purpose of confirmation of the presence of illumination is preserved in the cross-eyed Squint. The receptors can point in any direction and serve that function, provided that their input feeds an and-gate. Turning cross-eyed, however, suddenly creates an interesting further opportunity for selective response. If the receptive fields of the two receptors overlap, then there is a focal region some distance in front of Squint, at point o. Squint will be particularly sensitive to a light source occupying that focal point.

From this simple beginning, Squint and its descendants enter a brave new world. Contrast the old Squints, including the wide-eyed Squint, with the cross-eyed alternative. Like any object, the earlier Squints were bathed in energy and information. The precursors detected energy from distant sources but could not discriminate between near and distant sources. As a result, they lacked the ability to coordinate their responses to objects in specific locations around them. They could not, in short, get beyond their own transducing skin. They were equipped to confirm, via multiple channels, how things were at the skin, and following differences from one transducer to another, could use that information to determine a trajectory. But specificity beyond that eluded them.

Now consider the cross-eyed Squint. It is the first instance of a device that can signal the presence of a stimulus at a particular distal location, the region o in the sketch. This is surely handy information. The present cross-eyed Squint still motors about on one wheel. Split the wheel, and the crossed field receptors could mediate a set of new responses. Once a stimulus sits in its cross hairs, a suitably wired cross-eyed Squint can respond with pursuit or avoidance responses tailored to an object right there, at o.

In addition, the cross-eyed vehicle preserves the enhanced functional capacities of its wide-eyed cousin. The two receptors still patrol the same distinct regions of space: x and y. But where T_1 monitored light in the vicinity of x in the wide-eyed case, T_2 covers that same region x in the cross-eyed alternative. That may issue in an internal variation of the vehicle of figure 3.5. The variation is shown in figure 3.9. In order for the light source on the right to drive the same-side wheel, the channel from the receptor sensitive to stimulation from that side will need to cross from left to right. Crossed eyes beget internal crossovers.[1] The net result is a vehicle equivalent in function to the wide-eyed Squint. But with the specialized innards, especially one or more and-gates, the cross-eyed Squint is capable of responding

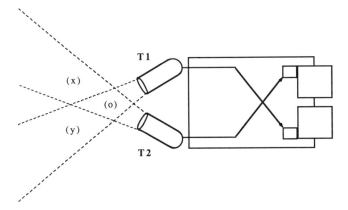

Figure 3.9
How crossed transducers might beget crossed connections.

to the presence of distal stimuli in specific locations, a great boon in the project of survival.

Synthetic Systems and Representation
So far I have described the rudimentary "evolution" of a device with some interesting emergent information processing capacities. Each stage of the evolution of that device was a near neighbor, a plausible mutation, of its precursor. It is highly unlikely that the evolution of the "nervous sytem" of the imaginary phylum *Squintae* recapitulates the phylogeny of any animal species. But the elaborations of Squint nonetheless modeled evolutionary resources and forces in two respects. First, biological versions of transducers, information channels, threshold devices (like the and-gate), and motor effectors are among the basic equipment of sensate, mobile organisms, just as in Squint. Second, reliability—the motive force in Squint variation—is essential to the survival of individuals, thus of species. Reliability includes safety from both false alarms and misses. Here I have stressed the escape from false alarms with nods toward false nonalarms, which can be accommodated by elaborating the basic framework of the cross-eyed Squint. By ringing the changes among those basic components, we observed a progressive improvement in reliability.

In section 3.3 and subsequent chapters, we will continue the breeding of Squint's descendants, assembling photodetectors into retinas, incorporating other kinds of transduction, and more. Presently, I suggest we pause to ponder the relationship of Squint (as sketched in figure 3.8) to the theme of representation. Consider the capacities of the cross-eyed Squint, wherein transducers with overlapping receptive fields provide input to a simple threshold device functioning as an and-gate. The basic inspiration for this functional architecture is the need for reliability in signal detection. If the detection of light is essential to Squint, then the multiple channel strategy improves Squint's abilities. We might say that the mechanism proposed affords Squint greater accuracy in its responses to the environment by reducing the risk of false alarms.

In enhancing accuracy, we created a system with increased specificity of response as well. In particular, Squint's crossed photodetectors provide one plausible model for mechanisms with linear selectivity. A single photocell cannot distinguish between a light source two inches away and a much brighter source at two feet, so it cannot carry information about the distance or the actual brightness of any source. But a device such as I've described not only serves to help confirm a signal, it is selectively sensitive to specific distal event types. When A is picking up information from both of its two input channels, then the upstream dependent event with the highest probability is the conjoint cause of both inputs, a light source at o. A multiple channel mechanism, in effect, focuses on its object.

Squint is the simplest case. Both accuracy and specificity can be further served by continued articulation of the basic information processing equipment. Relatively simple transducers (no more complicated than rods or cones) can be be harnessed to drive subtle and sophisticated detectors of distal environmental properties. In their internal sophistication, perhaps these devices can produce complex, articulate outputs. But the addition of secondary channels still follows the strategy of the simplest case, backing up the primary channel with secondary channels, all integrated by a single mechanism. Whatever integrative processes go on, their functional genesis might trace back to the conjunctive signal confirmation of the simple multiple channel mechanisms.

Whether simple or complex, devices like Squint are selective in another way: Only light can provoke T_1 and T_2, and thus A. The device is insensitive to many features of the stimulus (its temperature, for example), and insensitive to almost every feature of the environment. It has, in other words, a perspective from which it responds. Complex systems can respond to more patterns and types of energies in their environments, but still their response will be conditioned by the idiosyncrasies of their construction and the limits of their transducers.

Although Squint is primarily sensitive to a light source at position o, it is still fallible. We can produce a false alarm by placing separate light sources in the receptive fields of each photocell (at x and y, for example). But the simple device responds as before, exhibiting, prima facie, a capacity for error.

Finally, note that we have put A to work, driving the wheels of a Braitenwagon. Of course, many other motor behaviors might equally be controlled by something like A. A mechanical moth, for example, might well be guided by such a device, which would tell it when it was close to the flame—but not too close. Thus, the "firing" of A could lead, in the vehicle, to "uptake" that is specific to specific stimuli.

Accuracy, focus, (potential) articulation, uptake: these capacities emerged from a simple imaginary "nervous system" following a plausible "evolutionary" history. But they all made an earlier appearance in the discussion of the concept of representation in chapter 1. This suggests the hypothesis that events in systems like this might be very primitive instances of representations. Can events in a device this simple really be representations? I will argue that indeed they are and that this is a rock bottom rock simple representing device. It doesn't do much, but it does what it needs to, by the lights of the metatheory of chapter 1—although just barely. Evolved representing devices will tend to be complex, subtle, and sophisticated, but I will suggest that it is worthwhile to see them as elaborations of this simple network. But before exploring these possibilities in thought and action, we need a clearer description of Squint's modest accomplishments.

3.2 The Theory of Representation: Some Details

The preceding section ended with some bold hypotheses; the business of this section is to interpret them and examine some of their support. Toward these ends, I will first introduce a few technical distinctions, three special terms that will figure in the definition of representation. Then I will state the sufficient conditions for an event to be a representation. The hundred or so words of that definition will, not surprisingly, call for a lot of discussion, which will begin in this section and proliferate for the rest of the book.

Effective Stimuli
The cross-eyed Squint will once again provide the synthetic physiology lessons, as an example from which to generalize. (See figure 3.8 for a representation of its anatomy.) The special terms we need can all be specified with reference to the transducers, the various devices wherein one form of energy is translated into another. T_1 responds exclusively to some forms of energy (e.g., light but not sound), and the sources of light must fall within its receptive field, an area radiating from T_1 through o and y. Thus, the events on which T_1's response depends must be light emissions within a certain area specified in relation to T_1—anything from a match at two inches to a supernova at two light years. We call the set of these events the *effective stimuli* (ES) of T_1. T_2 has a set of effective stimuli that overlap with that of T_1, reflecting the difference in T_2's position and field of view. Its ES include light flashes in the field radiating from T_2 through o and x.

Each transducer has its unique set of ES, differing from all others according to its sensitivity and position. For any set of two or more transducers, we define the *mutually effective stimuli* (MES) as the intersection of their ES sets. The mutually effective stimuli of a set of transducers are the events that generate responses in all the transducers in the set. We can group the transducers any way we please, but here we are most interested in groupings according to downstream effects—we will be watching the sets of transducers whose outputs are integrated by devices like the threshold devices introduced in section 3.1. In T_1 and T_2, several sorts of events compose the mutually effective stimuli. The most conspicuous is light emission in the vicinity of o, the zone of overlap of the two receptive fields. But several composite events, for example simultaneous light emission at x and y, are also among the MES. Anything goes, as long as the events involved are of the right sort (in energy and location) to nudge both transducers.

The mutually effective stimuli can be further divided. On the one hand, the MES include single events—like light emission in the neighborhood of o. On the other, many of the events in the MES set are composite events, including the conjoint illumination at both x and y as well as many more baroque concatenations. I suspect that this is not an arbitrary division but rather reflects our conception of natural events (as introduced in chapter 1). Here the basic mereology of modest realism manifests itself. A natural event is a whole composed of parts, and we refer to it as a single event. An artificial event, on the other hand, is a concatenation of two or more natural events where the two events are not themselves part of a more inclusive natural event; we refer to it either with a plural noun ("the earthquakes"), a conjunctive phrase ("the earthquake and attendant tidal wave"), or with a special term coined just to cover the composite event. Among the mutually effective stimuli, some are natural events, and characteristically, single events. These we call the single mutually effective stimuli (SMES). "Single" is slightly misleading, however, if it suggests that there is only one member in the SMES set. There may be many events that are single mutually effective stimuli. But each of them is a single, natural event. A light source just to the right of o in figure 3.8 is a member of the SMES, as is a light source just to the left of o (assuming that each falls within the receptive fields of both transducers). But the pairing of light at x and at y is not among the SMES, since that is two events.

What a Representation Is
Now the theory can be stated. What follows is a recipe for representation that describes the conditions under which an event is a representation. To grasp the origin and import of the conditions, it might help to remember the architecture of the cross-eyed Squint: its multiple transducers directed at a common focal region, the and-gate wherein the transducer information is integrated, and the motor that the and-gate controls. Each of these is about to make a more formal appear-

ance. Squint's function was described in terms of dependencies between events (where dependency is understood probabilistically, as in chapter 2); dependency will be central to the abstract definition as well. Like other formal definitions, this may not be easy reading. Explanation and paraphrase, however, follow immediately.

A natural event r is a representation if it meets these conditions:

1. *The multiple channel condition* There is a set of at least two events, $\{v_1, v_2, \ldots, v_n\}$, such that r is dependent on the concurrent conjunction of at least two events in the set. (For example, r is a state change in an and-gate or a "majority rule" threshold device, as discussed in section 3.1.)

2. *The convergence condition* Events v_1 through v_n are further subject to the constraint that there is a set of single events, $\{u_1, \ldots, u_n\}$ (the single mutually effective stimuli), such that all of v_1 through v_n depend on each element of $\{u_1, \ldots, u_n\}$. The object of a representation is the element of $\{u_1, \ldots, u_n\}$ with the highest conditional probability, given r. (When conditional probabilities are tied, the representation is ambiguous.) (In practice, all the events occurring along the multiple channels depend on single sources.)

3. *The uptake condition* Event r has the capacity to cause either another representation or a salient behavioral event.

Each of the three conditions invites comment, following which we turn to some positive support for the theory. As a preliminary, however, it might be helpful to note that each condition concerns a specific part of the network of dependencies which are essential to representation. Figure 3.10, a schematization of the information flow through a vehicle like Squint, locates the joints. A closer look:

1. The multiple channel condition: This condition concerns the rela-

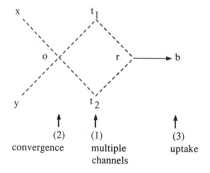

Figure 3.10
Three conditions sufficient for representation.

tion of a representation to "upstream" or afferent events. It states that there are several upstream events, and that the representation depends on two or more of them and will not occur otherwise. In other words, there are multiple information channels leading to the representation, and the representation integrates these input channels. That is, it takes input on two or more channels to bring about the representing event. Event r, a characteristic state change, occurs only if some concurrent conjunction of antecedent conditions is met. The antecedent events may begin at different times, but they must overlap for a time, and r occurs only following the overlap, the concurrent conjunction. Note, however, that although the antecedents need to be concurrent with each other, they need not be concurrent with the representation. It may take time, milliseconds to months, for the information from the concurrently occurring multiple channel events to seep through to their integrating device.

The definition describes conditions met by certain events, but we might talk equally of mechanisms in which these events occur. Such mechanisms might be called *representing devices*. When an object has the capacity to change state, and when the state change meets the conditions of representation, then the object is a representing device (R). Note that representing events and devices are described only by their dynamic relations to other events. The multiple channel condition, however, constrains R's function. Nothing fancy intended here: R's function is simply its statistically normal behavior. It may be that what R does is also what R is supposed to do, either by design or natural selection, but that is not a part of the present account. The functional constraint is straightforward: R is an and-gate or a majority rule threshold device.

The constraint is simple, but restrictive. Not everything is an and-gate or majority rule threshold device. Although any event can be described as the consequence of a conjunction of events—with conjoint events sufficient for its occurrence—not every event has particular event conjunctions as a necessary condition. And not every device operates in the way specified by condition 1, exhibiting a characteristic change of state when inputs arrive over multiple channels.

The presence of multiple channel devices is not by itself sufficient for representationality. Representations are dependent in special ways on other events. The multiple channel condition thus operates in tandem with a second condition.

2. The convergence condition: Installing an and-gate at the confluence of this watershed provides an indicator when conjunctions of antecedent conditions occur, but this is representationally useless without a further condition. The convergence condition picks out a

special circumstance, one in which we find, among the upstream watersheds of antecedent divergence, at least one instance of convergence. That is, there is at least one single mutually effective stimulus that can cause the multiple channels to fire, and thence cause the firing of the representing device. In other words, the convergence condition requires that the multiple channel device be uniquely situated so that sometimes one event (mediated by various channels) is sufficient for its activation. In this respect, the multiple information channels "focus" on a single event.

Of course, often there are many events among the single mutually effective stimuli, $\{u_i\}$. These are ordered by their conditional probabilities, given r (the representation). The u_i with the highest probability is, to a first approximation, the content of the representation. The essential difference between the multiple channel intermediaries and the unitary poles is the difference between many and one. Unitary endpoints are linked through a *collection* of mediating events. Specifically, between the u's and r lie a colony of intermediaries, multiple information channels, $\{v_1, \ldots, v_n\}$. *All* of $\{v_1, \ldots, v_n\}$ are necessary conditions for r (and there are at least two v_i). Thus, in ascribing representation to a system, we attend to two separate aspects of the whole: the *multiple parallel channels* and their divergence from and convergence to *unitary origins and termini*.

3. The uptake condition: This is directly motivated by the pretheoretical requirement that the content of a representation make some difference to the system. Now we are in a position to see the respect in which an effect (in a system) is content-driven: Effects are content-driven whenever they are caused by a representation. Our definition picks out a set of events via their relations to contents. Whenever these events occur, they have a specific, theory-dictated content, and they never occur otherwise. Thus, their effects automatically "respect" their content. Of course, such events have many effects. Here, we harness some of those effects within the representing system. In Squint, and in figure 3.10, the representing device drives a behavioral response directly. But in a more elaborate network, the output from r might be one of the inputs to a further representing device. We will examine examples of these more complex networks below.

For ease of reference, we should give the theory a name. A colleague, Yingti Xu, has observed that the central process I have described is dialectical: Multiple channels, each with a slightly different "point of view," are synthesized in a single integrative device, in which changes represent single events. The process of synthesis can be repeated, with representing devices contributing their output to further downstream representing processes (a main theme in chapter 5). Let us dub this the "dialectical theory of representation." (Whether that makes me a dialectical materialist is another question.)

Squint can provide a brief illustration of the application of the three conditions of the dialectical theory of representation. To begin, we apply the proposed definition of representation to the system consisting of the cross-eyed Squint and a light source at the convergent focal point of T_1 and T_2. The three conditions apply as follows: (1) Event r, the state change of A, is assumed to be robustly individuated—it is a natural event. We imagine an and-gate, and in so doing specify a device that we could individuate in many contexts. The intermediaries include events at N_1, C, and at T_1 and T_2. The conditions require that all must be realized in order for event r to occur, and Squint approximates this: N_1 is activated when T_1 is activated. C is activated when T_2 is activated. And R_1 is activated only when N_1 and C are activated. (2) But events in both T_1 and T_2 are dependent on the occurrence of the light source at o. Since we have assumed that the light source is a single object, and hence its illumination a single event, it meets the second clause of the triad. (3) Event r activates the motors and sets Squint wheeling but only when the Squint system is representing the presence of light at its convergent focus.

Why Is the Theory True?
Read in one way, all of *Simple Minds* is devoted to the direct and indirect support of the dialectical theory of representation. That support is distributed over the eight chapters. The lesser effort is indirect. It includes the challenging of alternative theories (the theme of chapter 2, with variations in section 3.3 and chapter 6). My main interest, however, is to put the theory directly to work. I will discuss the dialectical perspective as it bears on empirical research in artificial intelligence and neuroscience (chapters 4 and 5) and as it illuminates philosophical issues concerning the language of thought, consciousness, and cognition (chapters 6, 7, and 8). Success in each of these applications and extensions should build confidence in the whole.

Of immediate importance, however, is the fit of theory and metatheory. One of the pretheoretical constraints discussed in section 1.2 flags the compositionality of representation—this issue must be tabled until we examine more complex systems. But the theory accommodates the other constraints. Each of the three conditions, in fact, captures an aspect of our aspirations for a theory of representation. The first, the multiple channel condition, is the dialectical handling of the demand for an explanation of accuracy. Dependency is fundamental, and the multiple channels function to increase accuracy. Indeed, the need for accuracy motivated the synthetic evolution of the exemplary vehicle of section 3.1. (Error will be treated below.) The convergence condition explains the origin of specificity, the ability of a representing system to focus on its proper objects. And the uptake condition, as discussed, explains how representations get put to work in representing systems.

Each of these applications is direct. But compartmentalizing the conditions obscures their most important feature—their synergy. The three conditions fit together and support each other uniquely. In one stroke, their confluence offers living systems what they need most from their information-processing capacities while offering behavioral explanation the theoretical leverage it needs most when considering those same living systems. We will begin with the latter issue, the explanation of behavior.

Why would anyone want to talk about representations in the explanation of behavior? The reason, of course, is the content connection. When representational explanation is successful, it illuminates a link between the behavior being explained and the content of the representations imported to explain it. (On this, see Pylyshyn 1984, Garfield 1988, Fodor 1986, Lloyd 1986.) Representation and behavior are both directed at the world, and when the former explains or interprets the latter, in some sense both "reach toward" the same objects, events, and situations. For example, suppose we decide it is appropriate to explain a favorite bit of toad behavior—snapping at prey—in terms of representations. The following might compose part of the explanation: The toad snapped at the bug at location o because (in part) it represented the presence of prey at o. Here the overlap between the content of the representation and the description of the behavior is evident. Without that connection, there would be little point in adding the representational component. (Contrast: The toad snapped at the bug at o because it represented the presence of a predator at location z.)

One task of a theory of representation is to make the content connection clear. A theory of representation is worth adding to the resources of psychological explanation only to the extent that it can show that there is something inside the toad that can be said, independently of the behavior, to represent the presence of prey at o, and that this something contributes to behavior that is tied to the content of the representation.

Now look at this issue again from the toad's "point of view." Toads have to eat. The need to eat, of course, is not a felt need for the toad, but it is nonetheless a fact about it. That means that when a toad zaps its tongue at some target, there had better be food there at least some of the time. Random snapping will not work. That is why toads have nervous systems—so that if prey crawls through some visible nearby location o, they can get the sticky tips of their tongues to precisely that location.

How do they do that? In chapter 5 we will look at the details, but for illustrative purposes we can consider a speculative proposal: Toads execute their behavior through the mediation of a representing system on the dialectical model. We have already discussed the need for minimizing false alarms, a need that will also be an important component of prey detection. But in this example, the animal not only needs to avoid false responses, but coordinate the true. Let us consider how a generic representational system might serve these ends.

Figure 3.11 displays again the stylized schema answering to the three requirements of the dialectical theory of representation. We now face two problems: First, how does the response b come to be coordinated with respect to an event o, rather than with respect to a composite event consisting of x and y? Second, if the organism is correct in keying its response to o, what explains its accuracy? After all, there is nothing about the pattern of stimulation, t_1 and t_2, that can distinguish among members of a set of mutually effective stimuli containing many elements.

We can answer both questions by appeal to the "informational architecture" sketched in the diagram and codified in the three conditions of the theory. Let us look first to the world of the system, events x, y, and o. Suppose that the independent probabilities of each of these are about the same (where, for example, $Pr(x)$ is the probability of a bug crossing through location x, $Pr(y)$ is a bug through location y, and so forth). Given that bugs might be anywhere, how does the system "decide" where to zap? The decision is built into the interaction of t_1, t_2, and r. Event r occurs in an and-gate; it requires a signal from both t_1 and t_2 to send its signal to b. Earlier we noted that the

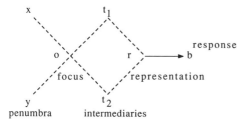

Figure 3.11
A representation and its necessary context.

multiple channel condition could be met by any of several mutually effective stimuli, of which o and (x and y) are examples. But note that even though o, x, and y are independently equiprobable, o is much more likely than the conjunction of x and y. I think the following generalization is plausible: By and large, single mutually effective stimuli events are more likely than complex (conjoint) mutual stimuli events. This is an empirical generalization, not a logical truth; but as we reflect on more complex cases (cases with more information channels and greater specificity), it seems more and more plausible.

Note what a handy generalization that is. It means, for example, that the toad could do worse than snap at location o. In fact, the toad is well served by taking r as the "go code" for the reflex sequence "snap at o." So also for many more complex systems. There seems to be a correlation between specificity, which is served by the addition of more channels between o and r, and accuracy, understood as the likelihood of a stimulus actually being present at o. Dialectical representation gives us that.

Thus the dialectical model answers the pressing needs of organisms to coordinate their responses with reality. At the same time, it answers the needs of a theory of representation to make sense of representational explanation. We will return to the issue of content ascription presently, but for now we can note that the dialectical schema provides an account of content (o in the schema) while explaining how that content comes to cause the appropriate coordinated behavior. For that reason, I think it is fitting to call this a theory of representation.

Indirect Support for the Three Conditions
To further support the proposed "dialectical" theory of representation, let us consider what happens when we remove each of the three conditions that together compose the core theory. First, suppose we delete the multiple channel condition. Figure 3.12 illustrates the results of a channelectomy. (We assume that r is no longer instantiated

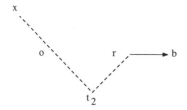

Figure 3.12
Life without multiple channels.

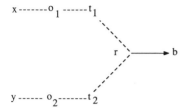

Figure 3.13
The network without convergence.

in an and-gate or majority rule threshold device.) The price of this deletion is high. In this case, the occurrence of r tells us nothing about the likelihood of any specific upstream event; it is equally an indicator of t_2, o, and x. We thus lose any special purchase on accuracy or selectivity, reintroducing the problem of linear selectivity discussed in chapter 2. Were our toad so crippled, nothing in its informational context would enable it to discriminate between a bug at o and a bug at x. If the toad continues to snap at o, then in a world where bugs might be anywhere, its success rate will decline, perhaps disastrously. And when we attempt to explain the toad's behavior, we will find nothing about the internal structure of the toad that indicates that o, as opposed to x, is a crucial determinant of behavior. Instead, we might say that the toad has a simple, nonrepresentational reflex: When t_2 occurs, the toad snaps at location o. The "content connection" is lost.

Figure 3.13 illustrates the network without condition 2, the convergence condition. Unlike the previous alternative, this is a network with an and-gate at r, but there need be no single stimuli among the mutually effective stimuli. Events x and y, that is, are independent. There is no obvious way to discriminate among the MES, which include elements like (x and y), (x and o_2), (o_1 and y), and (o_1 and o_2). They lack the natural and probabilistic beacons that informed the dialectical model, distinguishing its proper object amid the stew of possible events. It is also hard to see the general use for networks like the above, which exhibit both linear and lateral sprawl. A toad receiving such ambiguous sensory information would face a compounded problem of underdetermination. It quite literally wouldn't know which way to turn, nor at what distance to zap.

Finally, in figure 3.14 we block the effects of r, rendering it inert. Two crucial conditions on representation are met, but what's the point? Event r is a dead end, so it cannot figure in an explanation of behavior, either directly (as in figure 3.10) or through its influence on other representations (recall that either sort of uptake is allowed by

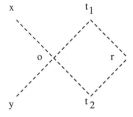

Figure 3.14
All dressed up and no place to go.

the third condition). Event r would be a curious one, but not a factor in any explanation of behavior and so not a strong candidate for a special role in psychology.

In sum, among the events on which a representation depends, the single mutually effective stimuli are the most probable of the mutually effective stimuli, probably the most specific, and probably the most apt to explain the behavior they probably provoke. The dialectical model of representation explains the context in which dependent events realize these conditions. This suggestive confluence wins it prima facie support.

Content Ascription
Our next task is the refinement of the concept of content in the theory of representation. Returning to the primitive "model system," the cross-eyed Squint, recall that I suggested as a rough first approximation that a representing device inside Squint represents the emission of light at an approximate location o. Suppose the light source situated at Squint's convergent focus happens to be a 40-watt GE soft-white purchased at the Star Market on the corner of Boylston and Killmarnock on March 18, 1988. Shall we say, accordingly, that what r represents is the illumination of a 40-watt GE soft-white purchased at the Star Market, and so forth? Yes and no. Recall that part of the metatheory of representation included a distinction between the extensional and explicit senses of the content of a representation. We are now in a position to illuminate the functional foundations of the distinction between those two kinds of content.

We begin with the light bulb. Like any other object, the light bulb can travel under any of an indefinite number of descriptions: "source of light 24 cm from each of T_1 and T_2," "40-watt GE soft-white purchased at Star, etc.," "object referred to in *Simple Minds*, page 72," and so on. These different descriptions and individuations work by assigning different properties to the one object, the light bulb in question. The light bulb instantiates each of these various properties, so it is a common element to each member of a set of events (recalling that events are understood here as property instantiations). So we have one object, many events.

Now let us consider the light bulb in its context, a context that includes Squint. We have defined the content of Squint's atomic representation in terms of dependent events, not objects. As imagined, only certain sorts of events make a difference that can be reflected in Squint's response—which is to say, only certain (instantiated) properties of the object figure in the determination of the content. Among these events: the conjunction of the emission of light and the location of the bulb relative to Squint's two transducers. Remove either of these conjuncts, and, other things being equal, event r—the representation—does not occur. The other events co-realized by the light bulb are not in this dependency. Let the bulb be made by GTE, purchased at Stop 'n' Shop, referred to on page 24—none of these has any effect on the occurrence of r. Accordingly, these events are not represented.

But the object that bears the property whose instantiation comprises the represented event is that light bulb of which (ex hypothesi) all of those descriptions (GE, Star Market, mention in *SM*) are true. So it too stands in a special relation to the representation. The coordination of this local metaphysics with the structure of representation is straightforward: The object or objects in which the represented event is instantiated is the *extensional content* of the representation. The event represented, that is, the event on which the representation depends, is the *explicit content* of the representation. So, Squint represents (extensionally) the 40-watt GE purchased at Star etc., and it represents (explicitly) the occurrence of light energy at the convergence point of its transducers.

Several other features of representational parlance fall into place around this partition. First, the extensional and explicit descriptions of content can be combined using representation-as. For example, Squint represents the 40-watt light bulb referred to in *SM* as a light source at its convergent focal point. Or, in general, any representation represents its extensional content (under any description) as an object described in terms of the properties whose instantiation is its explicit content. Second, the distinction between extensional and explicit content enables us to capture the metatheoretical representational capacity of perspective. The perspective of a representation is defined by its explicit content. What a representation represents are those features that can make a difference to it, on which it depends. That idiosyncracy is its characteristic perspective.

Extensional and explicit content differ along another axis as well. Suppose we switch one 40-watt bulb for another, indistinguishable bulb, both in the same focal location. Now we find that after the switch, event r's extensional content has changed—originally it represented (extensionally) bulb A, now bulb B. But its explicit content has remained constant—it still represents the flux of light flowing from its focal point. It is explicitly blind to the switch in extensional reality. This, I suggest, is an effect of perspective. The perspective of a representing device limits its ability to discriminate tokens of the particular type defined by the properties whose instantiation it can detect. So, explicit content is coarse grained. But extensional content is not so limited. Any tactic of discrimination can be brought to bear in the individuation (from our third-person point of view) of extensional content. So, extensional content ascription is as fine grained as our language and intellect will permit.

Error
With these distinctions behind us, we can next survey the logical geography of error. We've already glanced toward one example: Instead of locating a single light source at Squint's convergent focus, we place two sources, each within the area of sensitivity of only one of the transducers (for example, at x and y in figure 3.8). Thus the transducers fire, and so does A. Does event r in A represent the two sources? Not according to the definition. The definition directs us to look for a single event as both the explicit and extensional content of the representation. Given an understanding of a particular representing device, we can specify the explicit content, as afforded by the perspective of the device. It will be the single event with the highest conditional probability, given r. The event specification, in turn, enables us to describe the extensional content, the object represented. It is simply any object bearing the property, where that property's instantiation is the explicit content. Since the content assignment depends on conditional probabilities, all of this content determination can be counterfactual. That is, we can talk about the content of representations even when the represented events do not occur and the represented object does not exist. We can even talk of the content of a representation when none of the mutually effective stimuli are present. In that case, we are talking of the content a representing event would have if it occurred in a given system. We might call this the *latent content* of the representing device or system.

Where two light sources are placed at x and y, accordingly, our content assignment to the Squint system is just what it was in the original case in which one source illuminated both transducers—event r in A represents a single light source at Squint's convergent focus. But that representation is false—there is no such source. Its falsehood is both extensional and explicit: Neither the event nor any object realizing the event exist.

Under the circumstances just described, Squint delivers a false alarm. Squint can also err by missing its target. Suppose Squint is navigating in a heavy fog. Suppose the light source is present at the convergent focus, but not enough light penetrates the fog to activate both transducers. (For simplicity, assume that no light source at the convergent focus could be bright enough to penetrate the fog.) A, accordingly, slumbers. There are two ways to describe the fogbound system. The first acknowledges that any net of dependent events can be called a system, so the interpolation of fog need not be considered an extrasystemic event. That is, we have two systems, Squint$_{clear}$, consisting of light source, channels, A, motor, all interdependent; and we have Squint$_{foggy}$ in which the light source is informationally out of reach of both transducers. The latter system, it seems, is not a representing system at all, since with the fog counted in, no single event can activate both channels. Of course, if the system can't represent anything, then it can't represent the presence of a light source at its focal point. The second interpretation of the socked-in system regards the fog as extrasystemic, an intervention in the various information channels of the representing device. In this case, all the conditions for representation are met, but at least one of the relevant channels is blocked. Once again, no representation occurs.

Which of the two interpretations one adopts is a subtle question, relying on some dicey judgments about what is normal for Squint and its environment. If Squint "evolved" in continuous dense fog, then we might prefer the first interpretation, under which Squint isn't a representing system at all. Then its crossed eyes would be functionally irrelevant, a mysterious appendix to a mechanical dinosaur. On the other hand, if the fog is an exceptional occurrence, then we might think Squint to be a representing system, hampered in the short run by fog. Possibly, the weather statistics over the life of the device will be enough to ground the judgment of normalcy. But possibly, what is normal may have a teleological force, traceable to the purposes, including the evolutionary purposes, which inform Squint's design (cf. Millikan 1984, Dennett 1987b). But this issue is beside the point. Under the purview of representational theory, our two interpretations have the same result: Squint fails to represent the light source at location o. And this too is a sort of error.

Ambiguity

From error we turn to a near kin, ambiguity. Imagine placing two light sources as close as possible to focal point o. Case 1: Suppose the two lamps are each sufficient and properly situated to activate both transducers and A. The illumination of each lamp is a single event, and the definition suggests that the most likely event is the content of the representation. Suppose, however, that the two occurrences are equiprobable. Then the representation is indefinite between the two possibilities—the distinction between them is beneath the resolving power of the paired transducers, and either event might be the explicit content of the representation. Accordingly, one cannot say which of the two light sources is the unique extensional content of the representation. The representation is ambiguous in extensional content.

Case 2: Suppose neither lamp alone is bright enough to activate either transducer, but both together are enough. The explicit content of the representation is the occurrence of a light source at o, and this event occurs. The transducers are blind, once again, to the extensional correlate. In this case, two objects underlie the one event. The explicit content is indefinite with respect to the two sources. The extensional content includes them both, since both underlie the event which is represented. The representation, in other words, represents two light sources as a single source.

In sum, a representing device like Squint is surrounded by a vast web of (actual and possible) dependent events. The effort of these two chapters has been to trim the web—to describe the nonrepresentational facts about the web that isolate certain events in ways that correspond to our cultivated intuitions about the content of representations. Whole classes of events could be cut off with a broad scythe, but when external dependent events emerged as the class of finalists, our thought-experimental technique had to approach surgical precision. On the one hand, we had to simultaneously respect several dimensions of specificity, both among the events themselves and among the descriptions under which the events were individuated. That required some extreme restrictions on admissable events, which restrictions were achieved by describing convergent functional networks and the and-gates that might exploit the special information opportunities of convergent nets. But, on the other hand, we had to avoid becoming too fine-grained. We didn't want to allow ascriptions of content to become more detailed than our simple representing devices could handle. And, equally, we didn't want to tie content inevitably to truth. We had to make room for errors of several sorts; this too, the multiple channel model of representation permitted. The question before us in this chapter so far has been whether multiple convergent channels are sufficient to meet the metatheory of representation. The answer, I suggest, is yes.

But our progress is Pyrrhic if we cannot go much further than this. The systems pondered so far are, at best, atomic representational systems and utterly incapable of supporting any interesting cognition. We must construct or discover representations, in the sense developed here, in more complex systems. Our interest in representation grows as we rise along the continuum of complexity that terminates, so far as we know, with human beings. Accordingly, with this sentence we turn a corner and attend to a zoo of complexity. First, in section 3.3, we expand upon some of the capacities of monorepresenters, kin to Squint. The following chapters confront multiple representers and various dimensions of complexity in synthetic and living representational systems.

3.3   The Components of More Complex Systems

Representation and Subrepresentation

We begin this section with another Braitenwagon, a hybrid of two considered in section 3.1. Figure 3.15 depicts "Sleuth." Like its ancestors, Sleuth is a worshipper of light sources. But unlike some of its precursors, Sleuth's responses are more sophisticated. First, Sleuth has two wheels, driven by two separate variable motors (M_1, M_2). The conditions under which the motors turn are complex: T_1 activates M_1, and T_2 activates M_2. Thus a light source at x, activating T_2, tends to make Sleuth turn toward x. Similarly, Sleuth will turn in pursuit of a light source at y. However, the output of T_1 and T_2 does not solely feed the two motors; it also branches to provide the input to a Squint-style representing device (R_1), in this case an and-gate in the func-

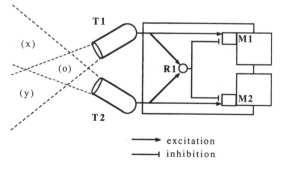

```
——————▶  excitation
——————|  inhibition
```

Figure 3.15
A more complex vehicle.

tional context discussed at length in the previous section. When R_1 is activated, as it is when a light source is present at about location o, it sends outputs to both motors. That output, however, is inhibitory. Thus, a light source at o will inhibit the ultimate response of the two motors.

Now suppose a single light source appears in the neighborhood of Sleuth. If the source passes into the receptive field of either transducer, Sleuth whirrs to life, heading in an arc toward the source. Just before Sleuth crashes into it, however, the source crosses through the focal point o. R_1 puts on the brakes and holds Sleuth in position as long as the source remains stationary. But if the source begins to move away, Sleuth will reorient to the moving source and follow, stalking it to the limits of its very limited capacities.

A few secondary cases round out our picture of Sleuth's behavior. First, Sleuth is easy to overwhelm. Two light sources, at x and y, turn it into Buridan's ass, stalled between two options. Similarly, in an environment characterized by light everywhere, bright enough to continuously activate both transducers, Sleuth is also immobile but poised. Then a shadow passing over Sleuth's transducer will cause it to stir, turning away from the dark patch toward the light. The circuit in Sleuth would be a useful one for a synthetic firefly, affording a minimal capacity for the nocturnal pursuit of other fireflies and an equally minimal capacity for evading threatening shadows by day.

Turning aside from the behavior, let us analyze Sleuth's representational architecture. Here we observe an overlay of systems, the first instance of a duality that will become important before we conclude. Sleuth is two systems in one: a *representational* system and an *informational* system. The representational system is familiar to us from the excursions with Squint: the characteristic multiple channels originating from a single source, exploited by an and-gate and driving, ultimately, some behavior. But in this case many of the same resources comprise an informational system that partly determines Sleuth's behavior, but does so without representations. The channel from T_1 to M_1 is part of this system. It is clearly an informational system, in that events at M are dependent on events within T_1's receptive field (as well as on many intermediaries). And it can be considered in isolation from the representational system; we might remove R_1 entirely, and still Sleuth would respond to light sources, though with a reduced range of responses. Representational systems, of course, are informational systems too, since a representation is informationally dependent on other events. But as this chapter has discussed at length, a representational system is informational and more. Accordingly, we might call the merely informational system a *subrepresentational* system.

In Sleuth, the shared resources of the two systems may obscure the important differences between them. The most important of these differences is the connection between events in the representational system and specific distal stimulus types. As we explored through the example of Squint, the representational system, even in that simple incarnation, has the capacity to "focus" on, or selectively respond to, light sources at or near a specific location. The informational system also responds to distal stimuli, since it too picks up distant light sources, but doesn't discriminate those stimuli as distant. It might equally respond to proximal stimuli, occurring right at the "transducer skin" of the system. From the perspective of the informational system, the light source could be anywhere. It will be just as responsive to stimuli exactly at the transducer surface as it will be to stimuli at a distance. Because the informational system is without specific or distal selectivity, we might say that to it, stimuli are indefinite.

Flexibility: Selectivity Without Specialization
The accent so far has been upbeat: Representing devices afford synthetic systems with specificity in distal representation, a useful capacity even in very simple environments. But there is a price: Selectivity entails specialization. A representing device like that at the heart of Squint or Sleuth is a special purpose device. How will the descendants of these simple vehicles get along in an environment where there were many distinct and significant stimuli? One possibility is to multiply the special-purpose transducers and representing devices, but this expansion comes at a price. Vehicles overladen with specialists and top-heavy with dedicated transducers require more resources to survive and could wither in a world of scarcity. The problem here is not fully met by the subrepresentational system—it has its work to do, but that is general purpose work. The earnest business of life in the nonsynthetic world demands considerable attention to details. How can special-purpose representing devices be put to the best use, while keeping the overhead low?

One key to optimal employment of representations is flexibility. At heart, the strategies of flexibility optimize the representational and informational resources by putting the available resources to many different uses rather than by multiplying specialists. But flexibility is a flexible concept, and there are many ways for systems to be flexible. We will tour a few of the apparent synthetic possibilities.

The first flexible mechanism is already prominent in Squint and Sleuth: wheels. Mobility permits the continuous repositioning of transducers, so from moment to moment the same system is re-positioned to detect and represent different distal events in its world. We might put this in terms of representational theory: Though the latent explicit content of the representations within Squint and Sleuth is fixed, the latent extensional content—the real objects scanned by the transducers—is constantly shifting. Naturally, the systems are tuned to keep objects of interest at an appropriate distance.

Occurrent and Stored Representations
A second route to flexibility is storage. So far we have pondered simple occurrent representing devices. These are active just during the event they represent—in Squint and Sleuth, R_1 is activated just while T_1 and T_2 are active. It's easy to imagine a device that would hold its activation state beyond the termination of the represented event: Suppose R_1 is a toggle switch, and the activation of the two transducers switches the toggle into its ON state. In this case, the event of instantiating the property of being on endures long beyond the event which is represented thereby. Yet the analysis of the system as a representing system is the same as that for an occurrent represen-tation: The correct functional dependencies are present; all that has changed is the duration of the representing event. The example sug-gests a general mark of stored representations: If a representational event r endures beyond the termination of its explicit content o, then r is a *stored representation*. (Otherwise, r is occurrent.) We can, for example, imagine a stored representation that begins with the onset of the effective stimulus, and that would encode the current or past presence of the stimulus. Or we could imagine a representing device that was activated just as the stimulus ceases, at its "offset." It would encode just the past occurrence of a stimulus.

Storage enlarges our concept of distal representation by suggesting the beginnings of representation of events distant in time (as well as space) from the representing event. But the basic mechanism of stor-age just discussed is extremely limited in its capacity for representing temporal relationships. (It resembles imprinting more than memory.) From the system's perspective, there is no record of when the repre-sented event occurred—no temporal specificity, in short. So with respect to plotting events on a time line, the stored representational system considered above has no more temporal specificity than an informational system with toggles but no and-gates. Nonetheless, we shall see over the next paragraphs and chapters that even simple stored representations can be the mediators of some surprisingly complex behavior.

Since a system with a stored representation has different response characteristics than one without, the capacity for storage enables one system to be two. Consider Pounce, a slight modification of the architecture of Sleuth, in which R_1 is replaced by a stored representing device, SR_1, with the following characteristic. SR_1, in its unactivated states (without dual inputs) nonetheless emits a steady-state signal which, as in R_1, inhibits Pounce's motor response. However, the activated response of SR_1 is to cease emitting its inhibitory output for two minutes. Its effect, in short, is the disinhibition of Pounce's motors. The resultant behavior: Pounce waits, poised for action but immobile, until a light source wanders into its convergent focus. At that second, it roars into action. Since SR_1 ceases its inhibition for the duration of its activation, Pounce's subrepresentational system takes the wheel. No matter which way the light source moves, Pounce careens toward it on a collision course (perhaps with its mouth open). The general point again: One way to regard SR_1 is as a switch that changes Pounce from one system into another. In each of its two states, Pounce is equipped for two environmental permutations: In the first, while no light sources are ready-to-hand, Pounce is a circumspect watcher. In the second, where a light source is near, Pounce is a pouncer.

The And-Accumulator

Let us now imagine a device for storing representations called an "and-accumulator" (AA). Like the other devices from the synthetic workshop, the AA is a threshold device, a device that changes state when it receives input above its threshold. But unlike the preceding and-gates and majority rule threshold devices, the AA has a *variable threshold*. That is, each time it receives input over both channels, it not only produces its characteristic output but its threshold decreases slightly as well. The decrease persists for a short time, after which the AA slowly returns to normal. Further, the threshold depression can accumulate. If AA picks up a succession of paired inputs, each leads to a further lowering of its threshold. As a result, there will be an ongoing record in the and-accumulator of instantaneous frequency of the joint occurrence of its input conditions. When its threshold is normal, we know it has not encountered paired inputs in the recent past. But when the threshold is very depressed, we know that the paired inputs have been arriving thick and fast. If we suppose that those multiple inputs arrive from a single source, then we might conclude that the AA is a representing device and its internal threshold depression a stored representation of the regular occurrence of a certain event in the surrounding environment.

Of what use might an and-accumulator be to a motile organism? As the threshold of the AA decreases, it may ultimately become sensitive to just one input, instead of its usual two. The sensitized AA might fire off its characteristic response, then, when just one input channel is active. (The AA is functionally similar to Braitenberg's (1984) "mnemotrix wire.") But in a system that needs to detect a certain event type in its environment, this hypersensitivity might be very useful. The lowered threshold is the sign that one sort of input has frequently appeared with another. In that case, it is a safe bet to jump at either input alone, as if both were present. It is as if, on the basis of one input, the system anticipated the other.

The analogy between this tinkertoy and associative conditioning is obvious. We might construct a vehicle inspired by Pavlov: It consists of two transducers, a "food-taste detector" and a "ringing-bell detector," both connected to an and-accumulator that activates a "salivator" (or whatever the Radio Shack catalog calls them). By repeated pairing of food tastes and ringing bells, the threshold of the AA decreases until the bell alone is sufficient to activate the salivator. Clearly, the analogy is imperfect, but it nonetheless suggests the utility of organic analogues to and-accumulators.

This is a new sort of dynamism: The same informational network drops from being a representational system to being a subrepresentational system. What once was a dual-channel device (and thus met the conditions for representing) now becomes a simpler single-channel device. In its sensitized response, this system does not represent anything, since only one channel is active. But it uses a (preestablished) representation (the threshold depression). Nor does it perform any inferences, since the system neither represents all the premises of any inference nor the rules governing the inference. So the "anticipation" we ascribe to it is not a peculiar internal state but rather a dispositional property inherent in the dynamics of the and-accumulator.

First- and Second-Order Dynamics
In sum, two kinds of flexibility help extend the behavioral repertoires of simple systems: physical flexibility (the literal rearrangement of transducers) and informational flexibility (the modulation of response properties of the informational and representational network controlling the behavior). The latter, internal, dynamism suggests two levels of understanding of a system: We can understand its first-order dynamics, the dynamics of its representational or informational networks at any given moment; and we can understand its second-order dynamics, the dynamics of changes in the first-order networks.

Higher-order dynamics are also possible. For example, over a long time SR_1 could become less readily activated, and as a result Pounce could lose its appetite for the chase. Accordingly, from the perspectives of different levels of understanding, we can talk of different systems. Pounce has two first-order dynamics, so we can think of it as instantiating, in alternation, two first-order systems.

These latest exercises in synthetic psychology only begin to survey the strategies for flexibility, but even this simple menu affords wide elaboration and permutation. Mobility, for example, need not be limited to the mobility of a whole (rigid) system. In addition, one can readily imagine mobile parts, including pivoting transducers, feelers, limbs. And the monomaniacs of representation so far considered, with their limited components and singular contents, only hint at the options available in sophisticated representing systems. The synthetic options are unlimited. It would be a wonderful project for someone with a large computer to create a simulated world of competing Braitenwagons, with a mechanism for mutating innards. I imagine that the results would be strange, and edifying.

Can Representation Really Be This Simple?
If you have been convinced by the foregoing, proceed directly to chapter 4. If not, perhaps you find the representations described so far to be too simple. "It can't be that these clunking little machines can represent!" This discomfort is not surprising, given the strategy of theory development employed here: I've introduced complexity with grudging stinginess, proposing and defending mechanisms that only barely do what they need to do. The method of synthesis is one that respects a corollary of Occam's razor—Occam's handcuff. Occam's handcuff warns us against the unnecessary invocation of complexity, complexity for its own sake. (Occam's handcuff, accordingly, prevents hand waving.) Of course, representation in the wild will be realized in systems of enormous complexity. But complexity as such is not essential to represention. Nonetheless, since the systems synthesized here barely account for the capacities of representation outlined in chapter 1, they will seem just barely plausible as the seat of genuine representation. I'll close this chapter, accordingly, by facing a few of the lingering doubts.

Recall, for starters, that the ambitions of the theory of representation are limited to accounting for mere representation. The representing devices I've described do not, and are not intended to, account for belief, desire, thought, and so on. Inner states like beliefs require the addition of many further conditions—for example, beliefs and ideas seem essentially to enter into inferences, and, ipso facto, to stand in coherence relations to other beliefs and ideas. (See Stich 1983 for discussion.) Those interrepresentational relations still lie ahead. Further, so far nothing has been said about consciousness. We have not established that dialectical representing systems have any form of awareness (we return to this in chapter 7).

However, the work so far has not been irrelevant to these advanced topics. The more complex states are nonetheless representational; that is, they are states with content or "aboutness." So representations must at least be part of their structure, and the work behind us constitutes an important part of the analysis of mind. Yet some may feel that even the limited target of representationality demands more complexity than the dialectical representers possess. Of course, very complex representations can be built from the simple components discussed, but some readers may feel that inner representations must be more complicated. Let us briefly examine the variations of the charge of oversimplification.

First, perhaps the demand is for increased complexity of internal structure. Basic representations can be internally simple, as simple as a flashing light or a spiking neuron. Shouldn't a full-blooded representation be at least as complex as, say, a sentence or a picture? That intuition can be challenged with a familiar round of thought experiments. First, recall the example of monkeys typing *Hamlet*; with world enough and time, random letter strings will duplicate not only the works of Shakespeare, but every other stretch of poetry or prose (along with a huge corpus of gobbledygook). Even though some letter strings look like regular sentences, the randomness of their creation suggests that they are not, since they are not appropriately hooked up to the community of language users. Similar examples arise with other forms of representation. Putnam (1981), for example, imagines a foraging ant tracing a likeness of Winston Churchill in the sand. The moral of these tall tales is simply that complex internal structure is not sufficient to make an object or event into a representation. Second, although most of the representations we encounter in public are rather complex, recall that they needn't be so. One could, for example, take a half-tone photograph of a small dot, producing a photograph in which one atomic dot represents another.

The cases of complex nonrepresentations plus simple representations are indirect reminders of a central theme of this study: Representations derive their content (and the complexity of that content) from the networks in which they are embedded. A representing device may itself be rather simple but reflect a complex set of conjoint input conditions, and so embody complex content.

Intuitions about complexity, however, may extend beyond internal complexity. Perhaps one could insist that to be a representation is to be intricately related to the rest of the representing system, not just to the objects of representation. One might, for example, suppose that nothing could be a representation unless it is understood as a representation by the user of the representation. Representations, according to this view, must be interpreted; certainly interpretation is a more complex business than simply standing in certain information relations to certain objects. The reply to this is to point out, first, that one can imagine uninterpreted representations (e.g., automatically produced photographs), and second, to note that some representations must be uninterpreted. That's because interpretation itself is a process that issues in representations; typically, the representations that comprise an interpretation are about the representations that are being interpreted and their relationship to their objects. Now if the representations that compose an interpretation themselves have to be interpreted, then there would be a regress of interpretations of interpretations. Our simple representing devices, on the other hand, are content-driven without the extra process of interpretation.

Interpretation imports additional (and unnecessarily) complex effects of representations. But perhaps the intuition of complexity may drive one toward additional complexity in the cause of representations. One may, for example, require that representations be the outcomes of a process initiated by a special intention. But once again, recall that there must be unintended representations, for the reason that an intention is itself a special sort of representation, its content having something to do with the state of affairs which results if the intention is fulfilled. If one must intend to intend, then we face a regress of intentions (Putnam 1981). So if there are some unintended representations, then intention cannot be a necessary condition for representation. This is not surprising. We would expect perception, for example, to be "data driven"—some representations, like those of approaching predators, must form by automatic processes.

In short, the theory of representation is constrained on two sides. On the one side, it must be complex enough to account for functions like the selectivity of representation. But on the other side, it must not be too complex, on pain of interpolating a secondary process that is itself representational. The minimal representing systems developed here are dumb, inarticulate, and automatic. Each of us may be an intelligent, conscious, intentional being, but our basic parts are not. Representations are basic; pondering them in their simplest form teaches us a great deal about their essential structure.

Many questions remain. A theory of representation is most useful when it can be applied and extended as an interpretive, organizing, and predictive tool in cognitive science and philosophy. Parts II and III of *Simple Minds* address some of the immediate issues that spring from the outline of the dialectical theory of representation. These questions include: What are the limits of synthetic system construction? Where are representations in actual nervous systems? Are there states of affairs that cannot be represented by natural representational systems? How are representations related to consciousness? How do representations interact in human cognition? How do representations compose minds?

PART II
Interpreting Neural Networks

Chapter 4

Parallel Distributed Processing and Cognition:

Only Connect?

All the materials of our thought are due to the way in which one elementary process of the cerebral hemispheres tends to excite whatever other elementary process it may have excited at any former time. The number of elementary processes at work, however, and the nature of those which at any time are fully effective in rousing the others, determine the character of the total brain-action, and, as a consequence of this, they determine the object thought of at the time. . . . Its production . . . is to be explained by a merely quantitative variation in the elementary brain-processes momentarily at work.
—William James (1890)

In the preceding chapter I set out to synthesize a basic representational system. The building blocks were devices of simple function, and we assembled them into equally simple networks. The systems built in the *gedanken*-lab, accordingly, were easy to conceptualize and appropriate for the first statements of a view of natural representation. But now that the theory has been outlined, we will want to set aside the toys. The theory of representation will illuminate the human mind only if it can encompass the complexity of its subject. That complexity manifests itself in two ways: in the complexity of cognition, both as observed in the lab and in ordinary life; and in the complexity of the central cognizing organ, the human brain. The remainder of this book addresses both dimensions of complex representational systems. Part II (chapters 4 and 5) explores representation within complex brains and brainlike networks. The final part extends the theory of representation to explore its fit with other aspects of our cognitive lives.

This chapter continues the synthetic exploration of the representational properties of informational networks but with an important twist: Now we begin to tighten the analogy between synthesis and nature by increasing the "neural inspiration" behind the networks we create. The integrative nodes of those networks will be upgraded to function more like neurons and less like simple logic gates, and they will be installed in larger networks with extensive interaction among them, again on the model of interaction in the brain. The result of these elaborations will be networks capable of tasks worthy of human intellect, genuinely "cognitive," as opposed to the simple pursuits of the vehicles of chapter 3. Here synthesis grows bold, and we could try many different sorts of networks, responsive to many constraints, hypotheses, and assumptions about cognizing brains. These new complexities make the outcomes of thought experiments uncertain, so we will aid the imagination with the power of computer simulation.

4.1   Connectionism, or Parallel Distributed Processing

These reorientations deliver us to the heart of a new and exciting branch of artificial intelligence and cognitive modeling: *connectionism,* also known as *parallel distributed processing* (PDP).[1] The central idea of connectionism is that cognition can be modeled as the simultaneous interaction of many highly interconnected neuronlike units. In this chapter we will tour the blossoming connectionist project and assess its prospects, especially in light of the theory of representation.

Connectionism is not at present a *theory* of mind. Rather, it is an "approach," a fairly loose array of well-informed hunches that have inspired several striking simulation models of diverse cognitive activities. In these salad days, both enthusiasts and doubters work to clarify the central commitments and the details of the connectionist approach (see, for example, Smolensky 1988 and the attendant commentaries). The free-for-all is exciting, but it undermines an author's hope of providing an Olympian overview. One must settle instead for a snapshot of a large, diverse, and rapidly evolving field. This chapter is such a snapshot, a report on connectionism as it exists at this writing. Only in section 4.5 will I turn to the possibilities for the future of connectionism.

Although the details of connectionism are still evolving, its broad outlines are clear. To see just how fresh the connectionist approach is, we might contrast it with the computer model of mind characteristic of classical cognitivism (the classical age flowers c. 1975 with Fodor's *Language of Thought*). The computer model of mind borrows several interconnected ideas from the computer model of computers:

> *Inner language* Thought is a representational process, and the representations are languagelike, with a big lexicon of distinct symbols and a complex syntax. (We return to this thesis in chapter 6.)

Stored programs Cognition, like computation, is governed by explicit rules that operate on explicit data (mental representations). The inner language is roughly an inner programming language. *Memory vs. processing* Like that of the computer, the functional architecture of the mind can be divided into a relatively stable long-term memory store and a dynamic processor, analogous to a computer's central processing unit.

Serial processing Thought is best understood by analogy with the step-by-step computation of a digital computer. It unfolds sequentially, one step at a time.

Discrete symbols A mental symbol is either present or not, all or nothing, and psychological processes are either engaged or not, by analogy with the discrete operations of a digital computer.

The computer model of mind has inspired a generation of artificial intelligence work, with some striking successes. (Most of us are no match for the best chess-playing programs, for example.) To its credit, the AI community has been forthright in identifying unsolved problems. Digital computers are very good at some tasks, like number crunching, at which we are fairly poor; on the other hand, even the best AI programs are weak at tasks like pattern recognition, at which we humans excel. There is a pattern of failure: Cognitive models in the computational style are generally poor at tasks that involve the simultaneous satisfaction of "soft" constraints (McClelland, Rumelhart, and Hinton 1986). Catching a frisbee is one such task. You must compute the trajectory of the frisbee, allowing for its familiar curves and drops, while moving toward an intercept (without running into anything) and positioning your hands for the catch. These various simultaneous constraints are "soft" in that none of the moves that result in a catch is mandatory. You can use two hands or one or twirl the frisbee around your index finger (on a good day). But all of the constraints interact continuously: If you do use two hands, you will have to turn toward the flying frisbee; if you stop short of the intercept, you will have to reach farther. A standard sequential computer program seems ill suited for coordinating this continuous self-harmonizing. The task seems better described by the interaction of several processes in parallel.

The computer model also contrasts with the function of the brain. One way or another, the brain is the implementation of the mind's program, yet no one knows how the hardware (or "wetware") supports the psychological software. To many it seems implausible that hardware like the brain could implement serial programs on the computer model of mind. Jerome Feldman and Dana Ballard (1982) have pressed this point with the observation that the brain is not fast enough to compute the functions ascribed to it by big AI models. A neuron performs its rudimentary calculation in a few milliseconds, and complex cognition (e.g., face recognition) takes a few hundred milliseconds. Thus the brain can pass through only about one hundred discrete program steps en route to its cognitive achievements. AI programs that model cognition with thousands or millions of lines of code seem implausible for that reason alone. Brains must work in parallel, computing many functions at once, not only at the biological but also at the cognitive level.

These problems for the computer model of mind presently motivate the connectionist alternative.[2] Against the computer model of mind, the connectionists recommend the brain model of mind. Accordingly, following neural inspiration, connectionists propose that cognition is implemented in networks of neuronlike basic processors. Specifically, these processing units share with neurons the following features: First, they are stupid. As processors, they are limited to fairly simple summation of their inputs. Their output signals are unarticulated. Far from emitting strings of interpretable code, a neural unit emits a signal that varies along only one dimension ("intensity," "frequency," or simple numerical value). Accordingly, the signals passed from neuron to neuron are continuous, unlike the all-or-nothing signals in a digital computer. But the brain exemplifies the fact that it is all right to be very stupid if you're well connected: Each neuron gets its simple-minded prods from many peers and sends its own simple signal to many more. Furthermore, neural nets operate in parallel. Many neurons are busy at the same time. Finally, the connections among neurons are plastic. A neuron changes in its dynamic properties as a result of the activity of other neurons with which it is connected. In an extensive network, changing connections could be one mechanism of complex learning. (See Smolensky 1988, Rumelhart and McClelland 1986, Hinton and Anderson 1981, Feldman and Ballard 1982.)

These differences in architecture lead to the main distinction between the brain model of mind and the computer model of mind, namely, the abandonment of the inner language idea and with it, the stored program idea. The activity of the brain is guided not by an explicit list of instructions in a hidden programming language, but rather emerges from the network and its connection strengths. It is in the connections, not in the code, and it is distributed over the simultaneous activity of many neural units in concert. The weights on the connections among the units tune the whole, producing the fluid harmony that seems characteristic of tasks demanding simultaneous constraint satisfaction.

Two Cautionary Thought Experiments

We will turn to the details shortly. But before we do, I offer two cautionary thought experiments. First, the "Total Brain Simulation": This science fiction tale has two stages. First, imagine that the golden age of neuroscience has arrived. We possess a thorough functional description of every neuron in the brain, one that exhaustively describes the sources and strengths of synaptic inputs, cellular responses to those inputs, and synaptic outputs. The dossier on each neuron includes not only these functional dispositions at the present time but also the cell's capacity to change those dispositions through the effects of growth, learning, damage, and fatigue. With this information we can predict the birth-to-death career of each of the hundreds of billions of neurons in the brain. With our vast library of individual neurobiographies, we proceed to stage two: Imagine that we use the assembled descriptions of neurons as a blueprint for a giant computer simulation. The descriptions of each aspect of a neuron's function are translated into commands or subroutines in an enormous computer program that keeps track of all of the activities and dynamic changes undergone by the brain it simulates. (Douglas Hofstadter (1981a) has explored this thought experiment in another context.)

All this would be quite wonderful, but the moral of the thought experiment is a bit somber. Even with our utopian program, we still would not know how the brain works. Where once we beheld the tangled neuropil, we now behold a staggering program listing; 10^{11} neurons have been translated into 10^{11} subroutines, and 10^{15} synapses have been rendered as 10^{15} subroutine calls. It would take years to trace even the simplest simulations of the program. Instead of that, our aim is first, a principled understanding of how the brain works, and second, a principled interpretation of our understanding of the brain that transfigures it into an understanding of the mind. The total brain simulation starts us down this path by providing a wonderful tool to tinker toward understanding; but in itself the program does not meet the aim, any more than photocopying an alien script amounts to translating it.

We shall follow that thought with another. This time let us imagine a much simpler device, without biological pretensions. Call it a Computational Associational Reactive device, or CAR for short. It will be another simulation of the brain but greatly simplified: Just as brains receive many inputs at once, so will the CAR device, which will have about ten distinct simultaneous inputs. These inputs are processed in parallel, as in the brain. CAR's outputs are also parallel and distributed, again varying along ten or so dimensions. All of this is mechanical; but under a suitable interpretation, CAR provides a model of a complex cognitive task—face recognition. Our interpretation of CAR maps facial features onto the ten input dimensions and name features onto ten output dimensions. For example, perhaps one input variable will stand for the height of the forehead and one output variable for the first letter of a simple name. Though the interpretation scheme is not obvious, with patience we can find a consistent scheme, supporting the interpretation of CAR as a cognitive model. It may not work just as we do, but it does "recognize faces" in that when a face is encoded along the ten input dimensions, an (encoded) name pops out. Face recognition is a cognitive task, so CAR looks like a system to study for insight into the brain and mind.

This is a cautionary thought experiment for the simple reason that CAR is an automobile. Its parallel inputs include specific quantities of air and gasoline, the state of the accelerator, gear shift, steering wheel, ignition system, and so forth. Its parallel outputs include exhaust, forward motion, direction of movement, and so on. One can also interpret it as a model of face recognition, but the unveiling of an old Ford Falcon ought to give us pause. We are warned against succumbing to the lulling rhythms of the language of cognitive science. These should be applied with circumspection; again, the call is for principles. Just because we can describe the behavior of a complex system with cognitive language does not make the system cognitive and certainly does not make the system a mind. (McDermott (1976) offers similar warnings about AI.)

The two cautionary thought experiments, the total brain simulation and the car, thus stake out two extremes to be wary of in pursuit of the brain model of mind. The first fails by underinterpretation. Nothing in the manifest complexity of the total brain simulation guides us toward an understanding of cognition. The second fails by overinterpretation. Almost anything can be interpreted as a model of a cognitive process. Again, some principled guidance is needed to make simulations and suggestive "models" into viable theories. The brain model of the mind thus must steer between these two cautionary thought experiments. They will be the Scylla and Charybdis of our inquiry in this chapter.

4.2   A Case Study: NETtalk

That completes the limbering up. The details of connectionism will unfold around a particular case, an extended example of a successful and fascinating network—NETtalk. NETtalk, the brainchild of Terry Sejnowski and Charles Rosenberg (1986, 1987), is, in the words of its creators, "a parallel network that learns to read aloud." That is, starting with random connection strengths among the units of a highly interconnected network, NETtalk acquires the ability to convert letter strings to phoneme descriptions with a reasonable likeness to correct (American) English pronunciation.

NETtalk Structure and Function
NETtalk consists of 309 neuronlike units and 18,629 connections among them. Figure 4.1 sketches a generic unit typical not only of NETtalk but of most connectionist architectures. Three of the many possible input lines to unit U_1 are shown along with just one of many output lines. We might imagine U_1 as an idealized neuron. I_1 through I_3 are upstream cells which synapse onto U_1. Their influence on U_1 depends on two factors: their firing frequency and the efficacy of the synapse between I_i and U_1. We let w_i stand for the latter, thought of as a weight on the input connection. A positive weight, accordingly, stands for an excitatory connection; a negative weight, inhibitory. (A weight of zero indicates no connection at all.) The output of U_1, the firing rate o_1 is a nonlinear function of these weighted inputs. Like a typical neuron, it has an input threshold beneath which it will be inactive. And it will have a maximum firing frequency. The cell's output, computed on the basis of its weighted inputs, then becomes input for further cells downstream. (For the mathematical details of NETtalk, see Sejnowski and Rosenberg 1987. Many variations appear in McClelland and Rumelhart 1986, Rumelhart and McClelland 1986, and Hinton and Anderson 1981.)

The 309 units of NETtalk are divided into three layers, as suggested in figure 4.2. The bottom layer is the input (or encoding) layer: 203 units in 7 groups of 29 each. The top is an output layer of 26 units. Sandwiched in the middle is a "hidden" layer of 80 units. Each of the bottom units connects to all of the hidden units; each of the hidden

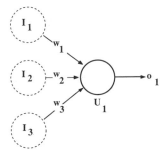

Figure 4.1
A basic connectionist processing unit.

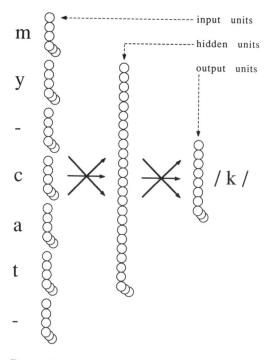

Figure 4.2
The architecture of NETtalk.

units in turn connects to all of the output units. Thus the network includes 18,629 connections, each with an associated weight.[3]

Processing in NETtalk proceeds from bottom to top (from left to right in figure 4.2), beginning with the seven groups of input units. One letter of an input string of seven letters is presented to each group. Each of the 29 units in the group is dedicated to one letter or to "." or "," or a between-word space. Thus, if the input to an input group is "a," the first unit of the group will be activated. If "z," the 26th unit will be activated. Since there are seven such groups, seven input units (one from each group) will be active during each cycle. Initially, all the weights in the network are set at moderately low random values. Thus the seven active input units have complex effects in the hidden units, activating some, inhibiting others. The active units in the hidden layer in turn have their effects on the output units, resulting in a pattern of activation among those units. That pattern is interpreted as a description of a phoneme. Seventeen of the 26 units encode articulatory features like the position of the phoneme in the mouth (labial, dental, etc.), the phoneme type (nasal, fricative, etc.), and vowel height. Other output units encode punctuation, syllable boundaries, and stresses. Once the output units have stabilized in their response to the input string, the output can be fed into a speech synthesizer to be rendered audible. Even though seven letters are input to the network, its output is only one phoneme. That is because NETtalk is designed to pronounce the letter in the middle of the seven-letter input string. So if the input string is "my-car-," NETtalk should produce the phoneme /k/. The three letters on either side of the target provide context information essential to determining the pronunciation (contrast, for example, "my-car-" and "-incite"). Note, however, that the seven-letter window includes only a limited context, less than that available to human readers and speakers in most situations.

Since the initial weights on all the connections are set at random, the initial performance of NETtalk is, of course, poor; it turns text into random speech sounds. But NETtalk has a second, learning, cycle, which has the effect of adjusting the weights in the right direction, thus incrementally improving NETtalk's overall performance. In order to do this, NETtalk first needs to know how far off its current response is. Thus it needs to be provided with a teaching input consisting of the *correct* text-to-phoneme transforms. Sejnowski and Rosenberg used a transcription of a recording of informal discourse, rendered as both standard English and phonemic English. The standard English provides the input for the performance cycle. The phonemic English transcription provides the teaching input. (As it happens, the canonical speaker for NETtalk was a first-grader. Besides making the subject of NETtalk's performance somewhat whimsical, focused on candy, little brothers, and bedtimes, that makes NETtalk's learning achievement more impressive, since NETtalk's teacher was himself no master of English pronunciation.) In the learning cycle, NETtalk runs backward, adjusting the weights governing each connection, from top (output) to bottom (input). First the teaching input (NETtalk's desired output) is compared with the actual output, to determine how far off NETtalk's last effort was. Then all the weights feeding into the output layer are nudged in the direction that reduces their contribution to the error. The nudging is back propagated: Incremental weight adjustment is passed back from layer to layer, adjusting the whole in the right direction, thus slightly improving performance. (See Sejnowski and Rosenberg 1987 for details.)

The forward and backward cycles repeat in alternation for the duration of NETtalk's education. One can think of the network as learning many lessons at once, coming to transform many different words into their various phonemes correctly.

One might compare the operation of NETtalk with that of DECtalk, a program (made by the Digital Equipment Company) designed for the same word-to-phoneme function. The heart of DECtalk is a dictionary listing of several thousand word-pronunciation pairs. DECtalk takes input text and looks for each word in this dictionary. If it fails to find the word, it applies pronunciation rules to the word seriatim. NETtalk, in contrast, has nothing corresponding to a dictionary and makes no distinction between familiar and unfamiliar words. Its memory and processing are in the same place, the network of connections between units. Further, in DECtalk both dictionary and special case rules are programmed by humans. But NETtalk acquires the appropriate connections through the learning procedure.

Performance

NETtalk is intriguing to listen to as it "learns." At first its droning is unrecognizable. But within seconds the droning alternates with abrupt consonant sounds and pauses—"babbling" (in the words of Sejnowski and Rosenberg). Shortly after that a few recognizable words emerge from the babble. At its peak, NETtalk still has a distinctly mechanical sound, a sing-song absence of the rising and falling inflections of whole sentences, as would be expected given the limited input window of seven letters. And the pronunciations are sometimes hard to understand, sounding like a speaker with a very heavy accent. In other respects the verisimilitude is striking, owing in part to two accidental features of the experiment: First, the voice of the synthesizer is set for a child's pitch and timbre; second, the text is informal speech, with its um's, ah's, and like, I mean, you know, informality. For most listeners, NETtalk is an audible success, comparable in its mechanical performance to DECtalk.

But the important measure of success is quantitative. In this respect, NETtalk's performance is impressive, especially considering that the network consists of a scant 309 units, each of modest abilities. After training on 50,000 words (a single text of about a thousand words repeated many times), the network produced the "best guess" on 95 percent of its attempts—that is, the network's output phoneme description was closer to the correct phoneme than to any other defined phoneme. Perfect matches (where all outputs fell within 0.1 of target values) were rarer, hitting 55 percent but still climbing after the training session. NETtalk was scanning familiar text as it achieved these rates, but its success with novel texts was not bad: 78 percent best guesses and 35 percent perfect matches on a text new to the network.

So NETtalk is a success at its assigned task and attracts our attention, first, because the task is seemingly cognitive—certainly when humans learn to read, we regard their achievement as cognitive. NETtalk's task is not exactly a human one (as Sejnowski and Rosenberg note), since it conflates learning to read with learning to talk and models both without modeling any aspect of comprehension in the reader. But the analogy with cognition is close enough. Second, we take notice because the computational resources of the network remind us of the networks in brains.

Unexpected Further Analogies between NETtalk and Humans
There's more, however: NETtalk also exhibits several striking and unanticipated analogies with the observed functional properties of real brains. Its "learning" resembles human learning both in general and in detail. Human rote learning in many domains is described by a power law: the learning occurs rapidly at first and slows with repetitions of the input, proportional to the logarithm of the number of repetitions (Rosenbloom and Newell 1986). So also with NETtalk. In addition, NETtalk's learning exhibits a "spacing effect." As college students know, rote learning of a single subject in a short time facilitates the recall of that subject for a short time after. But the crammed learning quickly fades. Better long-term recall results if the learning sessions are separated by other tasks, including other learning. NETtalk shows this same effect (Rosenberg and Sejnowski 1986). A few thousand repeats of a single word facilitate the short-term performance at pronouncing that word, but other learning quickly interferes, resulting in erosion of the learning of the original word. But if the initial learning is spaced among other learning, the long-term performance is improved. Moreover, as noted above, NETtalk generalizes to novel texts with good accuracy, suggesting that what it captured were the regular features of pronunciation, again reminiscent of human learning.

Furthermore, NETtalk displays characteristic errors and difficulties in learning that parallel those of children. For example, children have difficulty learning the pronunciation of the soft c, as in "cite," compared to the relative ease with which they pick up the hard c, as in "cake." So also in NETtalk: c → /k/ is a rapidly acquired skill, but c → /s/ follows rather slowly.

Finally, like other connectionist networks, NETtalk exhibits the capacity for "graceful degradation." Like brains, but unlike digital computers, damage to NETtalk does not bring it crashing to a halt. Instead, lesioning units or introducing random perturbations throughout the network produces an overall decline in performance but no catastrophic failures. A network thus damaged is quick to recover, relearning what it once knew faster than during initial learning.

Some suggest that graceful degradation implies that networks like NETtalk are models of inebriation; be that as it may, this piece of biological verisimilitude supports the plausibility of NETtalk as a model of brain and cognition.

NETtalk versus the Total Brain Simulation

I have spoken so far as if NETtalk's units and lines were real, but it is time to disclose another accidental fact about the state of the connectionist art: NETtalk, at this writing, is simulated only. It runs on a Vax computer—just like DECtalk. This is a properly inessential fact, since NETtalk simulates the behavior of a real network with the properties described above. However, as a digital simulation of a complex network, it nonetheless reminds us of one of the cautionary thought experiments—the total brain simulation. NETtalk is not much of a brain (its unit count is about 3 percent of the number of neurons in a garden snail). It accomplishes a lot on a shoestring, but its importance is not in what it says but how it says it: The connectionists have a theoretical understanding of NETtalk that distinguishes it from the boggling pit of the total brain simulation. The main contribution of connectionism to the science of the mind is the postulated formal treatment of highly interconnected networks of simple units. Most connectionists see their creatures under the following descriptions: All of the inputs to the system can be numerically represented as an input vector or ordered list of numbers. The activation states for the many units in the network, and resultant output values, comprise activation vectors and output vectors respectively. The whole set of weights on each line between units can also be given a uniform mathematical representation as a matrix. With these vectors and matrices in hand, connectionists can write general equations that describe the behavior of networks as a whole, both the fast dynamics of momentary shifts in activation states and the slower dynamics of incremental improvements in performance.

Two equations are crucial, corresponding to the two aspects of NETtalk's operation: First, the activation equation describes the changes in the activation state of each unit and the system as a whole, over time. In one general form:

$$a_i(t + 1) = F(\Sigma w_{ij} o_j(t)).$$

The equation states that the activation value of unit i at time $t + 1$ is a function (F) of the summation of the products of the outputs (o) of upstream units j and the connection weights between each upstream unit and unit i (w_{ij}) at time t.

Second, the learning equation describes the changes in weights on each of the many connections between units. Here is a general form, applicable to single-layer networks. The equation is often called the *delta rule*. (The learning equations for multilayer networks are more complex. See Rumelhart and Zipser 1986, Hinton and Sejnowski 1986, Rumelhart, Hinton, and Williams 1986.)

$$\Delta W_{ij} = a_i B(z_j - \Sigma W_{kj} a_k).$$

The equation describes the change of weight or connection strength between unit i and unit j. As above, a_i is the activation value of unit i; B is a learning rate adjustment, allowing for incremental change; z_j is the teaching input, the target value for a_j; and $\Sigma W_{kj} a_k$ represents the current contribution of all upstream units k to a_j. In short, straightforward numerical equations describe NETtalk at the level of first-order dynamics (the activation equation) and the level of second-order dynamics (the learning equation).

Thus, the whole system can be explained within a familiar scientific framework known as deductive-nomological explanation. The evolution equation is a covering law. With it, plus the current activation vector, weight matrix, and input vector, one can calculate a new activation vector (a complete account of the current state of the machine) and a new output vector. The learning equation similarly governs the process of back propagation that leads to incrementally improved performance. That equation, together with the target (or teaching) output, actual output, and current weight matrix enable one to compute a new weight matrix. Thus, two equations completely define the dynamics of a PDP system like NETtalk.

Thus, the contrast between the connectionist project and the nightmare minutiae of the total brain simulation is now apparent. The TBS came without a users' manual, no overview of operation. Ringing its changes in theory required a laborious computation of the separate dynamic shifts of each neuron (or something smaller), represented in its idiosyncratic uniqueness. Relative to that, a PDP system is elegant, coming with a slim guide for the perplexed. Two equations, a few numbers, and an interpretation of inputs and outputs, and one has the centerpiece in the explanation of system behavior. Once again, we see the virtue of synthetic psychology. Two equations make quick explanatory work of a PDP net for the simple reason that it was designed according to those very rules.

But elegance and (neural) inspiration must be tempered with circumspection. Our aim is the understanding of mind. We have supposed that representation is crucial to that goal; thus connectionism will clarify psychology only if its dynamics somehow clarify the dynamics of representation. The dynamics of a PDP system might illuminate the representational mind directly by literally describing the interaction of representations or indirectly by accurately describing a dynamism (that of the brain) from which representationality emerges. Neither application should be assumed; here we examine both. It turns out that there are steep hurdles between current connectionism and genuine hypotheses about representational minds. One hopes that these hurdles can be cleared, and quickly, for connectionism promises fascinating leverage on the mind.

4.3   Connectionism and Representation

Since connectionists are striving for new models of cognition (as opposed to mere neural modeling), they have a lot to say on the subject of representation. Although they do not go so far as to define representation, they nonetheless distinguish types of representation within networks. The discussion here will begin with the distinctions most common in the literature of PDP. From there, we will turn to the simple-minded questions of representationality (of any style) in connectionist networks.

Three Styles of Representation

The first strategy of interpretation is a direct extension of the interpretations of the simpler systems of the last chapters. Braitenwagons like Squint and Sleuth also housed simple versions of neurally inspired basic units, and these, I argued, were representations if their input and output information channels met a few specialized dialectical conditions. Connectionists call such interpreted units *local representations*. Under a local representation scheme, individual units have fixed interpretations. Each is dedicated to one content—understood as a proposition or hypothesis—and the activation value of that unit indicates how "committed" the system is to the truth of the representation. NETtalk does not cleanly illustrate a local representation scheme, but another network does: Gluck and Bower (1986) used a simple connectionist network to model a hypothesis confirmation task. Subjects were asked to diagnose imaginary patients on the basis of four symptoms, each of which had a certain likelihood of association with either of two imaginary diseases. The network representation of the task appears in figure 4.3. Each node has an independent propositional interpretation, and it is dedicated to the representation of that content. The node for disease 1, when it is lit, can only mean "disease 1 is confirmed," and similarly for each of the assigned interpretations of the other nodes. Even though each unit is itself simple, its content can be complex—a lesson carried over from our discussions of representation in previous chapters.

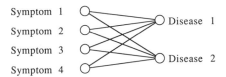

Figure 4.3
Gluck and Bower's model of a simple diagnosis task.

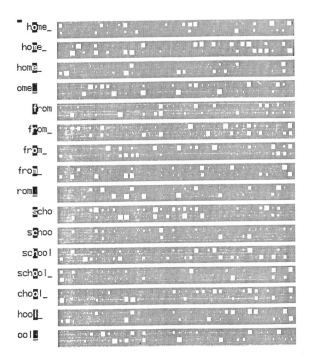

Figure 4.4
Activation patterns in NETtalk hidden units during processing of "home from school."
(Reproduced courtesy of Terry Sejnowski.)

At the opposite extreme, PDP systems can be designed without tidy local representations. Connectionists refer to this alternative as *distributed representation*, and the 80 hidden units of NETtalk provide a good example. Figure 4.4 is a "Hinton diagram"—the activation values of the 80 hidden units as the network makes its way home from school. Each gray oblong in the figure represents the entire hidden layer as two rows of forty units each. The active units appear as white squares, and the size of the square corresponds to the activation value of each unit. As we watch the activation states of the hidden units of NETtalk, we observe an evanescent pattern involving many units, with different activation values from moment to moment. In general, no one unit is exclusively associated with either a specific input or a specific output; if we are going to interpret anything, we must interpret all of the active units at once.

Connectionists generally restrict the debate about the preferred representational style to the two alternatives sketched above—local versus distributed representation. Yet I think there is a third alternative style of interpretation midway between the local and fully distributed. Let us call this third way *featural representation*. In connectionist theory, distributed has two senses that will correspond to the proposed distinction between fully distributed representation and featural representation. Paul Smolensky writes:

> In some [distributed] models . . . patterns are chosen in a deliberately arbitrary way, so that the activity of a single unit has no apparent "meaning" whatever—no discernible relation to the conceptual entities involved in the cognitive process. (1986:390. Similarly, Smolensky 1988; Rumelhart, Hinton, and Williams 1986:346.)

This describes a fully distributed representation of the type just illustrated by the NETtalk hidden units. Contrast that statement with the following:

> When we speak of distributed representation, we mean one in which the units represent small, featurelike entities. (Rumelhart, Hinton, and McClelland 1986:47. Similarly in McClelland, Rumelhart, and Hinton 1986:10; Hinton, McClelland, and Rumelhart 1986:80; Rumelhart, Smolensky, McClelland, and Hinton 1986:8.)

This style of representation, I suggest, is featural. For example, consider the output layer of NETtalk. Each unit in that layer encodes a feature of a phoneme (in its context). No unit, in isolation, represents a full phoneme; thus it is not appropriate to think of the output layer using the local representation of phonemes. Like a distributed representation, the patterns of activation of the whole layer are themselves significant. But at the same time, the output layer is not a fully distributed representation either. Individual units are interpretable—each is dedicated to the representation of a feature of the phoneme, and that interpretation remains constant over time. It seems that the output layer of NETtalk is an intermediate style of representation—hence, the positing of featural representation.

Thus we have three potential styles of representation: local, featural, and distributed. There is a lively debate within the PDP community over which style of representation is most desirable. The decision among them is partly motivated by computational consequences—certain styles of representation favor certain network behaviors over others. For example, nonlocal (featural and distributed) representations exhibit several attractive properties that follow from content being spread over many units. Among these benefits:

> *autogeneralization* A group of representations with similar contents will automatically settle into similar activation patterns, such that new inputs can be classed with similar existing patterns. ·
> *pattern completion* An incompletely specified input activates the complete internal pattern, that is, the network fills in the missing nodal activations.
> *fault tolerance* Just as in pattern completion, the network tolerates departures from perfection. As we discussed with NETtalk, damage to specific units only incrementally undermines the performance of the network.

Proponents of nondistributed (local and featural) representation celebrate the relative ease of interpreting nondistributed representation and fault distributed networks for failing to support more than one representation at a time and for failing to clearly represent relations or other logically complex contents. Modelers accordingly work out compromises among the various alternatives, including the incorporation of modularity in networks. (A modular network designed by Geoff Hinton is discussed below.)

Three Styles of Cognitive Model
Since cognitive models incorporate representations, the style of representation adopted by the modeler has important implications for the form of the resulting model. How do the three representational styles effect cognitive modeling in PDP? Suppose that cognitive models following the connectionist approach each used one sort of representation throughout. The models would thereby fall in three groups. I will survey each briefly.

PDP as a model of cognition: Suppose that all representations were local. The interactions of units would then correspond directly to the interactions of propositional representations, and the dynamics of unit interaction would be the dynamics of thought itself. If we were to interpret connectionism thus, then we would see in high relief the contrast between connectionism and computationalism, as outlined in the computer model of mind. Under this interpretation of connectionism, thoughts lack articulate structure, the same functional architecture supports both memory and processing, and there is no recognizable stored program. The activation and learning equations thus describe inference (and the dynamics of inference are associative—see Lloyd 1989).

PDP as a model of microcognition: If units are representations of the features of concepts, then whole thoughts (propositional representations) comprise ensembles of units—vectors—and their interactions are complex interactions among various patterns of activation, as determined by the weight matrix. But at the same time, interactions of individual units can still be interpreted. Thus, beneath the level of cognition is an interpreted level of microcognition and microinference. PDP systems are defined at the microcognitive level, and the cognitive level is emergent.

PDP as a model of subcognition: If representations are all distributed, then the interactions of individual units are uninterpreted. Cognition emerges only at the level of the behavior of the whole system. In this case, it might be appropriate to describe everything at the unit level as the implementation of cognitive processes, which are correctly defined at higher levels. If PDP is subcognitive, then it is not necessarily inconsistent with the computer model of mind. The computational mind may, in that case, be a virtual machine made out of PDP hardware (or then again, it may not: see Smolensky 1988). On this interpretation we may expect an ultimate cognitive science to be framed independently of PDP. However, PDP will importantly characterize the primitive (uninterpreted) operations available to the emergent cognitive machinery (Rumelhart and McClelland 1986b).

Thus, from three styles of representation emerge three different interpretations of connectionism. Each interpretation charts a very different course for the understanding of the mind. The more representation tends toward the local, the more the dynamic of thought is directly manifest in the dynamics of individual units. And since those dynamics are distinct from the dynamics of the computational mind, the more representation tends toward the local, the more the PDP model of cognition conflicts with the computer model of cognition.

Interpreting Representations in NETtalk
Thus the nature of representation in PDP models has important consequences for cognitive explanation in the connectionist image. By now, I presume NETtalk is something of an old friend. What sort of model is it: cognitive, microcognitive, or subcognitive? We answer this question by analyzing the representations, if any, internal to the network. This analysis, in turn, requires a theory of representation,

some principled way of identifying representations and their contents. Fortunately, we have such a theory at hand in the dialectical model of representation developed in the previous chapters. Now we will put that theory to work.

Since the work is hard, one inclines toward a quick fix: Why not just stipulate the content of representations? Such stipulations are innocent enough in cognitive modeling. For example, consider another famous AI toy, SHRDLU (Winograd 1972). SHRDLU "manipulates" blocks on a table—or at any rate, it would if it had a mechanical arm, sensing devices, blocks, and a table. SHRDLU's "environment" consists, instead, of a simulation of these things. SHRDLU is none the wiser, and its creators' purposes are met. SHRDLU can report and reason about its simulated blocks world just as it might about a genuine playroom, so it does not matter that SHRDLU's running commentary on its world does not really represent anything. Likewise, we can excuse the connectionists from the task of providing their models with perceptual/representational front ends. We can readily see how such front ends might work and recognize, I think, that they will not change much of the inner dynamics of the system.

But we cannot solve all our problems by stipulating their solution. Dynamic systems in nature represent, if they represent, without stipulation. The question of the form of their natural representation must be resolved on natural grounds, presumably through the use of the dialectical theory of representation (or its successor). If connectionism models natural systems, then we will be particularly concerned with how representations evolve within the connectionist models. Thus our analytic techniques ought to be the same as those we might apply to a natural system.

In sum, then, we can assume, with Sejnowski and Rosenberg, that NETtalk's input layer comprises a featural representation of seven-letter input strings, and its output layer comprises a featural representation of a stressed or unstressed phoneme. We turn, accordingly, to representation in the hidden layer.

Representation among Hidden Units: Local?
Concerning the hidden units, I will pursue two questions. First, are there individual local representations among the flashing tracery? Second, are distributed representations really representations? To get started, we assume that the input layer is truly representational and that the standard interpretation is correct. Next, we examine whether the hidden units exploit the information which passes through the input units to comprise a second layer of representations. We can see that at least one condition is apparently easy enough to meet: each

unit in the hidden layer can receive input from all 203 input units—that is 203 separate information channels potentially available to feed some deluxe and-gates or majority rule threshold devices in the hidden layer. Are those hidden units and-gates? It depends on their threshold. If the threshold is high enough that no single input is sufficient to fire the unit, then that unit will behave like an and-gate, requiring multiple inputs to fire. We have established, then, that the units can be individuated (that is taken for granted), that they can behave like and-gates, and that they have multiple information channels for inputs.

The rub comes when we seek salient unitary origins (single mutually effective stimuli) upstream from the hidden units. We know that within NETtalk the 203 separate information channels originate from 203 separate sources, one for each letter-position pair. Here, the network shows its disanalogy from the representing systems considered so far. The synthetic systems of chapter 3 were characterized by convergent knots, common origins for the multiple information channels. These common origins NETtalk lacks.

The search for local representations is not over quite yet, however. If we allow the content of a representation to be a relation, then it may be that among the input letters are certain significant relations among letters that NETtalk learns. Are there such patterns among input letters? Given NETtalk's task, we know that NETtalk must respect relational properties of input strings—consider the context dependency of the pronunciation of "e," for example. Since the hidden units are each connected to all of the input units, a particular hidden unit could respond selectively to relations among letters, producing a signal only in the presence of a complex pattern of letters.

We know from NETtalk's competence that, as a whole, it responds in ways that reflect higher order patterns like the rules governing the pronunciation of "e." But it is another question, and a hard one, whether the hidden units include representations of those higher-order patterns. The difficulty emerges from the complex array of patterns that arise in the trained network. Let us look at an example, a Hinton diagram of the weights (as opposed to the activation values) on the input lines to an arbitrary hidden unit in NETtalk (figure 4.5). In contrast to the previous Hinton diagram, in this illustration each row of squares within the gray rectangle denotes the weights (not the activation values) from each of the seven groups of input units—thus each row is dedicated to one of the seven letters in the input window, and the fourth row is assigned to the central letter, which the network attempts to pronounce. There are 29 squares in each row. The first 26 denote the letters a through z, the remaining three stand for punc-

abcdefghijklmnopqrstuvwxyz,.-

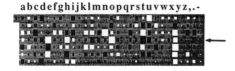

Figure 4.5
The weights on connections from input units to a single hidden unit. (Reproduced courtesy of Terry Sejnowski.)

tuation or word boundaries. White squares indicate excitatory connections (positive weights), and black squares inhibitory (negative weights); the size of the square indicates the magnitude of the connection. The square on the tab attached to the upper left corner indicates the threshold, an inhibitory weight that must be overcome in order for the unit to fire.

Suppose the input string is the sequence "big-biz." To determine the response of the unit in question, we find the weight on each of the input lines from the seven particular units that encode "big-biz." We start with the second from the left on the top row, "b," which is moderately positive. The letter "i" arrives at the second row, ninth slot from the left—also somewhat positive. G: third row, seventh position—positive again. And so forth. Only the between-word space, the last square in the fourth row, is inhibitory. Since the rest are excitatory, we can predict that this particular hidden unit will fire for "big-biz." When the input string is "carrot-," on the other hand, most of the inputs are negative, and the overall tendency is to depress the unit's activation value.

"Big-biz" and "carrot-" were deliberately chosen to provoke or depress the unit in question. "Bbbabab" and "ccccacd" would exhibit similar qualitative tendencies, along with many other alternative excitors or inhibitors. If we are to describe the hidden unit as a representation, however, the pattern it detects needs to be individuable as a single entity to us, the interpreters of the system. Looking at the diagram, one sees that the patterns to which the unit responds are complexly disjunctive. Perhaps there is a pattern there that can be succinctly stated as a single salient relation (and perhaps there are other hidden units that plainly exhibit a saliently determined response), but for now, none has emerged. This negative result must be counted as prima facie evidence against local representation in the hidden layer of this exemplary network.

Representation in Hidden Units: Distributed?
One open question begets another: We turn next to the issue of distributed representation in the hidden layer of NETtalk. So far we have

examined what would be necessary for an individual unit to be a representation and found no such unit in NETtalk. This would not disturb most connectionists, however, since they are primarily interested in distributed representation. A distributed occurrent representation in the hidden units would be a pattern of activation of those 80 units that, like any other representation, was itself robustly individuable, had multiple input chnanels, and a unitary origin. The representation, in other words, is no longer restricted to specific units within the hidden layer. Rather, we now ponder the possibility that a pattern over the entire layer is itself one representation. With 80 lines between the layer and each letter-position combination of inputs, there are plenty of input channels and many separate origins to choose from. Nonetheless, we will be perplexed again by the daunting complexity of the patterns of activation. These must be individuated before we ascribe representationality. Otherwise, talk of representation is just so much hand waving, as ill-advised here as with the CAR device.

We are unlikely to ever perceive distributed representations by the examination of Hinton diagrams, but the mathematical resources of connectionism may enable us to discern complex patterns that otherwise elude detection. Recall that the activation pattern in NETtalk is numerically represented as a vector with 80 elements. The elements of the vector can be conceived as coordinates of a point in an 80-dimensional coordinate space. That permits vectors to be compared in location in this 80-dimensional mathematical space. The distance between two vectors can be a precise measure of the difference between them (Sejnowski and Rosenberg 1987).

Measuring the distance between vectors may ultimately enable us to read the content of distributed representations. The program for accomplishing this will have several stages. First, something like a vector grammar will be developed: Roughly, the 80-dimensional space will be carved into regions, thereby categorizing the activation vectors. Then the inputs to various "well-formed" vectors will have to be analyzed for single events, though possibly single events with significant internal structure. Vector grammar may help there as well by indicating groupings among inputs that can be robustly individuated. With NETtalk, these input groupings would constitute, one supposes, phonological kinds, typical letter configurations that map onto particular phonemes during the process of reading aloud. At present, this daunting interpretive program is just starting. But many connectionists have recognized the importance of interpretation of distributed representations, and there is no reason to suppose that such interpretations are impossible.[4]

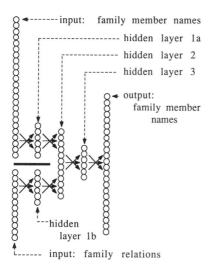

input: family member names
hidden layer 1a
hidden layer 2
hidden layer 3
output: family member names
hidden layer 1b
input: family relations

Figure 4.6
"Kin Net" architecture.

Featural Representation in Action
Having examined local and distributed representation in hidden units in NETtalk, we turn to featural representation. To illustrate what featural representations might look like and how they arise, I will turn from NETtalk to a simpler case, a network designed by Geoffrey Hinton (1986). His network learns family relationships in particular families (and generalizes to other families with similar family trees). For example, the network will learn that "Colin" has an aunt "Jennifer." Hinton has no ready name for his net; since it concerns familial relationships involving marriage and offspring, call it "Kin Net."

Figure 4.6 represents the structure of Kin Net. Each unit in each layer is connected to all units in the adjacent layer and activation passes in one direction from bottom to top, as in NETtalk. The 24 input units encode family member names from two families of twelve members each. The family trees are isomorphic, differing only in the apparent nationality of names in each—one is English, the other Italian. The family relations, encoded in a second set of input units, include father, mother, husband, wife, son, daughter, uncle, aunt, brother, sister, nephew, and niece. Both input layers match input terms and units one-to-one, as in NETtalk. (The two input groups and hidden layers 1a and 1b do not interact before converging on hidden layer 2.)

Here is the family tree of one of the two families learned by Kin Net:

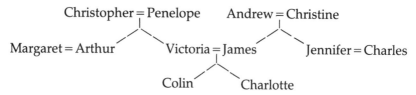

The goal of Kin Net is to demonstrate the network's ability to learn the familial relationships diagramed in the family tree and to generalize to new cases, again like NETtalk. For example, during training, the units for "Colin" and "has-aunt" will be turned on. Following a back propagation error correcting procedure, the output units for "Jennifer" and "Margaret" activate correctly—these are Colin's aunts. Kin Net does well at this learning. At present, however, we are concerned not with performance but with the details of representation. All of the above exegesis prepares us for opening the black box: We will examine the weights from the family name inputs to hidden layer 1a, as represented in the Hinton diagram of the weights on all the input lines to the six units of hidden layer 1a (figure 4.7).

The six gray boxes represent the six units in hidden layer 1a. Each receives input from all of the family name input units—each of the solid squares that dot the interior of the gray boxes corresponds to one input line. Thus, within each box is the representation of all 24 input units. The top row in each box is the family diagramed above and labeled by name in this diagram. The bottom row indicates the second family, which we will not be discussing here. As with the

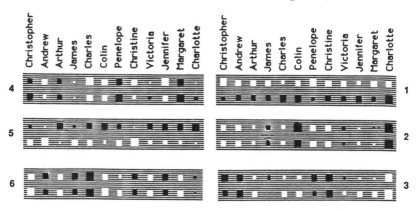

Figure 4.7
Weights from family member input units to all six units in hidden layer 1a. (Reproduced courtesy of Geoffrey Hinton.)

diagram of the NETtalk hidden unit, a white square indicates an excitatory (positive) weight, and a black square an inhibitory (negative) weight. The size of the square indicates the magnitude of the weight on the connection. So, for example, hidden layer unit 4, in the top left corner, is fairly inhibited by Penelope, but considerably excited by Charles.

The connections to the six units were originally set at low random values. But as we examine the Hinton diagram, we see that as the network learns, the hidden units begin to exhibit patterns in their responses. Unit 1, in the upper right, clearly indicates which of the two families include the activated member. That unit is on if the family is the one diagramed above (the English family), off for the second (Italian) family. Unit 2 encodes the generation of the input family member. The first generation (Christopher, Penelope, Andrew, and Christine) excite the unit, whereas the third generation (Colin and Charlotte) strongly inhibit it. The six characters in the middle evoke only slight responses in either direction. The family also has two branches, Victoria's and James's, and these seem to be roughly encoded in unit 6: Victoria's side of the family excites the unit, while James's inhibits it. The remaining three units exhibit the rough inverses of the three just discussed: Unit 3 is an approximate inverse of 2, 4 inverts 6, 5 inverts 1.

This analysis of the hidden units enables us to begin to interpret an overall activation pattern of hidden layer 1a in Kin Net. Suppose we observe this pattern in the layer: units 1, 2, and 6 on, units 3, 4, 5 off. We would expect the input to be a member of family 1, the older generation, Victoria's side. In fact, the input is more specific than that, but the interpretation seems to be on the right track. Our interpretive efforts have provided a partial grammar of layer 1a. We can now say, at least in part, what pattern inflections are significant, and we can identify which patterns are well-formed. The pattern just considered is well-formed. The pattern of 1, 2, 3, 5 on and 4, 6 off is ungrammatical—given the weight matrix diagramed above, no input could produce that activation pattern.

Distributed Representation and Charybdis
With this partially successful interpretation in hand, we may ponder some general conclusions about representation in networks like NETtalk and Kin Net. The complex Hinton diagrams preceding have suggested that establishing the presence of a representation in a PDP network is not easy. There is no all-at-once gestalt switch that enables us to read distributed representations. Indeed, we face in practice the glop problem raised in theory in chapter 2. Our closest approach to

reading a distributed representation revealed that the uphill labor began with an interpretation of individual units. Identification of a fully distributed representation lies in the future.

The fact that questions of representation in a PDP system are so difficult is itself a datum: Notice how similar the questions we now ask are to those posed concerning living brains. Our synthetic understanding has given out—NETtalk and Kin Net join the ranks of all those other brains, and understanding them demands a patient mix of (simulated) neurophysiology and (simulated) perceptual ecology. That the innards and outards are all simulated only simplifies the laboratory preparation—the challenge to theory construction is just as steep. Yet the challenge must be met if any of these networks is to lead to understanding the mind. Their sound and fury signify nothing if we cannot find representationality therein. And the elegant laws of connectionism will not inform psychology until we can see how those laws animate the interaction of representations.

Mixed Interpretation

Every dynamic system has levels of interpretation, and brains are no exception. Although one can begin with subatomic particles, the psychologically interesting properties of brains first emerge at the level of physiology at which we describe the neural hardware—the function of individual neurons and their interconnections. But we can also interpret the physiological interaction of neurons as neural signals, thereby interpreting the brain at the level of information. At this level, we find a different style of description of the same organ, one that abstracts from synapses, axons, and dendrites, to talk instead of information sources and channels. But not every information handling device in a nervous system is a representing device, so there is a third level of description—the level of representation. At this level we reinterpret information channels, sources, and receivers under a theory of representations and their objects.

In the explorations of the last two chapters, we have witnessed frequent level shifts among these three topologies, the physiological, the informational, and the representational. But even as we slide from one aspect to another, we should acknowledge that the entities that we refer to at one level of description are often beneath the purview of the next higher level translation. In the last chapter, we moved from informational topology to representational topology. In the next, informational topology will be abstracted from the available physiology and representational topology further abstracted from that. In this chapter, PDP presents a clean object lesson about the next level of distillation and the translation from information to repre-

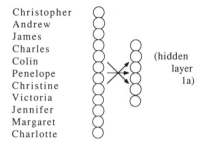

Christopher
Andrew
James
Charles
Colin
Penelope
Christine
Victoria
Jennifer
Margaret
Charlotte

(hidden layer 1a)

Figure 4.8
Kin Net informational topology.

sentation. These systems show that what is salient in informational topology is not necessarily salient at the representational level.

The different styles of representation invoked by connectionists illustrate the point. At the level of information transmission and manipulation, all units are created equal. Each has a similar informational/computational task to perform. But at the level of representation, different units play different roles. In local representations, one unit is dedicated to a single representation, which it affirms to the extent that the unit is active. In nonlocal representation, individual units participate in many representations.

One can also view that distinction from the direction of representation. With local representation, each representation comprises one unit. With nonlocal representation, each representation is made of many units. In the latter case, the difference between different representations is not a function of which units are used, but rather of the pattern of activation of a set of units shared by several representations.

However, except for systems using only local representations, PDP systems commonly use both styles of representation. Consider, again, the bottom rungs of Kin Net, reproduced in figure 4.8. This standard map captures the informational topology of the network. Compare it with a map of the representational topology, as shown in figure 4.9.

Each family name representation has one unit assigned to it, so the representational topology and the informational topology correspond in the input layer. But in the hidden layer, salient representations do not correspond to the salient units. R3, for example, represents the family name occurring in Victoria's branch of the family. Its pattern includes the activation of hidden unit 4 and inhibition of unit 6. R4, corresponding to James's branch, is the opposite pattern in these same two units. So the representational topology is every bit as

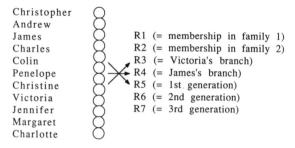

Figure 4.9
Kin Net representational topology.

complex as the informational topology, but, despite a superficial similarity, is distinct from it. In sum, just as physiology is subinformational, information topology is subrepresentational.

The learning and activation equations, however, describe interactions at the informational level only. Once again, we must ask how the informational dynamics will translate into psychological (representational) dynamics. Even if the informational dynamics are thoroughly accounted for—as they are by the dynamic equations and the vectors and matrices they govern—there remains an additional interpretive task and a new challenge to dynamic theory when one rises to the representational level. Representational descriptions are emergent from lower level descriptions, but connectionism will not afford a quantitative science of representation until the emergence is fully understood. This is a task that lies ahead. Shirking it leads directly to the problems exemplified by the total brain simulation.

Suddenly the effort to sneak by Scylla (the CAR device) seems to deliver us into the whirlpool of Charybdis. As the perplexity surrounding the interpretation of NETtalk mounts, one might be reminded of the total brain simulation: is it progress, if in our efforts to understand the brain we make machines which we cannot understand? We turn next to yet another hurdle for PDP modelers. After that, we can turn to the positive lessons of connectionism.

4.4   Connectionism and the Brain

The issues raised in section 4.3 concerned connectionism at the high end: its positing of representations, and their uncertain emergence from the interaction of units. Now we turn to the low end, the units considered apart from their representational interpretations.

Connectionism is fueled by neural inspiration, but the units in a PDP system are at best approximations of neurons. This is appropriate since no quantified science could get off the ground without imposing idealizations on its domain. The risk here, however, is that the idealization might ignore or falsify a dynamic feature at the unit level which in reality might ramify and accumulate to determine an important property of patterns of activation of the whole system. For example, as I described above, learning in PDP involves back propagation, running the system backwards to adjust weights. So any connection in such a system is a two-way street, passing signals forward on its activation cycle and backward on its learning cycle. But neurons, in contrast, are entirely one-way. Only in the laboratory, with current applied through intracellular electrodes, do neurons signal antidromicly, in reverse of their ordinary direction (P. S. Churchland in conversation, Smolensky 1988). So in this respect the dynamics of PDP systems are strikingly different from the dynamics of brains. Francis Crick and Chisato Asanuma (1986:360) list several other properties of units appearing in PDP models that have not been observed in any living system:

- Neurons that excite some cells and inhibit others.
- Neurons that merely change sign. For example, a neuron that accepts excitation from one neuron only and whose output produces inhibition on one neuron only.
- Neurons that connect to all other cells of the same type. . . .
- A neuron that, by itself, can fire another cell. This does occur in the cerebellum. . . . It is not certain that it does not occur in the neocortex, but the available evidence suggests that it is not common.

Each of these contrasts could be accommodated within connectionism by adding constraints to the architecture and function of networks. But there are further departures from apparent neural reality which question connectionism at its heart.

Uniformity in PDP
Connectionism is generally, though implicitly, committed to a principle of uniformity. The principle is simply this: one pair of equations, the activation and learning equations, applies in the same way to all the units and connections in a network. This commitment follows from the PDP style of explanation, which capitalizes on linear algebra and the two equations to model the behavior of many simple devices in concert—I urged (in section 4.2) that the application of those equations legitimates the whole approach, preserving it from the inexplicable morass exemplified by the total brain simulation.

The uniformity in question here is uniformity in second-order dispositions, or the principle of uniform plasticity. This principle concerns the weights on connections between units and their capacity for change—their plasticity. To understand uniform plasticity, it helps to recall the distinction between first-order dispositions and second-order dispositions. Solubility is a typical first-order dispositional property, issuing in familiar effects in familiar circumstances. A second-order disposition, on the other hand, is a disposition to acquire or change a first-order disposition. The marooned children in *Lord of the Flies* arrived on their island with assorted typical first-order child dispositions—timidity, meanness, curiosity, playfulness, and the lot. But unbeknownst to them, they also arrived with a nasty second-order disposition to acquire the first-order disposition of savagery. That latter disposition became manifest only as time progressed. Similar distinctions apply to connections. Their first-order dispositions are various and variable, changing with the weights on each connection. In their second-order dispositions, however, connections are uniform: given a certain initial weight and specific inputs (error messages), connection weights undergo specific changes. In other words, weight change on a connection is defined by a function over initial weights and certain other variables. The learning equation defines the function. The crucial point is that the function is the same for all connections—they are uniform in the way they change, in their second-order dispositions, even though their particular instantaneous weights may vary.

Are neurons in fact uniform in their second-order dispositions? Even if each neuron and each synapse never varies in its own second-order dispositions, there will be a problem for the uniformity assumption if one neuron or synapse is different from another, for in that case the learning equation will not apply uniformly throughout the network. If a single mechanism explained the function and plasticity of synapses, then there might be some distant hope for the uniformity assumption. But there are more than fifty known neurotransmitters mediating many varieties of synaptic function. It is too early even to guess at the number of mechanisms which underlie synaptic plasticity, but some estimate of their variability has been described by Ira Black (1986):

> It is now apparent that a single neuron may use multiple transmitters simultaneously, varying the actual transmitters employed, depending on environmental information [Black et al., 1984]. The elaboration and use of multiple transmitters, many (if not all) of which are subject to environmental regulation,

endows the neuron with plastic capabilities heretofore unsuspected. The expression, metabolism, and function of different transmitters in the same neuron are independently controlled by different regulatory molecules, each with distinct, characteristic time courses of action. Consequently, even the single neuron can store information for *varying* periods of time, using multiple transmitter systems. Employing these systems alone, a single neuron may store immediate, short-term, and intermediate-term information (seconds to weeks), dictated by the *kinetics* of the regulatory molecules involved. Moreover, the apparent *combinatorial capabilities* confer degrees of *temporal specificity* and *precision* that have yet to be fully characterized.

On the basis of neurotransmitter diversity alone, the uniformity presupposed in the connectionist covering laws is unlikely. Further, the differences in synaptic plasticity are directly observable. Some synapses are plastic, and some are not. This is amply borne out in the study of the neurobiology of learning, in which the entire aim is to locate the sites of learning, that is, to distinguish those cells which change with experience from those which do not (see Byrne 1987 for review). That study is in its infancy, but early successes suggest that in fact neurons do differ in second-order functional properties, in contradiction to the principle of uniform plasticity.

In short, these questions underline a contrast between existing PDP networks and brains: The connection systems are homogeneous in ways that brains are not. Or: Brains are modular and variable over time and from unit to unit in ways that connection nets are not. The examples I have presented challenge the principle of uniformity.

This suggests a dilemma. On the one hand, connectionism needs its neural inspiration. The neuron-like basic units provide the advantage that recommends the connectionist approach over the computer model of mind. To explain this, we might imagine a scoreboard in the match between the computer model of mind and the connectionist alternative. For each we find various strengths and weaknesses, but I will hazard a few generalizations. First, each proposes models of aspects of cognition, and in the tasks they confront, each does moderately well. By the time these words see print, the computationalist countercharge should be well under way, and each of the bold initiatives of the connectionists will be the site of a pitched battle. Thus, the two approaches cannot be absolutely ranked as models of cognitive competence and performance. Is there a second front along which one view might catch the other? There is, in the neural inspiration unique to the connectionist approach. The connectionists, it seems, hold the monopoly on plausible implementation, and theirs are the first accounts of how real cognitive tasks might be implemented in real brainlike hardware.

But these same inspiring neurons get them into trouble (and here the dilemma emerges). On the one hand, the connectionist approach initially captured our interest by its clean explanatory principles. These principles assumed idealized neurons, but apparently the idealized units are also oversimplified in contrast to the dynamics of real neurons. So we win robust explanations at the expense of neural reality. Oversimplified neurons, dynamics, and architecture lead to models that, robust or not, may be simply false. Such models confer no special advantage over competing models following the computer inspiration. Of course, connectionists can embrace more of the neural details, as the next generation of PDP models surely will. But unfortunately, attending to the neural details leads us, by various routes, to the hazards caricatured in the total brain simulation. The representational dynamics of PDP systems quickly boggle our efforts at interpretation. And the more realistic and brain-based such models become, the more difficult becomes the interpretation. Finally, dismay on dismay, those brains we would like to model are shrouded in mystery. We know we need more details to fulfill the promise of PDP, but those details may be generations away.

Two sections of doubt might be summed up in a short list of soft constraints that connectionism should satisfy as it grows toward theory. Connectionism should offer:

1. Elegant central principles
2. Successful models of significant cognitive tasks
3. Theoretical foundations for the appeal to representation
4. Dynamics that operate at the representational level (P. S. Churchland 1986:297)
5. Respect for all of the features of neurons that determine the dynamics of neural networks
6. An account of the relations between neural dynamics and representational dynamics

So far only (1) and (2) seem well met. But many people are currently researching cognition within the connectionist approach, and many more will soon join in. Relations among them are congenial. With all these connections, the network of researchers may rapidly settle on cogent theories in all six categories.

4.5   The Future of Connectionism

But what is to be done now? There are two responses to the dilemma outlined above. Both are feasible, though difficult.

PDP and Neural Modeling

First, connectionists might pick up the burden of neural inspiration and bring their implementations more in line with real brains. To take this low road, connectionists descend from the ivory tower of idealization into the nitty gritty of neural modeling. This enterprise will never converge on an ideal neuron, nor even, probably, on a typical one. Thus laws with the grace of the laws of thermodynamics may never emerge. (I could be wrong on that. There may be a level of description relevant to cognitive science at which neurons are completely uniform.) But low-road connectionists nonetheless can engage in legitimate science without covering laws. Like psychologists and especially like biologists, neural connectionists can contribute to the explanation of the brain by functional decomposition. Under this paradigm of explanation (described in Cummins 1983 and Haugeland 1978; see also Millikan 1984, 1986), one explains the behavior of whole systems by reference to the functional components of the system and their connections. The components in turn are further decomposed into other functionally characterized units. The emerging result is a rich explanatory network linking phenomena at high levels to lower level, ultimately subneural, phenomena.

If one's research follows the low neural road, the simulation of human cognitive performance may be premature—we just do not know enough about constraints 3 through 6 to span from bottom to top. Neural modelers might do well to turn to networks that are well understood physiologically and biologically—the explored neural circuits of humbler animals or the subsystems of larger brains, like the cerebellum. This enterprise is continuous with the explorations described and undertaken in the next chapter.

PDP and Brains in General

And the high road? Connectionists might, alternatively, cast off from the tangled neuropil and continue to explore the idealized systems that have afforded such successful demonstrations and promising laws. There are two ways of characterizing the high-road enterprise. We might call it the study of massively parallel computation (a branch of the theory of computation) with fairly obvious technical and theoretical payoffs. Or, more provocatively, we might call it the study of brains in general (see Smolensky 1988).

Once again, we invoke the helpful image of synthetic psychology. Brains, from the simplest to the most complex, are knotty, parallel, and modular, and so are PDP systems. Again, the neuronal inspiration is central, but here it informs a different enterprise. On the high road, connectionists should no longer characterize themselves as modeling the cognition of any living species. Their achievement should be understood, instead, as creating (not modeling) artificial brains. The systems they create will have cognitive interest in themselves, especially to the extent that they can be interpreted representationally. Just as genetic engineers are creators of new life forms, connectionists are the creators of new "informavores" (to borrow a term from Miller 1984).

For example, Hinton's Kin Net bears no particular resemblance to any brain in nature (as far as I know). It nonetheless displays at least two intriguing properties. First, it learns to encode salient properties in its domain—no programmer installed the sortals we saw at work in hidden layer 1a. Furthermore, we saw that it encoded each concept twice, once in a unit excited by the presence of the property, once in a unit inhibited by it. Are there general principles underlying this configuration, principles that would hold in any parallel, modular, and plastic system? Even as we dream of the laws of representational interaction in parallel circuits, however, we may feel upbraided by Kin Net itself: Both of the generalizations just presented do not fully apply in Kin Net—inflections in its weight matrix must be doing work in ways not obvious after superficial inspection. Kin Net would make an interesting ongoing study, especially since its life in RAM permits ready breeding of a specimen population.

In some respects, what I am calling the high road amounts to a simple reinterpretation of what connectionists are already doing. I suggest, in short, that study be directed at PDP systems a cappella, in the hopes of generating deeper principles of interpretation and operation. Then one can ask the further question about whether any of the parallel processor's biological peers can be explained through similar principles. (See, for example, Lockery 1989a.) At that point, high-roaders and low-roaders confer.

If there is indeed a methodological distinction between high-road and low-road connectionism, then much of the high-road data are already in. Every PDP system counts, once one has demoted it from being a model of human cognition and reconsidered it as a new informavore. Looking over the enthusiastic reports of early success, can one discern any general principles relevant to brains as such? From my armchair, I see at least two general lessons. They will be the topic of the final section of this chapter.

4.6   The Lessons of Connectionism

Articulated Representation

The first lesson can be briefly summarized because it has been implicit in much of the preceding discussion. In Section 1.2, I suggested that an adequate theory of representation must account for the articulation or compositionality of representations. The simple systems of chapter 3 were not complex enough to exhibit compositionality, but in this chapter we have seen several examples of (potential) representing systems with (potential) grammatically structured representations. Featural representation, in particular, meets the need for articulation, since the representation of any single feature can be used in many distinct complex representations. Indeed, if inner representations must be articulate, and if connectionist models are similar to the human brain, then some representations must use nonlocal representation. In short, this look at connectionism adds another support to the dialectical theory of representation by showing how brains might make and use articulate inner representations.

The Representation of Rules

The second moral for brains in general is one connectionists themselves are fond of drawing. It concerns the governance of PDP systems by explicit rules. One of the central planks of the computer model of mind is the stored program idea, which is that the operation of minds, like the operation of computers, is governed by a stored list of explicitly represented rules. This the connectionists deny. PDP systems, they maintain, can be described by various rules, but the systems are not controlled by those rules. On the other hand, committed computationalists might dispute the connectionist claim, pointing to some aspect of a PDP system as the locus of represented rules: the internal distributed representations or the pattern of weights on all the connections. As we shall see, it is a disagreement with important consequences. And not surprisingly, it turns once again on representation.

The central distinction in this debate is between rule-described systems and rule-governed systems. Consider the represented rule "If X, then Y" or "X→Y" for short, and a system, S, with the following causal dispositional property: When it is in state X, it tends to move into state Y. Let us abbreviate this with the following expression: S:X →Y. A system is rule-*described* if "X→Y" describes S:X→Y. A system is rule-*governed* when "X→Y" *causes* (as well as describes) S:X→Y (cf. Bennett 1964, Stabler 1983). That is, the explicit representation "X →Y" causes the system to acquire the causal disposition, S:X→Y. In neither case is the exact form of the representation important, as long as it is interpreted as meaning "X→Y." A computer exemplifies a rule-governed system. Somewhere in the computer on the table before me is an explicit rule, a representation or set of representations which can be interpreted (by programmers) as meaning that when ctrl-N is typed, execute a line-feed on the screen. Because that rule is there, inside the computer, the computer has the disposition to respond to ctrl-N with a line-feed. Given a different program, the behavior of the computer would have been different. In contrast, the planets are familiar exemplars of a rule-described system. The laws of gravity describe their behavior, but they do not move as they do because those laws are inscribed somewhere. Those laws need never have been represented anywhere, and the planets would move just as they do.

The issue before us, then, is whether PDP systems are rule-governed or (merely) rule-described.[5] Let us return to the case of NETtalk. After graduation, NETtalk displays this dispositional property: Presented with the letter k, NETtalk produces the phoneme /k/. Abbreviating NETtalk as N, we say that it is in the dispositional state N:k→/k/. Given that it displays this disposition, we ask what caused it to do so? Prima facie, one might say straight off that no rule caused NETtalk to become N:k→/k/. We know, after all, what the inputs to NETtalk are: letters at one end, and during teaching, phonemic descriptions at the other. These inputs determined NETtalk's dispositions. Sift through both, however, and you will find no rules.

But this is too quick. It ignores the possibility that NETtalk "learns" the rule "k→/k/" on the basis of its explicit inputs, just as one might learn the rules of solitaire by watching it being played. The rule "k→/k/" might be represented either in the activation pattern of the hidden units (analogous to the representation of inputs in the activations of the input units), or it might be represented by the pattern of weights between the various layers of the network.

Representations and Causes

These are plausible conjectures, but on what grounds do they rest? What grounds could there be, other than that NETtalk exhibits the causal disposition k→/k/? In other words, it behaves as if the rule "k→/k/" governed it. But look at this reasoning, generalized as the following principle: When a system is S:X→Y, then it is governed by the explicit rule "X→Y." If this is the principle by which NETtalk is a rule-governed system, then we are in trouble, for the same principle makes the planets into a system *governed* (vs. merely described) by the laws of gravity. In short, basing the ascription of rule governance on exhibited causal dispositions destroys the distinction between rule-governed and rule-described systems. On those grounds, every system turns out to be rule-governed.

We can make this point indirectly as well. Suppose that NETtalk does represent the rules that describe its behavior. What, in NETtalk, is the representation of "k→/k/"? The answer must be "the current state of the hidden units and/or their input/output connection weights." And if we further ask what are the causal properties that embody the disposition N:k→/k/, the answer is the same. But remember that the definition of rule governance is that the representation causes the dispositions to be as they are; if the representation and the disposition are identical, then we have landed in an absurdity: NETtalk has states that cause themselves.

Is the Weight Matrix the Representation?
One might urge (as Randy O'Reilly and Marc Intrater have in conversation) that the representation that governs NETtalk is not the actual connection weights, but rather the weight matrix, the numerical description of the connection strengths between units. To press the case, suppose that NETtalk had been programmed by hand, that Sejnowski and Rosenberg had started with the weight matrix written out before them and laboriously entered its values into NETtalk. Then the matrix (an array of numerals on a piece of paper) would cause the system to have the connection weights it does, those weights being the causal property underlying the disposition N:k→/k/. Thus, NETtalk would be rule-governed after all.

Still, I would stress the enduring disanalogy with a programmed computer. Next to the handwired version of NETtalk we set a home-built word processor: I build my very own digital computer on the basis of an explicit representation, a circuit diagram that is the moral equivalent of a weight matrix—it shows the necessary connections and their electrical properties. Down at the science fair, Sejnowski, Rosenberg, and I compare efforts. We each followed rules in wiring our respective systems, so in some sense, whatever our systems do is rule-governed. Then we turn our products on. Sejnowski and Rosenberg's proceeds to impress the judges by turning text into phonemes, while mine does—nothing. I have yet to program mine, which is to say, the behavior of my device needs a further set of explicit rules inside it in order to exhibit its characteristic causal dispositions (as a word processor, or whatever). Table 4.1 dissects these distinctions.

Table 4.1
Systems with and without Rules

Digital Computer	PDP System
Program code (public, for us)	Weight matrix (public, for us)
represents, describes	
Stored program (in memory)	represents, describes
causes	
Causal dispositional properties	Causal dispositional properties
causes	causes
System I/O behavior	System I/O behavior

Cognition without Mediating Representations
I have argued that PDP systems like NETtalk lack the stored program layer of the sandwich, in agreement with the widespread assertion of the connectionists. If that is correct, then connectionist networks are manipulating representations noncomputationally. That is, there are black boxes in PDP systems which have representations as inputs, representations as outputs, but nothing representational in between. The last argument, concerning the representation of rules, supports this, as do the doubts and difficulties surrounding distributed representations.

We shouldn't be surprised by this conclusion, since it also follows from a familiar a priori argument: If every process that involves the manipulation of representations must be governed by a representation, then we face a budding regress. That is because the application of rules to a process itself involves the manipulation of representations, demanding the application of rules determining how the rules are applied, and so forth. To block the regress, we must assume that there are some representational manipulations which involve no mediating representations (Fodor 1975: chapter 2, 1987:23; Dennett 1978d, 1982c). This must be true of any representational system, thus it must also be true of brains.

Thus, connectionism is a study of great value even if connectionist models are poor shadows of the brains—provided that suggestive analogy is not mistaken for perfect isomorphism. But if the gap between PDP networks and real brains is respected, we find that most of the serious questions about the function of brains as representing organs are still open. It is time, accordingly, to exit the fast lane of the high road and see where the low road of real neurons might lead.

Chapter 5
The Biology of Representation

Why have cognitive scientists persisted in attempting to model sub-systems with artificially walled-off boundaries (not just language understanders, but nursery-stories-only understanders, for instance)? Why are they not trying to model whole cognitive creatures? Because a model of a whole human being would be too big to handle: People know too much about too many topics, have too many interests, capacities, modalities of perception and action. One has to restrict oneself to a "toy" problem in a particular domain in order to keep the model "small" enough to be designed and tested at a reasonable cost in time and money. But . . . why not obtain one's simplicity and scaling down by attempting to model a whole cognitive creature of much less sophistication than a human being? Why not try to do a whole starfish, for instance?
—Daniel Dennett (1978b)

The two preceding chapters have been devoted to the study of synthetic representing systems. These imaginary and computer-simulated networks served two functions. First, the synthetic psychology of chapter 3 provided a setting for the initial statement of the dialectical model of representation. In that conceptual laboratory, we saw how a physical system might be organized to meet the standards of representation (as set out in chapter 1), and we further explored the straightforward hardware modifications that might give simple representing systems the ability to "remember" and "learn." In chapter 4, synthesis served its second function. By looking at more complex (but still thoroughly specified) systems, we examined a few of the complexities of representational analysis, and we witnessed the more sophisticated capabilities of larger networks. They performed tasks that struck us as cognitive, and they did so without representing explicit rules to govern their computations.

Taken together, the two preceding chapters have suggested how representation might occur in living brains. But do brains really work this way? The synthetic excursions were inspired by aspects of neural function and organization. But it remains to be seen if any natural system closely conforms to the dialectical and connectionist style of representation and cognition. In this chapter, I will take the conclusions of the previous chapters and apply them as hypotheses, questions to be put to nature. Do representations à la *Simple Minds* occur in animal brains?

The aspiring representational analyst faces two basic questions regarding any representational system: Where are the representations located, and what is their content? These questions are answered via the conditions stated by the dialectical model of representation, which provides a checklist for candidate representations and the biological devices in which the representations occur: (1) The multiple channel condition: Does the device function as an and-gate or a majority-rule threshold device? (2) The convergence condition: As we trace the upstream inputs to the device, do we encounter a (set of) single origin(s) upon which the representation focuses? (3) The uptake condition: Does the representation have the capacity to contribute to another representation within the system, or to a salient behavior? Positive answers to these questions signal the presence of a representation. Its content can be identified by first tracing the upstream route from the representational device, describing the properties of the sensory transducers at the afferent periphery, and ultimately describing the features of stimuli that can give rise to the inner representations. That enables us to pinpoint the explicit content of the representation. From there, the physical context of the representing system leads us to the extensional content—what, in reality, sits in the representational cross hairs?

Since axons and dendrites are reasonably good information channels in brains, neurophysiology may lead to the discovery of concrete internal representations. Representing devices can conceivably exist at any appropriate junction of neural pathways and be realized in subtle modulations of pre- or postsynaptic membranes or intracellular biochemistry. A complete bottom-up representational psychology, then, may be exceedingly fine-grained and detailed. Furthermore, if representing devices are indeed functionally characterized by their position in information transmitting networks, then identifying representations involves identifying connections between sensory neurons, interneurons, and motor neurons. These are tall orders for human brain science at present. What should students of neural representation do between now and the Golden Age?

One suggestion is to attempt an ethological rescue. The strategy is simple: If human brains are too complex (for now), begin with the brain of a simpler animal and develop a representational psychology for it (cf. Dennett 1978b). The work on relatively simple systems can in turn suggest methods and hypotheses for approaching increasingly complex brains. Ultimately, representational neuroscience will merge with representational psychology, as future researchers formulate increasingly abstract descriptions of neural representational processes. (For a circumspect discussion of this strategy, see Lockery 1989b.)

In this chapter I propose to begin to follow this optimistic strategy, considering two animal species whose neurophysiology has been studied extensively. Readers should be forewarned, however, that the ethological rescue is neither obvious nor easy. Despite the painstaking and ingenious research of a generation of neuroscientists, even simpler brains remain hedged in mystery. At present, we face a practical dilemma. On the one hand, the brains we most want to understand are those that are most like ours—but their complexity eludes us. On the other hand, although simpler brains are easier to unpack, they exhibit much less cognitive sophistication, showing less of the mindfulness that excites our wonder and, in the end, motivates this book. Here I have sought a compromise. I will review work on two vertebrate species that balances neuroscientific detail with cognitive accomplishment. In section 5.1, I will examine occurrent representation in amphibians of the order *anura* (which includes frogs and toads). In section 5.2, I will turn to memory and learning in the mammalian brain, particularly the brain of the rat. (A similar examination of two invertebrate species appears in Lloyd 1987.) The animals I will discuss have brains so much simpler than ours that one may question the whole effort. Nonetheless, I will argue that they meet the functional standards of representational systems and thus invite our scrutiny. Furthermore, attention to them as representational systems highlights specific questions of representational neuroscience—we might call them "neurosemantic" questions.

5.1   Occurrent Representation in a Vertebrate Brain

We might begin our discussion where the neuroethologists do, with a description of some toad behavior. The fixed action patterns (Ewert 1980:58) of toads and frogs are behavioral responses that can be reliably and repeatably evoked, permitting thorough behavioral and (ultimately) neurophysiological study. Frogs and toads have been snapping at simulated prey and fleeing from artificial threats for some thirty years now, affording a detailed account of key stimuli (Ewert 1987), the stimuli configurations that provoke a toad toward one response or another (reviews include Ewert 1980, 1984, 1987; Arbib

1987; Ingle 1976; Grüsser and Grüsser-Cornehls 1976). The study of anuran sensory neurophysiology and especially interactions in its central nervous system have developed in parallel with anuran ethology. The emerging big picture is not only fascinating but concrete enough to warrant consideration here.

In the preceding chapters, I suggested that hypothetical nervous systems consisting of tens or hundreds of simulated neurons were the plausible embodiments of rudimentary representations. Against that background, the 16 million (or so) neurons in the average frog (Kemali and Braitenberg 1969) provide many opportunities for representation. We will pursue that possibility in some detail in the toad, concentrating on occurrent rather than stored representation. The survey of toad neurobiology will be confined to the study of possible representation along one sensory-motor pathway, that leading to a sequence of responses involved in prey capture. The prey-capture response is in fact a sequence of several distinct behavioral subroutines: orienting (the animal turns to face the prey), approach, fixation (taking aim), snapping with its long tongue, gulping, and wiping its mouth with the back of one forelimb. The sequence from snapping through wiping seems automatic, running off whether or not the toad catches any prey, but the prior sequence (orient, approach, fixate) can begin at any stage, and loop (if the toad is stalking rapidly moving prey (Ewert, Burghagen, and Schürg-Pfeiffer 1983)). I will not only restrict our attention to this one sensorimotor routine, but ruthlessly simplify or extrapolate where the composite account is complex or incomplete.

Information Processing in the Vertebrate Retina

In a classic paper, Lettvin and colleagues (1959) asked, "What does the frog's eye tell the frog's brain?" Tempted by the analogy between the eye and a camera, we might propose a quick answer: The frog's lens projects a tiny image of the world onto the frog's retina. If a photograph is a representation, then so also is this biological camera obscura image. This is too quick, however, since we require of natural representation that it be put to use in a representing system, and the play of light on the retina does not qualify if nothing downstream happens as a result. In an early approach to answering their question, Lettvin and coworkers recorded from the optic nerve of a frog placed before a color photograph of its native habitat, taken from lily pad height. They discovered that what the frog's eye told the frog's brain about that pastoral scene was—absolutely nothing. With the complacency that only a simple nervous system can achieve, the frog visual system turns an almost blind eye toward everything stationary (see also Grüsser and Grüsser-Cornehls 1976). So much for the naive hypothesis, including the part where the little image gets sent along to the brain, where the homunculi (or in this case, anuranculi) go to work on it.

Three Relevant Retinal Ganglion Cells: R2, R3, R4
But when stimuli change or move, Lettvin's group discovered, the axons in the optic nerve crackle into life. By varying stimuli and recording sites, the researchers identified four functionally distinct retinal ganglion cells, R1 through R4, located in the frog retina, with axons projecting into the frog's brain. The retina is paved with such cells, with overlapping areas of sensitivity. Thus, each cell patrols a narrow alley of visual space radiating out from the eye.

Three of the ganglion cell types observed in frogs (R2, R3, R4) have also been discovered in toad retinas, so we will begin with them, examining their response properties, the upstream retinal circuitry that dictates their responses, and finally their downstream projections in the toad's brain. All three cells have two general features in common: First, as with many vertebrate ganglion cells, the receptive field (the area of the retina to which the cell responds) has a characteristic bull's eye structure, with a central ring of stimulation surrounded by a halo (or annulus) antagonistic to the central region (figure 5.1). That is, in the toad, stimuli in the center of the receptive field (the excitatory receptive field) of any ganglion cell tend to excite the cell, while stimuli off-center, falling in the antagonistic halo (or inhibitory receptive field) tends to inhibit the cell. (Stimuli that cover both the center and surrounding ring produce a weak excitatory response, a summation of the excitatory and inhibitory tendencies.) Second, as just mentioned, all known toad ganglion cells are exclusively detectors of motion. Together with the first feature, this means that the

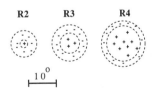

Figure 5.1
The receptive fields of three types of ganglion cells in the toad retina. Each has an excitatory receptive field (ERF) surrounded by an inhibitory receptive field (IRF). A change in the amount of light falling in the ERF tends to fire the cell, whereas a change in light falling in the IRF tends to inhibit firing. The diagram reflects the difference in size of the receptive fields of the three cells. Actual fields are not as sharply defined or regular as the diagram suggests. (See Grüsser and Grüsser-Cornehls 1976 for details.)

best way to drive a toad ganglion neuron is to move through its receptive field a stimulus that is exactly the width of the field's excitatory central region.

The ganglion cell types, R2, R3, and R4, differ most significantly in the size of their receptive fields. The overlapping fields each cover a small region of the retina; thus each is responsive to light from a specific region of space relative to the toad's eye. The width of that region depends on the size of the receptive field. That width is measured by the angle subtended by the stimulus from the point of view of the toad's eye (a worm at two inches and a tractor-trailer truck at two hundred feet might subtend the same angle). The excitatory receptive field of R2 cells is about 4°; of the R3 cells, about 8°; of the R4 cells, about 12°–16°. There are other differences as well, which I will not discuss (see Ewert 1984, Grüsser and Grüsser-Cornehls 1976).

Ganglion Cell Inputs
This summary of ganglion cell receptive properties makes it clear that what the toad's eye tells the toad's brain bears little resemblance to the image projected onto the toad's retina. Rather, the retina is already in the business of information processing (Ewert 1980:135ff.). Where there is information, there might be representation—accordingly, we will unpack some of what is known about the vertebrate retina, called by one of its preeminent explorers, John Dowling (1987), "an approachable part of the brain." How do R2, R3, and R4 cells work?

Like many other parts of nervous systems, the retina has a counterintuitive organization (see figure 5.2). The famous rods and cones lie in the retinal layer farthest from the surface of the retina (and from light), overlaid by two layers of specialized neurons and their processes. The receptors themselves comprise a layer known as the outer nuclear layer (because the cell bodies, or nuclei, of receptors are found there). The next stratum up (toward the center of the eye) is called the inner nuclear layer, consisting of horizontal cells, bipolar cells, and amacrine cells; the third and topmost stratum is the ganglion cell layer, tenanted by the R-cells in question. Between these layers of cell bodies lie the layers of interaction, regions dense with dendrites and synapses; between the ONL and INL, in the outer plexiform layer, receptors interact with horizontal and bipolar cells; between the INL and GCL, in the inner plexiform layer, bipolars interact with amacrine and ganglion cells. Axons from the GCL lie on top of all, ultimately collecting in the optic nerve. For ease of interpretation, I have indicated in figure 5.2 that synapses occur between nerve fibers and cell bodies, rather than between fiber and fiber; thus

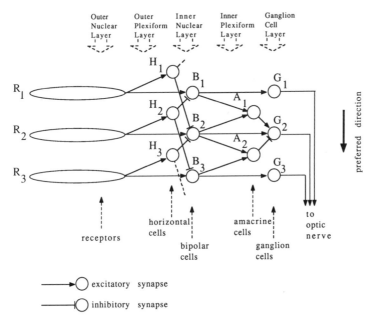

Figure 5.2
The vertebrate retina, greatly simplified, showing a few examples of the main types of cells. Receptor R_2 tends to fire ganglion cell G_2 while tending to inhibit G_1 and G_3. The other receptors would inhibit G_2 through other horizontal cells. G_2 is more responsive to stimuli moving from top to bottom, owing (possibly) to the amacrine cells. Whether ganglion cells are members of class R2, R3, or R4 depends in part on the extent of receptors that excite them, and the horizontal cells which inhibit them. (See Dowling 1987: chapter 4; Poggio and Koch 1987; Masland 1986.)

the diagram contradicts retinal anatomy. It also falsely suggests that each receptor is matched one-to-one-to-one with a bipolar and a ganglion cell. In reality, several receptors synapse onto each bipolar, and several bipolars synapse onto each ganglion cell. Again, ease of interpretation is the aim, and this infidelity should not distort the very general points illustrated by the diagram.

Let us begin with the outer plexiform layer, where photoreceptors, horizontal cells, and bipolar cells interact. We can think of this layer as its own information processor with photoreceptor input and bipolar output and internal interaction mediated by horizontal cells.[1] Each bipolar cell has a field of photoreceptors which excite it—the activation of the photoreceptor is correlated with the activation of a bipolar cell. At the same time, the receptors are also exciting horizontal cells that branch horizontally through the plexiform layer, and these have the effect of inhibiting bipolar cells (and possibly photoreceptors) that lie further away. Thus, the inner plexiform layer has the functional dynamics to account for part of the ganglion cell dynamic, namely, the presence of an excitatory target with an inhibitory surround. "On" photoreceptors activate their nearest bipolar cells while inhibiting more remote cells (through the mediation of inhibitory horizontal cells). The size of the excitatory center would be a function of the field of receptors making direct excitatory connections to bipolars, whereas the size of the antagonistic surround would depend on the stretch of the inhibitory horizontal cells. Beyond that, all the bipolars need to do is pass their information along to the ganglion cells (R1, R2, or R3) to be turned into action potentials, the common currency of the central nervous system.

Bipolar cells do some of that, passing signals from the outer plexiform layer through the inner nuclear layer to the inner plexiform layer; but there is more to the story. Interactions just reviewed may account for a large part of the bull's eyes of receptive fields and antagonistic surrounds, but we have not yet accounted for the toad's eye preference for motion over stationary stimuli. Apparently this transformation is mediated by bipolar cells, amacrine cells, and ganglion cells primarily in the inner plexiform layer. But the story to follow is somewhat speculative: There are about 30 varieties of amacrine cells (Masland 1986) possibly mediating as many functions. Furthermore, the data on retinal function come from intracellular recording from cell bodies and anatomical studies. The interactions that underlie motion detection in the retina may involve synaptic interactions in the dendritic arbor and not appear in cell bodies. Nonetheless, here is the proposal (see Dowling 1987; Torre and Poggio 1978; Reichardt and Poggio 1980; Poggio and Koch 1987; Masland 1986): Motion detection involves the timing of excitatory signals along roughly parallel paths through the retinal layers. Let us return to ganglion cell G_2 in figure 5.2. Bipolar cell B_2 excites the ganglion cell, as does amacrine cell A_1. But amacrine cell A_2 inhibits G_2 (this is the crucial difference). The signal from receptors R_1 and R_2 tends to excite G_2, while R_3 inhibits it (via amacrine cell A_2). Now imagine a stimulus moving across the receptors. Whether G_2 fires or not depends on which receptors fire first. If it moves from top to bottom, a wave of excitation arrives at G_2 and provokes a spike before any inhibition can stop it. But if the stimulus moves from bottom to top, the inhibition (from A_2) arrives first, temporarily shutting down G_2, blocking it from sending a signal to the brain. Thus G_2 is directionally sensitive, preferring motion from top to bottom. The assembly detects movement from top to bottom by virtue of the timing of propagating signals along convergent paths.

A mechanism of bipolar, amacrine, and ganglion cells still does not quite match the functional properties of the toad ganglion cells. The latter were responsive only to motion, whereas the grossly oversimplified mechanism just described would also respond to a stimulus parked over the top bipolar receptive fields—as long as the bottom inhibitory bipolar remains unstimulated, the signal gets through. A possible modification to produce mechanisms exclusively sensitive to motion would multiply the basic mechanism just described, preserving the top-on, bottom-off pairing, and require the motion sensitive ganglion cell to receive several uninhibited signals before firing itself. The race between excitatory and inhibitory stimuli would have to be won by several excitatory cells in succession to fire the ganglion cell. So a stimulus parked over just one bottom-on cell would be insufficient to rouse the ganglion cells.

Representation?
I have edited the details of retinal processing (for which, see Dowling 1987), resulting in, at best, a crude approximation of the vertebrate retina. But enough has been surveyed, I think, to determine if any of the functions just narrated involve representation.

The horizontal, bipolar, amacrine, and ganglion cells receive various combinations of excitatory and inhibitory signals over a bundle of distinct information channels (one for each input synapse). But this by itself is not sufficient for representation. The multiple channel condition requires, in addition, that the representing device integrate the various inputs by functioning as an and-gate or majority-rule threshold device. This might happen in either of two ways. First, if an individual cell has a threshold that cannot be exceeded by any single input channel, it will require two or more summed inputs to fire. Thus it will meet the multiple channel condition. Second, a neuron (or synapse) can meet the multiple channel condition if it lies at the nexus of excitatory and inhibitory inputs and is "tuned" so that the cell will fire only when it is excited and not inhibited. Here too there are two input conditions that must be met: excitation (on one channel) and disinhibition (on the other).

The idea that quiescence should count as an input is unusual physiology but perfectly acceptable from the point of view of information transmission. For example, if your doorbell is operating normally, its present silence tells you that no one is at the door (or at any rate, nothing is pushing the button). The channel exists in any case, so the relevant conditional probabilities among events all hold. The two exclusive events at the source (button pushed/unpushed) are echoes in an exclusive pair at the receiver (bell ringing/silent).

Do any retinal cells meet either of these conditions? Answering this question is complicated by the fact that horizontal, bipolar, and amacrine cells do not communicate with all-or-nothing spikes (unlike ganglion cells and most other neurons), but rather by smoothly graded changes in membrane voltage. Further, retinal cells all receive many inputs, making it very difficult to ascertain when the multiple channel condition is met. We might nonetheless sample a representational analysis of the simplified retina depicted in figure 5.2.

The bipolar cells and the ganglion cells are the first in the sequence (according to the diagram) to meet the multiple channel conditions. Let us consider, first, the bipolar cells. B_2 in the figure, for example, responds when R_2 is active and when R_1 and R_3, in the inhibitory surround, are inactive. If this is physiologically correct, we turn to the remaining conditions—the convergence condition and the uptake condition. Do the inputs to B_2 originate from a single source? That is, could a single stimulus give rise to the response in B_2? A stimulus might well cause R_2 to fire, but we must also look at the other channels integrated by B_2, namely R_1 and R_3. These must be inactive, and the condition they report is the absence of stimuli in their receptive fields. Thus there are three distinct events: a stimulus present in the field of R_2 and stimuli absent in the fields of R_1 and R_3. There is no obvious convergence, or focus, on a single stimulus event. Thus the convergence condition fails; the bipolar cells are not representing devices.

Note that the addition of more excitatory channels does not change the representational analysis of the bipolar cells as long as disinhibition is a necessary condition for cell response. Disinhibition will remain a sign of the absence of stimuli in a part of the receptive field, and this event will be distinct from the presence of stimuli anywhere else, no matter how many channels are active.

We turn next to the ganglion cells. If it is true that motion detection arises in the inner plexiform layer by a mechanism like the one described above, then are ganglion cells the sites of simple representations? The first interpretive issue to arise concerns whether ganglion cells are functional and-gates or threshold devices that require more than one input to fire. As with the bipolars, each receives multiple inputs, and some of the inputs are excitatory, some inhibitory. Further, there must be activity among the excitatory inputs, and there must not be activity on the inhibitory lines—in short, like the bipolar cell, the ganglion cell must be both excited and disinhibited.

If ganglion cells are and-gates, and hence candidate representations, are there single mutually effective stimuli on which the various inputs focus? Following again the simple retina of figure 5.2, we see

background (light/dark or dark/light) (Ewert et al. 1983; Borchers, Burghagen, and Ewert 1978; Ewert, Arend, Becker, and Borchers 1979; color perception is reviewed in Grüsser and Grüsser-Cornehls 1976). Each of these variables makes some difference to the toad's response readiness, but none reverses the basic preference for the wormlike. Importantly, the toad's responses reveal size constancy. That is, the toad can tell the difference between a meal worm at four inches and a garden snake at four yards, even though the image of either might cover the same extent of retina, and thus cause the same pattern of retinal stimulation (Ewert 1980:73). Somewhere along the line, it extracts and uses size information, indicating that it has information about the distance of stimuli. We will return to this point below.

If we compare this to the messages available at the toad's retina, we note a few important differences. The retinal ganglion cells are not particularly responsive to wormlikeness. In particular, the length of stimuli in the worm configuration (moving parallel to the long dimension) makes no difference to ganglionic response—R2 and R3 cells respond just as well to squares as to worms—but makes a marked difference to behavior. In addition, ganglion cell responses display no size constancy. Instead, their excitatory and inhibitory fields are defined by visual angles. Larger stimuli at a distance have the same effect as smaller stimuli closer by. Thus, while the toad's retina detects (and represents) moving edges, it does not represent prey. Indeed, it is doubtful that the toad ever detects prey—that is our concept. Yet it nonetheless uses a more elaborate scheme for prey detection than that provided by the retina alone. There is more to be processed, so we will follow the information from retina back into the animal's brain.

Into the Toad Tectum

For the most part, axons from each retina project to the contralateral side of the brain. Among their several destinations, the most important will be the optic tectum, a layered knob of neurons crowning the anuran brain (Grüsser-Cornehls 1984). Ganglion cell axons terminate in several layers there, each of which maps the spatial layout of the retina with a fair isomorphism—the retinotopic map in this brain is more regular than that in mammals (for example) because the anuran eye lacks a fovea, a central retinal fixation point of particular acuity (Gaze and Jacobson 1963). Since the tectum includes several separate layered retinal maps, when we refer to particular locations in the tectal map of the toad's visual world, we are referring to a particular sensory column penetrating each of those layers at the same place. The visual map projected in the tectum is not the only such map in the toad's brain, nor is it the only destination for retinal afferents. Among the other terminals, we shall also be particularly interested in the retinotopic projection into another part of the brain, the thalamus—but later.

Nine main classes of neurons are found in the optic tectum; these are identified T1 through T9. Each has a different pattern of response. T1, for example, is driven by binocular stimuli, receiving inputs not only from the retina, but also from the contralateral tectum (Ewert 1984:263; Fite 1969). It has a receptive field of 15° to 30°, and responds to motion within that field. T3 cells, in contrast, are mainly quiet when objects move around the toad. But they respond when an object approaches the toad, looming in the visual field. Of the classes of tectal neurons, one is particularly important, T5, because its response characteristics are most like those of the whole toad. T5 cells have been further divided, on a functional basis, into two subclasses T5(1) and T5(2). T5(1) and especially T5(2) display a marked worm-preference (and antiworm reluctance). Ewert expressed their response preferences qualitatively in inequalities comparing cell responses to worms (R_w), antiworms (R_a), and squares (R_s). For stimuli between 2° and 20° along the long dimension, the cells behaved as follows:

T5(1): $R_s > R_w > R_a$,

T5(2): $R_w > R_s > R_a$.

Both cells are active during prey-catching, and lesioning the tectum or disabling the T5 cells resulted in complete extinction of all prey-catching (Ewert 1984:359). These are cells which may well be doing interesting work. What gives them their orders?

At this point, we turn to another retinotopic map, one found in the thalamus. There, Ewert (1971) found ten different cell types, TH1 through TH10 (TH for thalamus). The responses of these cells are complex, some involving nonvisual input. Ewert has selected one of particular interest, TH3. TH3 has an excitatory receptive field of about 30° and is sensitive to moving objects, with these qualitative gestalt preferences:

TH3: $R_s > R_a > R_w$.

Do TH3 cells play a role in prey-catching? Their preference ranking and receptive field suggests that they are far more selective of predators than of prey. But there is evidence that thalamic cells have an

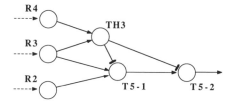

Figure 5.5
A possible neural network underlying prey detection.

important function in prey-catching, namely: Thalamic lesions transform ordinary animals into attack toads, who snap at anything, including large and irrelevant objects like their own limbs, other toads, and hands. However, T5(2) responses after the lesion continue to co-occur with attack behavior. In other words, the thalamic lesion disinhibits the T5(2) cell.

This is slender evidence, but suggestive. On its basis, Ewert (1974) proposed a network suggesting the neural interactions that drive T5(2). Figure 5.5 shows the interactions in one sensory column (now superimposing the tectum on the thalamus). Figure 5.5 is an abstraction from the available neural details, depicting the flow of information through the network. The pathways between the neurons may involve other interneurons, but this is nonetheless an intriguing hypothesis in the present context. First, Ewert suggests that T5(1) cells are driven by R2 and R3 retinal cells (the small- and medium-field cells), whereas TH3 is driven by R3 and R4 (medium and large fields). In support of these hypotheses, Ewert details the response properties of T5(1) and TH3 cells in comparison with the retinal ganglion cells. Since we are less concerned with the theory of the total toad and more with the exemplification of possible neurorepresentational strategies, I will omit that discussion (see Ewert 1984, 1987). The cell type in question here is T5(2), and Ewert fields an ingenious proposal for its input. Here, again, are the response preferences of the involved cell types:

T5(1): $R_s > R_w > R_a$,

TH3: $R_s > R_a > R_w$,

T5(2): $R_w > R_s > R_a$.

Ewert proposes that T5(2) is excited by T5(1) but inhibited by TH3. The rankings above suggest part of the functional support for the proposal. The following table describes, in rough and ready qualitative terms, the responses of each of the cell types of worm, antiworm, and square stimuli. Plus and minus signs in T5(1) and TH3 reflect the excitatory or inhibitory effects of the signals sent to T5(2).

	Worm	Antiworm	Square
T5(1)	+ + + +	+ + +	+ + + + +
TH3	−	− −	− − −
T5(2)	+ + +	+	+ +

The table suggests the integration of T5(1) excitation with TH3 inhibition, giving rise to the observed qualitative preferences in T5(2) responses. We might think of the network as performing simple arithmetic on input signals: T5(2) = T5(1) − TH3.

Interpretation
Again, we seem to be observing a multiple-channel device whose output depends on the simultaneous presence of excitatory input and occurrent disinhibition, not unlike the output of retinal ganglion cells. TH3 cells act like a filter of T5(1) cell output, and through this interaction T5(2) cell output reflects some of the central gestalt features of prey. Thus, the conditions on representation are met by the T5(2) cells. Their representational content is defined in terms of the features of stimuli that excite them—"wormlikeness," a configuration of shape and direction of movement, characterize their nonextensional content. Wormlike objects tend to release prey-catching behavior, whereas larger objects—squares or antiworms—do not release prey-catching. The extensional content of T5(2) excitation depends on what turns out to be typically wormlike in the toad's world. Probably what toad T5(2) neurons most often represent, in their native habitat, is worms.

From Perception to Behavior
The story of anuran representation is incomplete, however. T5(2) output is not in itself sufficient for determining behavior. Among other things, the circuit described above does not yet account for size constancy, since it makes no provision for the computation of distance from the toad (Grüsser and Grüsser-Cornehls 1976; Roth and Nishikawa 1987). The size of the stimulus makes a great difference for the toad's response, however. Further, the presence of an internal worm detector only begins the story of behavioral control, since toads engage in several different responses to prey stimuli, including orienting, approaching, fixating, and snapping. All of these involve the visual identification of a stimulus, but most involve further discriminations to control their initiation and sequence.

Ewert's proposals for the "command releasing system" follow a similar strategy to his proposal for prey detection: seek combinations of neural responses that mirror the observed behavior. For example (from Ewert 1980):

T5(2) + T4: Orient,

T5(2)' + T2(1) + T1(1): Approach,

T5(2)' + T1(2): Fixate,

T5(2)'' + T1(3) + T3: Snap.

He expands his interpretation as follows (Ewert 1987):

> Command elements may be compared with a keyboard (to use an analogy of Hoyle's, 1984) on which certain combinations elicit specific responses: "stimulus moving somewhere in the visual field (class T4)" and "stimulus recognized as prey, n degrees outside the fixation area (class T5(2))" yield the command to orient; "stimulus moving in the frontal visual field (class T2(1))" and "stimulus recognized as prey (class T5(2))" and "stimulus far afield (class T1(1))" yield the command to approach; "stimulus recognized as prey near the fixation area (class T5(2)')" and "stimulus close to the toad (class T1(2))" yield the command to fixate; "stimulus recognized as prey inside the fixation area (class T5(2)'')" and "both retinae adequately stimulated (class T1(3))" and "stimulus within snapping distance (class T3)" yield the command to snap.

Ewert suggests that these various input channels are integrated in neural and-gates, cells or assemblies further downstream that are selectively sensitive to inputs along their constituent channels, from ensembles of particular precursor cells. The representational interpretation is obvious. If there is an and-gate in charge of orienting, then its content concerns the direction and preylikeness of the stimulus, as does the and-gate in charge of approach.

Representational Systems: The Toad's Teaching
There remain many unanswered questions in the understanding of the toad brain and many more uncovered topics in my compressed review of a few of its highlights. But we can nonetheless step back and coordinate the lessons of *anura*. The result is a better grasp of representational dynamics in general, an emerging agenda for neurosemantics—the biology of representation. In the light of the above discussion and biological examples, we can begin to fit the toad into the general enterprise of cognitive science.

Have we, in tracing the circuits, also been tracing the ground floor of cognition? For one central reason, the answer is positive: Representations mediate the toad's behavior. That they are representations was the burden of chapters 2 and 3. That such representations occur in the toad seems to be supported by the work of the neuroethologists. The representations analyzed shared resources, in that the output of one representation comprised an input channel to another representation, downstream from the first. Thus, T5(2) cells might be called *mediated representations*, where mediated means mediated by other (upstream) representations. Where there are no upstream representations, as in the retinal ganglion cells, the representations are immediate—no representations mediate between R2, R3, or R4 cells and the objects of representation—they are the first sites of information convergence that meet the standards for representation. But in addition to these basic distinctions, the discussion above suggests some interrelated conclusions:

1. *Representation in the toad is not fully distributed.* Individual neurons seem to be representations in the anuran brain of features of stimuli, and these featural representations are fixed in explicit content by their place in their neural networks. In another context, H. B. Barlow (1972) has recommended featural or local representation as a specific "dogma" of brain science:

> At progressively higher levels in sensory pathways information about the physical stimulus is carried by progressively fewer active neurons. The sensory system is organized to achieve as complete a representation as possible with the minimum number of active neurons.

If Ewert's proposals are correct, then this claim seems to be true of the toad. But even though single neurons can be representations, there is no suggestion that only one representation is active at a time. Instead, many representations at many different levels clamor simultaneously in the brain, and many of them have concurrent roles in the determination of behavior. Grüsser and Grüsser-Cornehls (1976) explain this representational dynamism with detailed application to the toad:

> The behaviorally observable invariants (prey, predator, hiding places) in the world of anurans are represented by the simultaneous or successive excitation of different classes of visual neurons. The activity of a single class of retinal ganglion cells can be interpreted as a "letter" attributed to a certain location in the visual field. Different combinations of the retinal "letters" represent different meanings. The different activity level of the

retinal neuronal classes leads to the activation of different classes of tectal and thalamic visual cells. Their activity is interpreted as a "word," which facilitates together with other nonvisual or partly nonvisual neurons the motor subcommands of a certain behavioral response. The "words" are still related to a certain location of the stimuli within the visual space. As the motor responses are performed, the visual stimulus changes (e.g., the prey image moves from a lateral part of the visual field to the binocular part). . . . The new stimulus elicits a different combination of "letters" and therefore activates a different set of central visual neurons, i.e., different "words" eliciting different motor subcommands. . . . The sequential combination of different words leads to a "sentence," i.e., the sequence of motor responses.

The metaphorical letters, words, and sentences are, in nonmetaphorical fact, representations.

2. Following from the above, *cognition in the toad is spread out throughout the brain.* There is no central locus of cognition, no seat of selfhood, no "middletoad" (to borrow a term from Dennett 1987c). Nor is there a privileged level at which everything representational occurs. Interactions occur between levels and within levels.

3. *Cognition in the toad is not obviously rule-governed.* All the toad needs, or has on call, are occurrent representations of stimulus configurations. Nowhere in the toad do we find representations with content (even in our terms) like this: "When T5(2)' and T1(2) neurons are lit, then FIXATE!" Instead, when the right representation lights up, the toad responds for the simple reason that the representation is hard-wired to the response. Variability in response arises not from choice in the toad but from the conflicting representations and the interaction from modulatory channels. This observation coordinates with the extended discussion of the representation of rules in chapter 4. Indeed, we might make analogous arguments here, switching toad talk for NETtalk talk.

All three of these statements are only first approximations, and we will return to the many issues implied by them in subsequent chapters. Taken together, they suggest that we will find no cognitive program governing the toad, no uniform, sequential, rule-governed piece of anuran software, the reading of which is the goal of psychology.

But then, who would expect something so cognitive in the toad? In toads, we have reviewed the complex effects of connections among occurrent representations in systems of moderate size (as brains go).

One might well argue that toads are still much too simple to offer interesting insights into human—or even mammalian—cognition. Let us then move on to more brainy cognitive systems.

5.2   Remembrance of Things Past

There can be little question that mammalian brains exceed all others in cognitive abilities. Their mass alone is enough to suggest their magnified representational capacities. But do the brains of mammals share functional properties with those of "lower" animals? How does the complicated hardware of a bigger brain support more sophisticated cognition? In this section, I will explore, somewhat briefly, a few of the hardware enhancements that might underlie more sophisticated cognition. We will look first at the effects of "more of the same"—the increases in representational ability that an increase in the sheer number of neurons affords. Then we will turn to two variations in physiology (plastic synapses and highly connected networks) and their representational effects.

Depth and Breadth of Representational Systems

Representational systems can be characterized, very generally, along several dimensions. First, we can describe the *depth* of a system by the number of mediating representations lying between the most mediated representation and its object. In our tour of the toad, at least three layers of representation emerged: the ganglion cells, T5(2) cells, and the various proposed command releasing units. Probably there are more mediating layers, but we can say that the depth of the anuran representing system is at least three. Similarly, one can speak of the representational depth of individual representations. In the toad, the ganglion cells lie at a representational depth of one, the T5(2) cells at (at least) two, and the command releasing cells at a depth of three. In more complex brains, we probably cannot expect orderly relations among representational layers; instead, some representations will likely be found at different depths along different channels.

Along with depth, one can compare the *breadth* of representational systems, the representational band width. Representational breadth can be measured by comparing the number of representing devices (properly situated threshold devices) at a given depth in a representing system. Two associated measures of systemic breadth might be called transducer breadth, the number of nonredundant transducers (sensory neurons or subrepresentational assemblies) available to the system, and the motor breadth, the number of nonredundant motor effectors driven by the system.

How do depth and breadth help a system? Intuitively, broad and deep systems are more sophisticated than shallow and narrow ones, and this sophistication is clearly manifest in the representational capacity of systems. Breadth and depth are both means of achieving greater specificity in representation. The toad illustrated the gain of depth. As we moved downstream, each representational layer integrated more information from upstream channels—an increase of informational convergence through each layer of representation. The final representations, those penultimate to the behavioral response, represented the most sophisticated integration of inputs. Theirs was the most specific content and afforded the most specific response.

Depth provides for specificity, but so does breadth—in two ways. First, a broad system might be one with many different parallel informational/representational pathways. Such a system is a bundle of perceptual and behavioral specialists, each on a slightly different patrol, each with slightly different duties. Systems with more parallel representational columns are accordingly capable of a greater variety of responses to a greater range of stimuli. Second, with breadth comes the opportunity for individual representing devices each to be connected to more input channels. This convergent connectivity has the same effect as increased depth, permitting more channels of focus and greater specificity of representation. In sum, more neurons afford more specific representations, hence more specific and elaborate behavioral responses. But this is not the only way to increase the capabilities of brains.

Natural And-accumulators

The original and-accumulator (AA, introduced in section 3.3) is a dual purpose device. It is first a threshold device that will fire when it receives sufficient input. But its firing threshold can change; in effect, the AA is a device of variable sensitivity. It begins with a high threshold, requiring multiple inputs to fire, thus behaving like an and-gate or majority-rule device. But if those multiple inputs occur together repeatedly, the AA's threshold decreases. Finally, input along a single channel is enough to fire it. The AA remains hypersensitive as long as paired inputs reinforce the threshold depression. But in the absence of paired inputs, it slowly returns to its original high threshold state.

Though synthesized for expository purposes in chapter 3.3, the and-accumulator bears more than a coincidental likeness to nature. Interacting neurons sometimes function like the AA. In this section, I will review one model of a natural and-accumulator and an intriguing proposal for its employment in the mammalian brain. My purpose here, as in section 5.1, is not to rule on the truth or falsity of the proposals but to display them as both neural models and representing systems. They exemplify the application of the dialectical theory of representation as a bridge between the brain's wetware and cognition.

If there are natural and-accumulators, they might be explained by a mechanism of neural plasticity known as long-term potentiation (LTP). LTP takes several forms, but all have a common result, namely, a facilitation of synaptic efficacy as a result of high-frequency stimulation of the presynaptic cell (Veronin 1983, Eccles 1983, Lynch and Baudry 1984). For example, less than one second of high-frequency axonal stimulation can produce an increase in synaptic response that can last for days to months.

LTP does not always require input over multiple channels to occur. In many cases, however, the long-term potentiation is more pronounced if several neurons converge on the cell that is potentiated (Abraham and Goddard 1984; Barrionuevo and Brown 1983; Gustafsson and Wigström 1986; Kelso and Brown 1986; Lee 1983; Levy and Steward 1979; McNaughten, Douglas, and Goddard 1978; Robinson and Racine 1982; Veronin 1983). When cooperation among inputs creates a long-term increase in synaptic efficacy, the cell in which LTP occurs bears a strong resemblance to an and-accumulator. But even where cooperativity is not observed, networks with the right properties could realize functional and-accumulation, depending on the threshold of LTP effects. In a circuit whose input lines have a normal firing frequency in the presence of stimuli that is less than the threshold for LTP, LTP effects will emerge only when multiple input lines are active. Thus, the potentiated neuron or synapse will change state only in response to conjoint inputs. But like an and-accumulator, the effect of recurrent conjoint inputs is an increase in the sensitivity of the potentiated cell or synapse. After LTP, the normal input along just one line is sufficient to fire the cell.

Well-Connected Brains
LTP effects have been observed in the hippocampus, cortex, and other sites in the mammalian brain (Lee 1982; Racine, Milgram, and Hafner 1983; Gerren and Weinberger 1983; Stripling, Patneau, and Gramlich 1984; Kelso, Ganong, and Brown 1986). Thus, the mammalian brain may well have an abundant supply of neural devices for storing representations—and-gates that change state and remain changed long after their inputs have ceased. Mammalian brains also have another resource, namely, myriad connections among neurons. The evidence for a high degree of connectivity is

indirect and depends on comparisons of brain size and neural population across species. As one progresses from small to large mammalian brains, increases in absolute brain mass are not matched by increases in neuronal numbers. Rather, the increase in brain size is disproportionately due to increases in mass outside the cell body. Rising through the ranks from mice to humans, one finds a larger proportion of the brain devoted to connections among neurons.

Gary Lynch (1986:19) has explained this progression by considering the resources required to expand two varieties of neural circuits, namely, topographic and combinatorial circuits. A paradigmatic topographic circuit is one in which each cell of one layer is connected to just one cell of the next higher layer, as illustrated in figure 5.6A. In contrast, in a combinatorial circuit, each cell of one layer connects to several (or all) cells in the next layer (B in figure 5.6). (Note that circuits A and B have equal depth and breadth, but that the latter has greater connectivity.) Now suppose we enlarge this hypothetical brain by adding more cells. We could do so while preserving the topographic wiring (as in C) or while preserving the combinatorial wiring (D). In the latter case, the high degree of connectivity demands that each added cell to the circuit travel with a nest of connections: Four interlayer connections become nine. Increasing the breadth to four increases the connectivity to sixteen, and so forth. In a system with maximum interlayer connections, the connectivity will be equal to $b_i b_j$, the breadth (b) of layer i times the breadth of layer j. But when connections are topographic, connections match the breadth of the interconnected layers.

Lynch suggests that the observed relationship of brain size and neuron count is a consequence of this geometric growth of number of connections in combinatorial circuits along the continuum from small

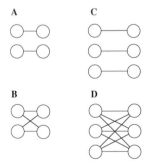

Figure 5.6
New connections outpacing new cells. A and C are topographic circuits, B and D are combinatorial.

to larger brains. In brief, what sort of brain wiring would require disproportionately more dendrites and axons with the addition of more cells? The idealized examples suggest that the enlargement of combinatorial circuits could account for the relation. Apparently evolution built better brains not simply by adding more neurons but by adding more neurons and by adding many more combinatorial circuits throughout the brain.

Lynch's ingenious argument for combinatorial brain wiring next informs an interpretation of the anatomy and physiology of those parts of the brain concerned with the sense of smell. The path Lynch sets out to trace begins with the olfactory bulbs at the forebrain of the rat and terminates with the fixation of long-term memories at different sites in the brain. He cites evidence for combinatorial circuitry in five different stages in the processing leading toward and through the hippocampus (1986:25ff.) In our terms, the depth of the olfactory combinatorial circuit is at least five layers. What follows here is a generalized examination of the processes Lynch discusses. Though some of his proposals are speculative (as are many of mine), his is a far better informed speculation. I recommend Lynch's monograph for the details, which are many and complex.

Plasticity Meets Connectivity
If each input neuron connected with all neurons in the next deeper layer and all the connections were equally effective, any particular input would, at the next deeper level, either fire all the cells at that level or none of them. Since neither of these effects is very useful to a brain, we would expect a neural combinatorial circuit to be somewhat sparse in connectivity. That is, buried interneurons must be selective among their input lines. Some might receive inputs from large banks of upstream neurons, and some from very few. The best circuits, presumably, strike a balance between topographic and combinatorial organization (on which, see Lynch 1986:36). A system with several such layers achieves the ability to encode complex ensembles of inputs—specificity in short. This is, again, the lesson of convergence, nicely illustrated by the toad. Whereas toads have a very low cognitive acuity, discriminating only certain relatively simple configurations, mammals do much better, harnessing greater depth, breadth, and connectivity to generate more specific representations.

What happens when the highly connected and-gates are traded in for similarly connected and-accumulators (as seems to be the case in the mammalian brain)? When and-accumulators are embedded to various depths in a rich network, the specificity of occurrent representation is matched by the capacity for storing highly specific representations. Such a system becomes sensitized to the co-occurrence of many separate features of stimuli. With increasing depth and breadth, a highly connected network can learn to discriminate increasingly specific stimuli.

Consider a general example. Suppose we characterize an object of perception O in terms of three distinct features—a, b, and c. These features can range widely over any combinations that the network can integrate. Perhaps, for example, the features are edges detected at specific orientations and positions in the visual field, or perhaps they are complex combinations of visual cues and cues in other sense modalities. Figure 5.7 depicts a schematized network for detecting objects of type O_{abc}. O detection is mediated by units T_a through T_c, each of which is a simpler feature detector. Although these may be as simple as transducers, they are more likely to be networks themselves, perhaps similar to the retinal and tectal feature detectors in the toad. Similarly, the individual units of the diagram may be an ensemble of cells in the brain. If N_{abc} is an and-gate requiring all three inputs to fire, then it is an O_{abc} detector—but it is a picky one, requiring that all three features arouse the relevant transducer/detectors at the periphery. But if it is instead an and-accumulator and the system is exposed to objects of O's perceptual type for some time, then the sensitivity of the unit increases until only some of O's features, perhaps even just one, is enough to spark the cascade of responses leading to the activation of the deepest unit. What we find is a stored representation (of stimuli of type O_{abc}) mediating a new informational pathway, one which need no longer be occurrently representational, since and-gates have modulated into or-gates. To put the transformation in Lynch's terms, we find memory in the service of recognition. A nest of and-accumulators enables a brain to become tuned to the regularities inherent in the objects that typify its perceptual environment. Networks like these enable brains to reflect, in their internal economy, the unity among diversity of the external world.

A network of and-accumulators additionally allows for flexibility in

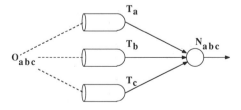

Figure 5.7
A simple network for integrating detected features to detect a complex stimulus.

the system's responses, a feature nearly absent in toads. Remove a toad from the world where prey moves and deliver it to a smorgasbord of inert but otherwise delectable toad chow, and it will go hungry. But mammals will do much better, thanks in part to the neural flexibility that allows them to get on in a changing environment, responding to new stimuli and adapting to changes in the old. Figure 5.8 expands the network shown in figure 5.7, in order to give some sense of this adaptability. In its starting state, such a network detects stimuli composed of adjacent features (O_{ab}, O_{bc}, etc., or O_{abc} etc.). But as it encounters these sorts of objects, and its and-accumulators become sensitized, it also acquires capacities to represent other feature combinations, like O_{abe}. At the extreme, some mammals take the same apparatus that equipped their ancestors for hunting mammoths and digging roots and retool it for parallel parking and catching fly balls.

Feedback and Modulation
Complex nets of and-accumulators, it seems, can encode complex information. Each element of the network exhibits the ability to alter its response, and these deflections can emerge, in the end, in modified behavior. But the processes described so far are data-driven in a strong sense. Signals propagate downstream, from input to output. However finely tuned and deeply integrated, a system built along these lines would inherit some of the simple-minded features of our earlier *gedanken*-beasts: Take away the stimuli, and this imaginary brain lapses into quiescent waiting, not just for Godot, but for anything. Lower animals, like the toad, may in fact reach these zen neural states, but the mammalian brain is always busy. To what do neural networks owe their industry, if not to external stimuli?

An obvious, but very general answer: Internal nervous activity is mutually or collectively self-sustaining. Even in the absence of

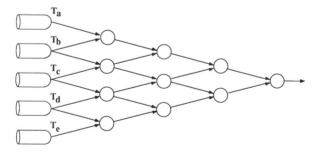

Figure 5.8
Larger and-accumulator networks afford representational flexibility.

stimuli, networks reverberate in a continuous brainstorm of mutual excitation. In general, this interneural resonance must be the biological basis of cognition, but how? There have been several proposals, none claiming universal acceptance (in addition to Lynch 1986, see the papers collected in Anderson and Rosenfeld 1988). Even a network as oversimplified as that depicted in figure 5.8, however, can provide the hardware needed to produce effects similar to recall.

To see how a neural network might break out of purely perceptual or data-driven processing, let us first add a capacity for feedback. For example, figure 5.9 adds excitatory feedback to the connections sketched in figure 5.8. The shallower input units excite the deeper units as before, but now the deeper additionally re-excite the shallower. In neural terms, postsynaptic neurons synapse back onto presynaptic neurons.

In a circuit of and-accumulators, this feedback can have interesting and variable dynamic effects. We will observe these dynamics in stages. In the beginning, the network is naive, with no units tuned by recurrent association. At this point, the feedback is redundant, flowing upstream toward units that are already activated en route to the representation, as in figure 5.8. This is, again, a finicky, sluggish network, requiring that all perceptual features are present before the higher-order units fire.

Suppose, however, the network is repeatedly exposed to features a, b, c, and d, and that the convergent synapses throughout the network have the properties of and-accumulators. As in figure 5.8, one or both of the converging inputs at each junction are potentiated, with the result that several connections become sensitized. For example, activity in T_a alone might fire N_{ab}. But the feedback circuits may also be enhanced, and as a result the firing of N_{abc} could fire the upstream cell N_{bc}.

Next we consider a sequence of activation in a highly tuned, hair-

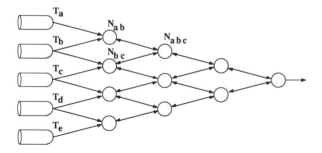

Figure 5.9
A simple network with excitatory feedback.

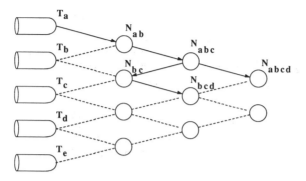

Figure 5.10
Feedback and rebounding excitation.

trigger network. In such a net, a single transducer event, say event a, will arouse several downstream units, including N_{abc} and N_{abcd}. Event a has become the cue to the detection of two stimuli, O_{abc} and O_{abcd}. The activation of the deeper units also has rebounding effects in the network. Unit N_{abc} propagates excitatory feedback back toward the input periphery, firing N_{bc} and ultimately N_{bcd}. The resulting chain reaction is shown in figure 5.10.

Now let us introduce the network to a new experience, this time, the conjunction of features b, c, d, and e. As in the earlier instance, feedforward and feedback to various and-accumulators sensitize a number of connections in the circuit. The set of cells implicated in the response to O_{bcde} overlaps with the cells responsive to O_{abcd}. Unit N_{bcd}, for example, can fire in response to either stimulus. This overlap extends the range of the rebounding activation, with a possible sequence shown in figure 5.11.

The crude depiction of the process suggests burgeoning chaos, a wild cascade of impulses leading to the simultaneous activation of several motor responses. But the brakes are built into the system at several points. First, the activation of the deepest neurons does not necessitate a motor response. Between unit N_{abcde} and the response lie several more layers of information processing, several more synapses. And where there are synapses, there are thresholds. At any point the spiking of any cell may be subliminal for the next cell downstream. So the neural ricochet may be sparse. Along with that, we might expect that there will be lateral inhibition among cells in the same layer, resulting in a dampening of neighboring responses. This suggests that for the rebound effect to be sustained, it must stretch beyond the inhibitory immediate neighborhood of any active cell. So the effect will be more pronounced in networks in which neurons have wider arborizations and where there is more depth; both enable

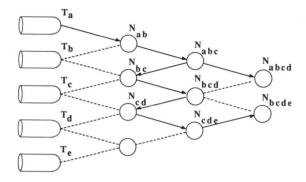

Figure 5.11
Extended rebound.

the feedback to reach far afield from the inhibition accompanying the initial feedforward. Finally, the overall liveliness of the brain is subject to an assortment of global and local neuromodulators. None of these biological constraints, lamentably, appear in the simple network, but they are available, fortunately, in animal brains.

When will the rebound be sustained, and what course will it follow? Whether propagating upstream or downstream, it will take the path of least resistance, i.e., lowest thresholds, i.e., greatest LTP, i.e., most sensitized and-accumulators, and it will continue as long as such a path lies before it. As a consequence the ricochet is an outgrowth of the experience of the organism. If neuron N_{ab} is sensitive enough for the feedback to fire it, that is partly because its inputs have often occurred together, and the association has potentiated N_{ab}.

How do we interpret the activity of the various spiking and reverberating neurons? By now, the interpretive drill is familiar and can have different results for each neuron. In figure 5.11 we observe a process in which event a triggers a stored representation of O_{abcd}. But this ultimately activates a stored representation of O_{bcde}. O_{bcde}, however, is not present as its representation activates. But the activation of N_{bcde} has been facilitated by the network's past encounters with O_{bcde}.

In its skeletal description, then, the process resembles recall. The process has been facilitated by the shared features of the two stimuli. The network, upon "seeing" O_{abcd}, was "reminded" of O_{bcde}. Note that the features these representations pick up might be various and complex and the content assigned to them accordingly diverse. An event might be a simple tone or light, or the smell of madeleines. The remembrance of things past these stimuli arouse can range from similar tones and lights to ten volume novels. Further, the features integrated by the representation can have various relations to one another. The features might be co-occurrent: with a nice ambiguity, the Beatles sing, "I've just seen a face I can't forget/ the time or place where we just met." Or the features might be presented sequentially. In the review of toad vision we saw how a mechanism for motion detection might work. A similar time-sensitive network could remember and recognize sequences of events. (Such a network has been modeled by Dehaene, Changeux, and Nadal 1987.) The ricochet of memory might lead one far afield from the initiating event. For example, Garcia Marquez opens *One Hundred Years of Solitude* with the following: "Many years later, as he faced the firing squad, Colonel Aureliano Buendia was to remember that distant afternoon when his father took him to discover ice." (Ice signaled Aureliano's first encounter with the world outside his village; the firing squad was his last.)

Of course, these elegies lie well beyond the 14 units of our examples. The memory excursion has been yet another bottom-up exercise intended to show how a physical system could in fact embody a cognitive process. Biological brains use many of the resources we have built upon, including long-term potentiation, multiple inputs, and elaborate feedback and feedforward. The networks used in the examples hardly began to exploit the resources of highly connected networks of neurons. Assemble a few hundred billion neurons, and stocking the storehouse of memory will come naturally.

Resemblance, Contiguity, and Cause-and-Effect?
In 1748, David Hume (1748 (1977):14) described the dynamics of the mind:

> To me, there appear to be only three principles of connexion among ideas, namely, *Resemblance, Contiguity* in time or place, and *Cause* or *Effect*.
>
> That these principles serve to connect ideas will not, I believe, be much doubted. A picture naturally leads our thoughts to the original; the mention of one apartment in a building naturally introduces an enquiry or discourse concerning the others; and if we think of a wound, we can scarcely forbear reflecting on the pain which follows it.

Interlayer rebound seems indeed to resemble the principles of classical association enumerated by Hume, since stimuli that are similar, contiguous, or sequential are likely to produce long-term changes in neural and-accumulators. But there are differences. First, there are constraints on the available associations due to the structure of the network. Some connections can never be made, regardless of the world outside, and some will be made even in the absence of empirical warrant. The structure and connections of the brain determines them. In the present framework, the brain, independent of all experience, is a repository of latent content, potential representations on call to the right combination of transducer outputs. The role of experience is to push the buttons, making the latent actual, both occurrent and stored.

A second difference is that the associated entities are not ideas. We have said nothing yet about introspection and have certainly avoided appeals to an ontologically distinct realm of the mental. Instead, associative connections emerge between different representations or informational states. These share with ideas the capacity to bear content but analyze the applicable sense of content in a thoroughly naturalistic way.

Perhaps these distinctions remove that sense of reinventing the wheel. We have, at any rate, explored the option of a retread. If this is progress, it is because we have worked to establish the basis in speculative physiology for the associations brains might realize. In chapters to follow, we will face some of the perennial problems shared by both vintage associationism and these efforts at rehabilitation.

These examples suggest, I hope, that natural representation offers a powerful framework for the description of information processing and integration in diverse living systems. Or, to put it another way, that systems using natural representations are capable of complex and sophisticated behavior. They are powerful systems in many respects. But at the same time, neurophysiology, computer simulation, and our synthetic imagination so far leave untouched several important cognitive faculties. These capacities are either our human monopoly, or at best only dimly present in other species. We humans speak, we experience, and we reason. How might natural representation illuminate these three capacities?

PART III
From Simple Minds to Human Minds

Chapter 6
The Languages of Thought

SOCRATES. It appears to me that the conjunction of memory with sensations, together with the feelings consequent upon memory and sensation, may be said as it were to write words upon our souls. And when this experience writes what is true, the result is that true opinions and true assertions spring up in us, while when the internal scribe that I have suggested writes what is false we get the opposite sort of opinions and assertions.
—Plato, *Philebus* 39a

This book began with a contrast between two approaches to the study of minds: the top-down and the bottom-up. Five chapters have been devoted to exploring the potential of the bottom-up approach. Part I harnessed philosophical intuition and synthetic imagination to describe physical representational systems in their simplest incarnations. Part II used the concept of representation developed in part I as an interpretive tool in the examination of complex information processing networks, some of them living, some simulated. If the dialectical theory of representation is correct, the behaviors of these networks and brains are mediated by representations. Moreover, as these networks became more complex, so did the behavior they exhibited. Some of this behavior seems, to a first approximation at least, to be cognitive, involving pattern recognition, memory, or perceptual-motor coordination. Parts I and II, taken together, suggest how physical systems might come to be representing systems, and how they might harness representations in apparently cognitive tasks. These physical systems thereby share some important properties with minds. They might be called simple minds.[1]

But even if the systems considered above are minds, their simplicity limits their application. The study of mind is inspired by the human mind, and it would be welcome if the simple minds approach were to illuminate us. The remaining chapters comprise three tentative forays into more human cognitive states and capacities. This chapter relates the dialectical representations of parts I and II to language. Chapter 7 examines consciousness, and the last chapter considers human reasoning and thought. Generally, the issue I will explore in these three chapters is one of continuity. In sophistication and complexity, human cognition and behavior easily surpass that of any animal or computer. Does our mental prowess reflect a fundamental difference between us and simpler minds? Or is our braininess just more of the same—are we super-charged simple minds?

I will explore the prospects for continuity by exploring how dialectical representing systems could display some of the main capacities of the human mind. So far I have been relentlessly building from the bottom up, but henceforth the analysis will be more from the top down, beginning with the behavioral displays of whole minds and analyzing the underlying capacities into processes a simple mind might undertake. At this stage, there is little hope of being correct. Instead, I hope the hypotheses are suggestive, leading to empirical tests and fruitful refutations.

This chapter begins with a collision of the dialectical theory of representation with another theory of representation, the "language of thought hypothesis" (LT). The LT hypothesis, sometimes dubbed "the only game in town," has been championed with tenacity, wit, and insight by Jerry Fodor (1975, 1981, 1987). Its application here is twofold: the contrast between the LT hypothesis and the simple minds approach reveal some serious limitations of dialectical representation, but the language of thought hypothesis faces some deep problems of its own. In this chapter, I will suggest a single solution to both problems.

The Basic Language of Thought Hypothesis
A large part of the doctrinal differences between the language of thought hypothesis and the simple minds approach trace to the differing motivations of the two views. Fodor begins with a consideration of what brains do, whereas I began with the question of what representation is. In many respects, we travel the same road, but in opposite directions. In brief, Fodor has argued that doing what brains do requires certain sorts of entities, mental representations. I have argued that certain sorts of entities are representations, and that they can do what brains do. Readers have heard enough about simple minds; let us turn briefly to Fodor's starting point, complex mental processes.

Fodor begins his argument for the language of thought with the observation that psychological explanations appeal to (among other things) capacities for behavioral choice, concept learning, and perception (1975: chapter 1). It is psychology's business to explain what happens when cognizers exercise these capacities. What must the explanations be like? Fodor describes them from a programmatic and schematic distance, revealing their common elements. For example, complex behavior is a multistage process wherein an animal perceives itself to be in a certain situation, believes it has certain options, each with a more-or-less probable outcome, ranks those options and outcomes in desirability, and executes a behavior that it believes to be number one on its short list. The account is unavoidably laced with belief-desire terminology; that is, it is full of talk of representational states. Fodor's account of concept learning and perception equally exposes commitments to content: Each process involves hypothesis formation and confirmation (for concepts or percepts)—hypotheses are, of course, representational. In sum, each of these central cognitive processes involves computation. Given Fodor's slogan, "No computation without representation," each process presupposes representation. (Also see the papers in Fodor 1981. An interesting generalization of the argument appears in Fodor 1986; cf. Lloyd 1986.)

In the aftermath of chapters 4 and 5, we might challenge part of the computational story—the part that conceives cognition as inevitably involving the application of rules to representations. In the previous chapters, we toured complex systems that represent events and regularities in the world but that perform their own internal processing without governing rules (as distinct from Fodor 1975:72; cf. Stabler 1983). Both living brains and connectionist networks are rule-described but not rule-governed. But the internal operations of these living and synthetic systems are nonetheless representational. So the general moral that cognition needs representation is compatibly supported by both Fodor's arguments and the discussions above. This does not yet say much about what representations are or how they get their content. Fodor's developed theories in answer to those questions more fully characterize the language of thought hypothesis.

Principally, according to Fodor the inner representational system uses a languagelike medium: Thought is the manipulation of internal symbols with cognitively relevant constituent structure. In the terminology of section 1.2, the structures of thought are articulate, having a syntax that describes how meaningful atoms compose contentful molecules, just as linked words form sentences. Like language, inner representations are constructed of parts whose contribution toward the meaning of the wholes they comprise is fixed. This compositionality is motivated by the flexibility of thought: We can entertain new thoughts, just as we can produce new sentences, until our dying day and not run out of representations. Though we hit some hardware limitations on the complexity of processing, we find no limits on the variety. Only compositionality of representation accounts for the productivity of thought.

Let us call this core theory about representation—entities with syntax and computational dynamism—the basic language of thought hypothesis, BLT for short (see the appendix to Fodor 1987 for a defense of this basic form of the LT hypothesis). BLT, so far, is ecumenical, consistent with many possible construals of inner representation. For example, the language of thought might well be a natural language like English or Russian. And at the other end of a continuum, the language of thought might also be a representational system like the more complex systems toured in the previous chapters. We have discussed ways in which neural systems can embody complex representations with combinatorial possibilities. Though the systems are lightweight contenders, they have some of the resources Fodor requires. The limits they hit, though they hit them quickly, are arguably analogous to the limits in complexity that our larger brains ultimately hit as well. Thus, to this point BLT coexists with the simple minds approach. And as the arguments above suggest, the philosophical support for BLT is strong.

The Radical Language of Thought Hypothesis

BLT, however, leads to further developments that are not so comfortable. The first and perhaps the most palatable is the assertion that LT is not a natural language. We are to think of it, instead, as "mentalese," a peculiar language "spoken" only in the hidden corridors of thought. At least two arguments work to establish the mentalese hypothesis, the one empirical and open to exceptions, the other not.

First, Fodor notes that we use the same sorts of behavioral explanations for many animals as we do for people, and so our commitment to content extends to them (1975:56; 1978). But they lack any natural language. Presumably their inner representational media are dialects of mentalese, a non-natural language. So the continuity of explanatory strategy employed toward us and them argues for a continuity of computational resources, one inner language for everyone. But the argument establishes less than the full-blown mentalese doctrine requires. It suggests that there are languages of thought in addition to the languages we humans speak, but it does not argue that mentalese (in its dialects) is the only language of thought. It remains possible that we are discontinuous with the animal kingdom in thought in exactly the way we are in behavior—we are the sole speakers and perhaps the sole thinkers in natural language. (The animals might make do with a basic language of thought, namely, dialectical representation.)[2]

Fodor's second argument for mentalese is much stronger and will lead to a characterization of mentalese that is more problematic (1975: chapter 2). The argument follows from broad considerations of language learning. Fodor's characterization of language learning is of a piece with his account of concept formation: Language learning is a special case of hypothesis formation and confirmation. In language learning the hypotheses confirmed take the form of truth rules. For example, when a native English speaker learns German, she will be forming and confirming hypotheses like the following:

"Schnee ist weiss" is true (in German) if and only if snow is white.

Or, more generally:

'Py' is true (in L) if and only if x is G.

'Py' is a sentence in the language being learned. But in what language is the rest of the truth rule? Obviously, the phrase "is true (in L) iff x is G" must be in some language the language learner already knows. Since this point is true of any language learning, it is true of learning a first language. The truth rules used to learn that first language, in other words, must be framed in a yet prior language. Thus, there exists a language that you know prior to learning any natural language—this is mentalese.

This same account of language learning entails three noteworthy features of mentalese. First, in expressive power the language of thought is equal to (or greater than) any natural language. That's because the predicate P in 'Py,' in order to be learned at all, must be mirrored by a coreferential mentalese predicate G—otherwise the relevant truth rule cannot be framed. (Which is why, by the way, one cannot learn a whole language beginning with a fragment of that language—unless the fragment is already as powerful as the whole language.) In short, mentalese is very rich. It includes the predicates (or the resources to construct the predicates) corresponding to everything we have ever talked about—from rain to superconductivity—and everything we ever will talk about—from ozmyrrahs to quettles.

Second, since we cannot speak mentalese, and since we really cannot even speak about it on the basis of introspection, the language of thought must be unconscious. In Freud's wake, this claim may not be so unpalatable. (The Freudian unconscious—demanding, infantile, stormy—stands in provocative constrast to the Fodorian unconscious—cognitive, rational, intricately structured.)

Conscious or unconscious, the representational resources of mentalese would be an embarrassment of riches if the following regress got started: Grant that we need mentalese to learn natural languages. By the same argument, it follows that we need a mentalese precursor to learn mentalese, and a preprecursor to learn the precursor, and so on. But, as Fodor points out, the regress gets rolling only if every language is learned. Thus he blocks it at its inception: mentalese is not learned—it is innate.

Let us call the doctrines following from the argument about language learning RLT, the radical language of thought hypothesis. RLT goes beyond BLT in its assertion that the language of thought housed in each of us is a rich, innate, unconscious, mentalese. Other views of language—notably Chomskian linguistics—posit innate structure underlying the language faculty, but RLT is stronger. The Fodorian vision of language learning exceeds the model of innate constraints on syntax. RLT is not just a set of constraints on possible languages we might learn; instead, it is itself a language from top to bottom. "Radical" is not a novel polemical adjective here. Like the argument at the heart of the *Meno* or the arguments for the existence of a prime mover, this argument has left many—Fodor included—squirming. On the face of it, RLT seems both extreme and extremely unlikely. But how else is language learning to be explained?

This bind, often called "Fodor's paradox," has been discussed by many authors, but I will omit a survey of those discussions. Instead, I will temporarily table RLT to turn to another batch of problems: those facing the dialectical theory of representation.

Limits to Dialectical Representation
By now, there should be no need to review the model of dialectical representation used in *Simple Minds*. It is clear, I hope, that both natural and contrived representational systems have the resources necessary to represent an indefinite range of events and situations. Indeed, an organism with the right transducers and right innards can represent any event on which it is dependent. But right there comes the rub: Dialectical representing systems can only represent events on which their inner states are dependent. But real people can represent much more.

A few examples: Suppose you are taking a swan census. You begin with your bedroom, and conclude, "No swans in here!" Represented in your brain are many things that are present in your bedroom, comprising a local (12-by-14-by-8-ft) plenum that, by implication, excludes swans. From the inactivity of your "swan detectors" one might infer that no swans are present, but that is distinct from the explicit thought, "No swans in here." Dialectical representing systems seem to lack the resources to represent explicit negation.

Universal generalization is perhaps even more troublesome. Suppose your swan census runs into the thousands, and you frame the hypothesis, "All swans are white." You may have represented many individual swans or perhaps a single swan prototype, but in either case the conclusion induced goes beyond the separate representations of many individual white swans. The event in question—the instantiation of whiteness by all swans—is not an event toward which you stand in a dependent relation. The dialectical theory of representation lacks the resources to express a universal generalization. Yet you can grasp the thought, "All swans are white," well enough.

These two cases are enough to make trouble, and behind them stand legions of thoughts that only complex sentences (hypothetical, counterfactual, merely probable, wishful, etc.) can express. It is a problem in the Fodorian spirit. The sentences we speak do seem to reflect the complexity of thought. A theory of representation without the resources to match that inner complexity seems unlikely to apply in human cognition.

Thus we have two problems on the table. First, there is the problem of RLT, the rich, innate, unconscious, hard-to-be-convinced-of mentalese. Second, there is an opposing problem of poverty, the apparent limitation of a representational system that is hardware-hobbled, associative, data-driven, and constrained in content to salient distal events in the immediate environment. How might these problems be solved? The next section introduces a feature of representation that will help, I believe, with both.

Metarepresentation
Pinned to a bulletin board in our house is a picture postcard depicting Velasquez's great painting, *Las Meninas*. The postcard originated with a photograph of Velasquez's canvas; it is a picture of a picture, a metapicture. As such, it pictures the painting in the same way the postcard next to it pictures the beach at Coney Island. But it has a curious further property of inheriting the content of the original painting. The painting depicts the Infanta, her attendants, and Velasquez himself, and so does the postcard. It depicts those people and their situation in addition to depicting the patches of pigment that, in the original, depict those same sitters.

Analogous phenomena appear in other representational media. A familiar case is quotation. "As Shakespeare says, 'Discretion is the better part of valor,' " I intone. I am quoting Shakespeare; thus my words represent Shakespeare's words. In quoting them, I may not mean what Shakespeare meant, but beneath the pragmatics of the utterance and my communicative intention is a kernel of meaning common to the words on both my lips and the playwright's. They are not mere sounds: I, like Shakespeare, am talking about discretion, using the word "discretion," not "disk retch shun" or other homophones. But I am additionally talking about Shakespeare's words. Similarly, the postcard may not convey what Velasquez wanted to convey with his canvas (the painting may have been a token of the artist's admiration for Philip and Isabella, but the postcard certainly is not). But in both cases we see signs of content inheritance from the representation to the object that represents it.

Let us call this phenomenon—a representation inheriting content from another representation—*metarepresentation*. (The term also appears in a related application in Rollins 1989.) The postcard reproduction offers a positive case. Contrast that, however, with the following: Suppose I represent *Las Meninas* with the words "Las Meninas." In one respect, this resembles the postcard example: "Las Meninas" represents *Las Meninas* and *Las Meninas* represents the Infanta and company. But this case does not exhibit inherited content. "Las Meninas" (the name) does not refer to the Infanta, even though the picture named does. Why not? A first glance leads to this suggestion: It seems that the metarepresentation inherited content from its original not merely by referring to it, but by virtue of reproducing the features of the original that gave it the content that it had. This first glance yields trouble, however—it will be difficult to say what features are reproduced from representation to metarepresentation. With respect to most visual features, my postcard is false to its original. Further, we can imagine a case of metarepresentation in which no features are common to representation and metarepresentation. For example, we might digitize the metarepresentation of the painting, like a half-tone photograph ready for transmission. Now we compare the painting to the string of ones and zeros that represents it—none of the visual features of the former reappears in the latter. Yet there is a scheme of interpretation that allows us to reconstruct an image of the painting from the number string. If on that basis we are willing to assert that the digitization represents the patches of pigment that comprise the painting, then it seems we should be equally willing to refer to the digitized representation of the painting's content, the Infanta. If we are not willing to freely metarepresent, then a lot of our pictorial behavior becomes weird, since the average newspaper photo has exactly the history just imagined—it is reconstructed from a digitized representation of a photograph. *The Times* would not have much interest in showing us representations of silver halide grains in various stages of darkening were it not that the presidents and prime ministers those grains represented were also represented by the tiny blots of ink on newsprint lying on the breakfast table.

The relation, in short, that makes metarepresentation is not the resemblance of features shared by representation and metarepresentation but rather the representation of original representational features by the metarepresentation. This suggests a general definition of metarepresentation:

R' is a metarepresentation of O if and only if R' represents some representation R such that R represents O, and R' represents R as having the properties by virtue of which R represents O (as opposed to some other content).

The phrase "the properties by virtue of which R represents O" is vague, but, I hope, vague in the right way. For example, *Las Meninas* represents the Infanta by virtue of being composed of certain patches of color in a certain arrangement. The elusive issue of which patches can successfully picture the Infanta need not detain us, since the important point is that some patches will not work—a black square on a red field would not count, in this world, as depicting the Infanta (though it might be a picture, and it might be a representation of the Infanta (by stipulation, for instance). See Lloyd 1982, Schier 1986). In order for my postcard or a digitization to metarepresent the Infanta, it must represent those patches. From the postcard, one can tell that the painting included the requisite patches, patches from which one could tell that the original represents the Infanta.

The representation of words offers a similar example. Suppose you are perceiving a photograph of some words—as indeed you are, since printing these days is mediated by photographs of camera-ready copy. You see through the photographic representation of words to what the words represent, but you can do so only if the photographic metarepresentation clearly depicts the features of the words that make them the words they are—the loops, ascenders, and descenders that distinguish letters and, hence, particular words. Blur those features, and these sentences no longer metarepresent the content of *Simple Minds*. Instead, they merely represent blurry shapes.

Note that metarepresentations represent the features of representations that make the latter the particular representations they are, as opposed to the features that make the latter representations (at all).

Words are representations because of their place in a complex conventional system—or something like that. Pictures are representations because of complex relational properties involving picture surfaces, perceivers, and objects in the world—or something else like that. Metarepresentations need not represent those complex relational facts about their subjects. That is, metarepresentations need not represent whatever it is that makes their targets representations. But given that the targets are representations, the metarepresentation needs to represent the distinguishing features that make the target representations have the content they have, and not some other content. Several issues can be left hanging: We need not worry about how either representations or metarepresentations represent their respective contents. Presumably there are several possible representational systems—language exemplifies one type of representation, pictures another. And a metarepresentation can be a representation in one system, whereas its target representation can be a representation in another (pictures of words, for example).

Metarepresentations at Work
The account of metarepresentation is so far a part of a general theory of representation, and a somewhat technical part at that. What use can it have when we turn to the brain? Here is the application: We have a process involving three events or objects (object, representation, metarepresentation) and two separate representational processes to link them. And we have a theory of natural representation developed in the chapters above. Suppose we put the metarepresentation in the head, facing a target representation in the world (which in turn represents an object in the world). (A similar proposal appears in Rumelhart, Smolensky, McClelland, and Hinton 1986; cf. Vygotsky 1930 reprinted in Vygotsky 1978:56.) Schematically:

O ←—— (is represented by) — R ←—— (is represented by) — R'
(external)   (external)   (internal)

If R' meets the standards of metarepresentation, then R' inherits the content of R, thus representing whatever R represents. As a result, we have just imported into the head something with the same content as an external, public representation. For example, let R be the printed word "no." Various marks are tokens of the word "no" by virtue of being the concatenation of the letters n and o, and they in turn owe their identities to their shapes. In order to be a metarepresentation, R' must be sensitive to those configural facts about "no," as it may well be, if R' is the last layer of a nest of visual feature detectors with combinatorial learning capabilities. R' has exactly the content of the English word "no." But R' is a token in another representational system, namely, the natural dialectical representational system described at length in these pages. As it is for "no," so also with "all" and "perhaps," not to mention "rain" through "superconductivity." A natural representational system can harness the representational capacity of any other representational system whose symbols it can discriminate. If we learn the symbols of English, for example, a small part of our inboard representational system will be devoted to metaEnglish, the inboard analogue of the outboard public language.

Metarepresentation provides a powerful extension to dialectical representation. For starters, the various intrinsic limits to natural representation alluded to above all fall in a stroke, since the content of any representation that can be framed in any representational scheme can be smuggled inside, if the representation in that scheme can be distinctly perceived. Metarepresentation is limited by the complexity of the physical symbol tokens we can perceive and discriminate. But those tokens can mean anything, according to the symbol systems of which they are a part.

Mention, Use, and Understanding
Suppose, now, I show you a token in a language you may not know:

In Chinese (I am told), the token means college, but suppose you do not yet know that. The theory of metarepresentation suggests that, nonetheless, after your intent study you now carry with you a metarepresentation of college, the meaning of the symbols. I could go on from there to inflict you with a fair number of uninterpreted Chinese symbols, perhaps a complete basic vocabulary of Chinese. Yet the metaChinese in your head would not yet comprise a language, and thus would not comprise a language isomorphic with Chinese. You would not, in short, be able to use your conned metarepresentations to think in Chinese.

What more is needed to make the body of tokens into an inner language? One central addition, I think, boosts a body of metarepresentations into the sphere of language. Consider an analogy: Suppose you learn to pronounce (or draw) the symbols above and several hundred like it. Would your ability to produce the list count as knowing the language? Obviously you must add to an ability to produce symbol tokens the ability to use them by and large correctly, in syntactically well-formed and semantically normal ways. Now draw the analogy inside, where instead of producing target representations in the public tongue we produce representations of those representations. The analogy suggests that to know those metarepresentations as a language, we need to be able to use them in ways that would be correct for the corresponding public target representations. That is, the internal concatenations of metarepresentations map onto grammatical sentences in the target language, and those internal representations are active in situations when the corresponding external representation would be applicable. These constraints of the inner tongue mirror those of the outer through the full range of language, ranging from matter-of-fact assertion through the whimsical, ironical, quizzical—even the philosophical.

Note that mastering the syntax alone is not enough. Milton, according to one of his biographers, taught his daughters Mary and Deborah how to read Hebrew and Greek aloud, but did not teach them what any of the words they read meant—thus anticipating NETtalk by 300 years. He might have added to their training the grammar of either language, enabling them to spot well-formed sentences; yet he would still not have taught them the language. Learning a language involves learning its semantics, and this project is "holistic" in its involvement with both big chunks of the language and big chunks of the world. Remove contact with the world, and the ability to speak meaningfully evaporates, a point to which I will return.

The importation of metarepresentation also gives us an attractive alternative to RLT, the radical language of thought hypothesis. Metarepresentation suggests an alternative account of both thought and language learning, one not committed to framing truth rules in an inner mentalese. This alternative account reconstrues the relations of the inner and the outer by reversing the priority and dependency relations in Fodor's account. The new account of language learning has these stages:

1. One encounters a public representation, e.g., the spoken or written word "ozmyrrah." The ability to represent the relevant properties of the word leads directly to a metarepresentation, an internal symbol with the same content as the word "ozmyrrah." (And this is repeated for other new terms.) Thus the natural representational system acquires the representational powers of external language.

2. One learns the appropriate use of "ozmyrrah." This is mediated by exposure to examples of correct and incorrect grammatical usage (e.g., correct: "Holding the barbeque in the rose garden resulted in a

striking ozmyrrah"; deviant: "I ozmyrrah on Tuesday only"), and by examples of truths and falsehoods including the word (true: "An ozmyrrah is a mixture of pleasant smells"; false: "Distilled water exudes an ozmyrrah"). All of these cases involve coordinating the public word with other words and perceived situations (of which the presence of a mixture of pleasant smells is the most important). The process of learning the use of the word may be subject to a variety of innate constraints. But importantly, none of the stage 2 learning presupposes an explicit rule linking the inner term with the outer. That link goes the other way, from the outer to the inner, and is already provided for in step 1.

3. The inner metarepresentations become an inner language when users deliberately model their inner use on the outer language. By this step, the inner medium, already equal in representational power to the outer (via metarepresentation), also acquires the computational power of outer media. Thus we learn to think linguistically in a meta-English, metaRussian, or another language. Likewise, we can learn to think cinematically, photographically, sculpturally, or along the lines of any other representational medium. The structures on which we model our thought can be both large and small and need not exhaust the combinatorial resources of the target media. For example, one can model one's thought on the *Critique of Pure Reason*—or on *People* magazine.

The inner, finally, can guide the outer. The inner discourse can simulate and anticipate the outer, making what we say cognitively dependent on what we think. (Though this is not obligatory. While it is possible to talk deliberately, i.e., as the result of a process of inner revision and rehearsal, it seems to be equally possible to think out loud, or simply talk without the corresponding inner discourse.)

Having outlined the resources of metarepresentation, I find it useful to detail the significant differences between metarepresentation and Fodor's view. First, I have stressed the fact that words and other public representations are physical objects, and that learning to use them is a task analogous to learning to produce or manipulate other physical objects. In some respects, this is a task like learning to cook (Wittgenstein 1953; Millikan 1984; Vygotsky 1930 reprinted in Vygotsky 1978:24). Fodor sees public representations as ordinary public objects too, but seems to see the relevant learning as fundamentally different. Though we are learning how to deploy these special objects, there is another sort of learning, namely, learning what the objects mean, which is central for Fodor.

Why should Fodor concentrate on this sort of learning? Perhaps he is motivated by the widely felt view that a full-blooded language ability comprises not only the ability to use the language correctly, but to understand what one is doing in so using it. To this, two replies: First, if understanding requires truth rule links between the language understood and some other language in which the understanding is realized, then we run another regress; this time, a regress of languages in which to frame the understanding of other languages. Fodor recognizes this threat of regress and blocks it by positing that mentalese is a language used without understanding—we just do use mentalese correctly, like an external language, and that is all there is to it (1975:67).

Those who stress the need for understanding as part of a full language endowment may not be pleased with Fodor's regress-blocking denial of understanding of mentalese. Surely, if there is one language we must understand, it is mentalese, the most intimate language of all. If we do not understand it, then we do not, for example, understand the truth rules, framed in mentalese, that constitute our understanding of natural language. That our understanding of spoken language should consist of the parroting of truth rules without understanding, seems at best a dubious step toward understanding understanding.

Instead, let us back up and reconsider understanding. The complete analysis of understanding lies beyond these pages, but nonetheless a few intuitions can come to our aid. The oft-exploited central intuition is this: Mastery of the closed system of language alone is insufficient. John Searle (1980) is the creator of the most familiar thought experiment on this front, the "Chinese room." We are to imagine a system in which a person manipulates symbols (in Chinese) according to an elaborate transformation table. This paperpusher has no knowledge of Chinese apart from the look-up table, and so, Searle asserts, has no understanding of the Chinese symbols he manipulates. Nor does the system consisting of the person plus rule book, paper, and pencil have any understanding of Chinese. What is missing? Fodor looks inward, to a separate process of language understanding involving translation into mentalese—thus encountering the problems just glossed. But the other resource for language understanding is the world at large, the complex, holistic conditions that govern the truth or falsity of representations. The suggestion—no more than that here—is that understanding be sought in that aspect of language mastery, a skill conspicuously absent in the tenant of Searle's Chinese room.

This point, the suggested defusing of the force of the somewhat obscure appeal to understanding, leads to a second divide between the Fodorian hypothesis and the approach suggested here. I am suggesting a reconstrual of the relations between inboard and outboard representational systems. Fodor has suggested that the meanings of predicates in the public language are derived from the meanings of predicates in the private language of thought. In opposition to Fodor, Sellars (for example) seems to be suggesting that the dependency runs the other way: The inner representational system derives its representationality from the outer.

My view is distinct from both. Various representational systems are completely independent of one another, and each would represent in the absence of the others. The system of natural representations, the main theme of this book, seems to me to be fully freestanding. Its representational powers are underived from other sources. Public representational systems are also independent; their representationality rests on other grounds. For example, the multiple channel hypothesis will fail quite miserably as an account of the representationality of individual words, since it ignores contextual effects. It may come closer when taken as an explanation of the content of some whole sentences, but even so regards the sentences as lacking significant internal structure, thus missing the common contribution of common elements within different sentences. Furthermore, public representational systems have powerful content-determining resources which cannot touch their inner counterparts: Convention operates freely and reliably in the public realm, allowing people to settle on powerful representational schemes in which standardized formal properties determine content.

But while conceiving various representational systems to be freestanding, I have also linked them. Metarepresentation enables natural representational systems to bootstrap without limit. In this respect, my speculations have been Sellarsian more than Fodorian: The outer language comes first; the inner language of thought owes its richness to the preestablished conventional richness of the outer representational systems.

A third difference separating Fodor and me has been a recurrent theme throughout: I have doubted the need for explicit rules to govern the inner processes of representation and cognition. In this chapter, I questioned truth rules explicitly, but they may join a crew in general exile. The net force of these chapters, I think, is to deny the computationalist model the status of "only game in town." Other means to the same complex ends are available.

Once computationalism is no longer the only game in town, then its tougher consequences—the doctrines collected under the RLT hypothesis—begin to look like counterarguments. I have questioned Fodor's account of language learning, substituting for it a composite account that takes advantage of metarepresentation. Without that premise, we no longer need to bite the bullet of the radical language of thought. Instead, we have a modest innate representational system, a basic language of thought, dependent on the structure of the brain, within which to build an indefinite number of representations of perceptual expectations and memories. This palatable innateness and plausible richness offer resources enough for us to become thinkers—metaspeakers—in inner analogues of natural languages. Those afterburners enable thought to streak to the far corners of the universe.[3]

Toward a Taxonomy of Representational Systems
Finally, to the animals again. What has emerged in this chapter is another distinction within and among brains. In chapters 4 and 5, I stressed a distinction between representational systems and (merely) informational systems, arguing that representational systems emerge from some informational systems. Both of those previous chapters surveyed ways of cooking up increasingly complex and flexible systems of both types. Now we have added metarepresentation to the stew and can further rank animal and synthetic systems by its measure. A basic metarepresenter has the capacity to represent objects as tokens of symbol types of some external representational system. That is rather basic indeed, but nonetheless affords a continuum that may make human public representational systems an exclusively human metarepresentational domain. As AI efforts at language understanding suggest, sentences are generally the most complex stimuli we can perceive and process. Pictures, on the other hand, seem easier—pigeons do a good job of sorting pictures by content (trees, bodies of water, specific persons) (Herrnstein 1979; Herrnstein and Loveland 1964; Herrnstein, Loveland, and Cable 1976). Consider, for example, this sentence, with at least one dependent clause of questionable relevance to the train of thought, and as you consider it, reflect upon the dimensionality of the stimulus and all the near variants of this sentence which might have exactly the opposite—or the same—meaning. In short, we are specialists at the metarepresentational processes involved in the representation of language and in this respect leave all other species far behind. But even the ability to discriminate sentences of great complexity is not the whole of the language faculty. I distinguished a separate stage of language learning where one learns to simulate speech and to deploy sentences internally, smuggling the ratiocinative powers of discourse inside for silent plotting—or perhaps just for telling limericks during department meetings. This capacity for inner speech (and the corre-

sponding capacity for inner imaging) might be a separate capacity than that for audible speech alone. But these speculations can be saved for another time.

As we rise toward more complex systems, we find more questions than answers. So in the interest of producing a finite book, I will have to be selective. This chapter discussed a capacity for inner speech. Suppose we do have such a capacity. Next question: Is anybody listening?

Chapter 7
Once More, with Feeling

We see, like those with faulty vision, things at a distance from us. . . .
When they draw near or are present our intellect is wholly at fault. . . .
—Dante, *Inferno*, X

7.1 A Taxonomy of Conscious Experience

Sometimes one makes progress on a big problem by reconceiving it as several smaller ones. That strategy guided the search for representation. We initially posed the problem of representation in terms of several separate aspects of representationality, and the theory fell into place incrementally. Now that theory has been developed and applied in several case studies and a speculative extension. But to many people the mind seems to contain more than representation alone can capture. It is time at last to address those dim states of awareness, those nagging pangs of doubt, those private reservations expressed to oneself, all about the subject of consciousness.

How can a physical system be conscious? I think that this is not one problem but several, for consciousness exhibits several distinct aspects. Our first task, accordingly, will be taxonomic, turning one impossible problem into several incredibly difficult ones. The concept of consciousness, as wielded by ordinary folk and spruced up by philosophers, seems to include four disparate phenomena: sensation, perception, reflection, and introspection. After sorting through the four, we will be in a better position to see what they have in common and why it is correct to regard consciousness as a tough problem.

Consciousness as Sensation

I drink a glass of cider, and then I hiccup. My states of consciousness during the episode include at least two sensations (or qualia, or raw feels)—the taste of the cider (in its most subjective dimension, nicely pinned by Dennett (1988) as the way the cider tastes to me) and that hiccuping feeling. The pains and tickles, tastes and looks in this familiar category of conscious experience seem to many to pose the central problem of consciousness (and not surprisingly, since these qualitative conscious states are singularly resistant to functionalism. See Dennett 1988; Block 1980; Churchland 1985; Shoemaker 1975, 1981, 1982). Among states of consciousness, sensations are uniquely contentless or nonrepresentational. Though certain stimuli commonly cause familiar sensations, the sensations are not about the stimuli in the way that a belief or other representation would be about its object. Sensations lack propositional content (no "pains that p") and intentional objects (no "pains of p").

At first, the claim of contentlessness seems odd, for we certainly link our sensations to objects all the time: My pain tells me I have pulled a muscle, and a sweet taste is not only an inner experience, but—somehow—a property of the cider (like the dryness of wine). But this is shorthand for the full story: Some property in my muscle causes me to feel pain, and some property in the cider causes me to experience that sweet taste. The sensation is a symptom of its cause, a different relation from representing pain in the muscle or sweetness in the cider, as though pain were a special somatic property in the same category, but distinct from, the strained fibers and sputtering pain receptors, or sweetness were a special property alongside the balance of sugar and acid. In speaking of sensations, we focus on the inner experiences, each of which has a distinct character but no content.

Consciousness as Perceptual Awareness
Sensations are thus logically distinct from states of perceptual awareness: I perceive that my cider glass is now empty. K. V. Wilkes is responsible for the crucial observation here (1984), that, unlike sensations, states of perceptual awareness are straightforward representational states, with either propositional content (expressible in "that p" constructions, as in "I see that the glass is empty") or representational objects. Thus, the phenomenologists' perennial slogan, "All consciousness is consciousness *of* something," indicates their allegiance to this sort of conscious experience (among others). Wilkes also flags some of the other distinctions between perceptual awareness and sensation: Sensations consist of isolatable episodes with clear beginnings and endings and distinct locations on or in my body. But perceptual awareness cannot be so readily pinned down in either respect. When did I first notice that the leaves had changed color, for how long was I aware of the change, and was I aware continuously through that time? Like a president charged with covert misdeeds, I may find those questions hard to answer. Indeed, Wilkes points out that perceptual awarenesses may have no qualitative, sensational

aspect at all—there may be nothing that it feels like to notice that I am the third person to arrive at a dinner party. This worldly orientation of perceptual awareness is not always obligatory, since I can have several sorts of straightforward perceptual awareness of myself—as the object with which I have the closest perceptual contact. I can see or feel that my knee is flexed, and this is nonetheless a different aspect of experience from the way it feels when my knee is flexed.

States of perceptual awareness, in short, seem to be states with content. As such, they permit a distinction between explicit and extensional content (a distinction introduced in section 1.2 and again in section 3.2). Macbeth's famous hallucination might be characterized as the perceptual awareness of a dagger, provided it is understood that the content of his experience is nonextensional—the explicit phenomenal content of the state of consciousness. But if Lady Macbeth is using a fly-fishing rod to dangle a dagger in front of her husband and he sees that, then he is aware of a dagger in the extensional sense (as well as the explicit or phenomenal sense). Presumably that standard philosophical thought experiment, the disconnected brain in a vat, is perceptually aware only in the nonextensional, explicit sense. But the disembodied brain feels sensations in the same rich full sense we allegedly normal people do (if the brain experiences the phantom body effects reported in Dennett 1978c).

Frank Jackson (1982) has invented a case which can be interpreted as a further illustration of the distinction between sensation and perceptual awareness. He imagines the brilliant scientist Mary, confined from birth to a single room but with access to all of the world's knowledge. Her room is done in gray tones, and all of her experience with the outside world is mediated by a black and white TV; as a result Mary has no direct experience of the color red. Jackson's argument has a particular point: Suppose, Jackson suggests, that part of Mary's intellectual achievement is the mastery of Golden Age neuroscience and the relevant parts of physics and optics of color vision. She would then know everything physical there is to know about seeing red, but, Jackson points out, there would still be something she does not know; namely, what red looks like, what it is like to actually see red.

The thought experiment of Mary's education is supposed to suggest that physicalism leaves something important out of its account of the mind; but Paul Churchland (1985) has observed that its moral is broader than that, provoking an intuition that afflicts any -ism, dualism included. To see this, suppose that Jackson is right, and there is an irreducible dualistic aspect to the mind. Let us grant Mary access, through her TV, to every fact of Golden Age dualism—let us imagine that she herself formulates the correct theory of mind and matter. The outcome of the experiment remains unchanged. Now Mary knows all there is to know about the flux of ectoplasm, but she still does not know what red looks like. The experiment undermines not only a physical account of the mind, but any theory of mind whatsoever.

The thought experiment makes better sense, however, as an illustration of the distinction between sensation and perceptual awareness. Mary has been provided, through her TV link, with everything perceptual experience can provide. That is, if perceptual awarenesses can be characterized by their content and the content stated propositionally or represented pictorially on Mary's black and white TV, then she can, one way or another, learn everything that perception can teach (including statements like "Apples are red."). But the sensation of red slips the net of perceptual awareness. Since it is contentless, whatever it is that makes the sensation of red the sensation that it is cannot be captured by any number of representations. The sensation of red lies beyond Mary's perceptual ken.

Experience might have aspects of both perceptual awareness and sensation—the distinction is fuzzy in practice. But the examples just discussed nonetheless suggest that the two are logically distinct even if they often occur together. We may set them up as two distinct hurdles for a theory of consciousness to clear.

Consciousness as Reflection
Both sensation and perception are data-driven and largely compulsory. I cannot help but taste the cider or feel the hiccup, nor can I help but see that the glass is empty if I look in its direction. Both are compulsory, too, in that, given that cider and that glass, I cannot choose to taste another taste or see a nonempty glass. That is quite different from the occurrent experiences of reflection, the discursive musing that happens on the side, with perception and sensation out of gear: I remember the ciders of yesteryear and the picnics of their consumption. This in turn stirs anticipations of the summer to come, followed by speculations about the concept of the picnic: Did the australopithecenes have picnics? (James Joyce has made these mental wanderings into art.) Like perceptual awareness, reflective states are fully content endowed, capable of truth or error, open to extensional and nonextensional (explicit) interpretation. These states of consciousness frequently use inner analogues of outer representational media. We speak to ourselves inaudibly, spinning out our local versions of Molly Bloom's soliloquy.

Consciousness as Introspection
Reflection becomes clearer in contrast to a near cousin, introspection. When I direct my attention to consciousness under any of the three previous aspects, that is, when I try to become aware of being conscious, I engage in introspection. "What are you thinking?" asks my friend. I reply, "How sweet the cider is," or "Time for a refill," or "Imagine *Déjeuner sur l'herbe* set two million years ago." In arriving at any of these answers, I use introspection.

Many have taken introspection to be the main issue in the study of consciousness as well (e.g., Lyons 1986). It is important, however, to see the distinction between introspection and the other aspects of consciousness and thereby to recognize why it is not the sole faculty of consciousness.

First, some comparisons and contrasts. Introspection is clearly a contentful state and in that respect distinct from sensation. But its content is one's own consciousness, and thus it is distinct from both perceptual awareness and reflection, since both of these are directed at the world or at oneself as an object in the world. Even though those other states are conscious states in themselves, they need not be about conscious states; but introspection is a conscious state, and is about conscious states as well.

One can understand how introspection might seem to be the whole problem of consciousness because it is central to the problem of the epistemology of consciousness. Through introspection we come to know how we feel, see, and think as we do; thus it seems that if we want to know how we know we are conscious, we must find out about introspection. But introspection is nonetheless logically distinct from the other states. This distinction is crucial to the understanding of consciousness, and much of the perplexity surrounding the topic arises needlessly from sliding among the various types of consciousness.

The distinction between introspection and the other conscious episodes is a precursor to a second important point, one that has been acknowledged only in recent years: Introspection is a fallible source of self-knowledge (Dennett 1988; Lyons 1986; P. S. Churchland 1986: 305ff; Millikan 1984). Being in a state of consciousness does not necessarily entail knowing that one is in that state. Examples of introspective derailment are commonplace, and people pay therapists large sums of money to arrive at the introspective truth about themselves. Those afflicted with sensory deficits or neurological impairments can add other examples—e.g., the facial vision experienced by blind people, apparently not a visual sense at all. Or there are the phenomena of blindsight (Campion, Latto, and Smith 1983). Patients with blindsight will seem to themselves to be completely blind, but when asked to point to specific objects in the vicinity, they do so accurately ("Just guessing," they report). Apparently, they are patients with no introspectable perceptual awareness, but who seem, somehow, to have retained an awareness to which they have no introspective access.

The distinction between introspection and the other conscious states and the fallibility of introspection both solidify when we ponder the alternatives. Suppose, first, that every state of consciousness C necessarily entailed the knowledge that we were in state C. Thus, attending every state of consciousness would be a second state, C', where C' is the state of knowing that one is in state C. C' must itself be a state of awareness, since otherwise our knowledge of our own states would not be an introspective (that is, conscious) knowledge. But if C' is itself a conscious state, then by the supposition it must travel with a state C'', the conscious awareness that we are in state C'. And C'' requires C''' and so on ad infinitum. No finite system could ever become conscious. Thus we conclude that there can be states of awareness of which we are unaware. Conscious states occur in us, unaccompanied by any introspection.

Similarly, let us suppose that every state of consciousness is (somehow) at the same time an introspective awareness of itself, and again, suppose this is a necessary feature of all states of consciousness. On this supposition, every state C = C', where C is the primary state of consciousness (for example, a state of perceptual awareness), and C' is the secondary state of awareness of C. This entails an absurdity like the above, according to which every state of consciousness is in fact an infinitude of distinct states, C = C' = C'' = ... It also seems flatly contradictory. State C might be a perceptual awareness, perhaps of the emptiness of a glass, while C' is an awareness of C. Those are two distinct contents and seem to preclude identification as a single state.

One last aspect of introspection of interest is that the states one can introspect include one's own (previous) introspective states. Introspection, in other words, allows for iteration. Thus, actively entertained memory is sometimes an introspective process, but sometimes merely reflective. Its category depends on its content: If the memory is of one's own conscious state, as a state of consciousness (a sensation or a previous introspective state), then the reflected memory is an instance of introspection. On the other hand, if the memory concerns the way things seemed (apart from one's consciousness of them), then the entertainment of the memory is a reflective state. Obviously, as in the sensation/perception pair, there will be fuzzy cases in practice. But, here as there, we should acknowledge the logical distinction. The moral is this: There are conscious states, here termed reflective states, which are neither introspective nor perceptual. (The reflective states can repeat, but not iterate.)

Thus we have four grades of consciousness or types of awareness and in their coordination, a taxonomy of immediate experience (immediate, because all of these states are occurrent). Table 7.1 summarizes the comparisons and contrasts among them.

7.2   Why the Problem of Consciousness Is So Difficult

The previous section suggests a practical reason why the problem of consciousness has seemed so hard: Consciousness has four distinct forms, so the problem of the physical basis of consciousness is four problems. A solution to one of the four is not likely to serve as neatly for the others. But in addition to the multiplication of the initial question, we are yet to survey two features of consciousness shared by all. These are the issues of subjectivity and transcendence, and they make the problem of consciousness difficult indeed.

Proximal to a Fault

Experience tells us that the more intimate something is to us, the better we can find out about it. Our own states of consciousness are maximally intimate, so one would think them maximally knowable. But intimacy turns out to defeat knowledge in this arena. Like the nose on each of us, consciousness is too close, too proximal, to be brought into clear focus. Our excessive intimacy leads us toward epistemic paradoxes, of which two are now familiar.

We meet, first, the problems of subjectivity, a property shared by all the conscious states. Since Nagel's (1974) classic article, the test

Table 7.1
Taxonomy of Types of Immediate Experience

	Sensation	Perceptual Awareness	Reflection	Introspection
Contentful?	no	yes	yes	yes
Extensional/ nonextensional distinction applies?	no	yes	yes	yes
Data driven (compulsory)?	yes	yes	no	no
About other conscious states?	no	no	no	yes
Iterative?	no	no	no	yes

question is: What is it like to be a bat? Nagel's question touches the intuition that there is something specific that it is like to be a bat, and that what-it-is-like-ness is a handy tag for bat consciousness. By extension, there is something that it is like to be you in each of your conscious states, and to be me in each of mine. Each state is inescapably bound by the particularity of our respective consciousnesses, our separate and distinct subjectivity.

From this observation, Nagel generates a problem for the attempt to place consciousness in a physical framework. The physicalist framing of consciousness, like the physicalist reach in general, involves sloughing off the merely personal and subjective in favor of the objective, acentric "view from nowhere." But the objective treatment of consciousness would entail the exclusion of its very subjectivity, so Nagel concludes that he cannot see how a physical account of consciousness could escape a kind of incoherence.

Nagel affirms, and most people seem to agree, that there is something that it is like to be a bat. Sometimes, however, he makes a stronger (and ambiguous) claim that there is something that it is like to be a bat *for the bat*. If the appended phrase has the force of locating bat consciousness in the bat, then there is no problem—where else would bat consciousness be? But if the addition attributes to the bat an apprehension of the fact that it is conscious, a consciousness of its own consciousness, then he has ascribed to the bat an introspective capacity which bats do not obviously possess. There may be nothing that it is like to be a bat for the bat. Bats may not be given to introspection.

But this skirmish leaves most of the problem untouched, since unreflective and nonintrospective animals like bats (presumably) nonetheless feel and perceive. Sensation and perception are their portion as well as ours. Bats aside, there is nonetheless something that it is like to be us for us, and the fourfold problem emerges there, close to home.

But Nagel's argument flushes out a more general problem, not confined to physicalism. Any account of consciousness that attempts to impose generalizations on its domain—that aspires to science— necessarily involves abstracting from the personal, the idiosyncratic, and the subjective. Again, we can imagine a sophisticated scientific dualism. What else can the sophisticated dualist hope for, if not an objective science of mind and matter? But the very objectivity of that account will subject it to Nagelian failure.

Subjectivity can thus be added to table 7.1 as a feature of each of the types of consciousness. As an analogy, consider the "subjective" and objective views of a camera. You might characterize your Polaroid in terms of the photographs it has taken, its "personal history" expressed via the contents of your photo scrapbook. Or you might give an objective view of the camera alone, the physical principles that determine its operation. One's theory of cameras could begin with attempts to build generalizations about the content of all of the photographs a certain class of camera takes. Or it could begin with an examination of all cameras of that class. Nagel sees a tension between the two analogous approaches to the mind, a tension to which we will return below.

The camera analogy can introduce a second can of worms: The one subject a camera cannot readily photograph is itself. Even shooting into a mirror distorts or obscures the essentials, since the apparatus of lens, shutter, and film plane (the heart of the camera) necessarily eludes the camera itself. The problem is that of the transcendence of consciousness: We cannot catch ourselves in any particular occurrent state of consciousness because the shift of consciousness to the act of catching involves abandoning the state of consciousness that we would catch. Consciousness transcends the consciousness that would apprehend it (see also Wittgenstein 1921 translated in Wittgenstein 1961:5.63ff). How can we ever know about a particular state of consciousness? Since the introspective consciousness directed at any other state of consciousness extinguishes that state of consciousness, it seems that we cannot.

Sartre was so troubled by this problem that he posited a third sort of consciousness expressly to meet the problem, as he put it, of consciousness unconscious of itself (1937, 1953). Two of the basic Sartrean types of consciousness correspond to the two categories of perceptual awareness and introspection—in his terms, the prereflective consciousness of things and the reflective consciousness of being conscious. The problem of transcendence forced him to adopt a third consciousness, the prereflective consciousness of being conscious. This third type of consciousness accompanied the other two continuously and was a part of them. It underwrote the ability to account for our thoughts immediately, without deliberate introspection, "prereflectively." But Sartre's solution seems ad hoc, tailored to slip in among the thorns of the problem. It also leaves one flank of the problem open since we do not know how we know about this third consciousness—does it have another prereflective consciousness of being conscious attached? Sartre accepts this circle as a basic condition of consciousness, but in fact it seems to be a regress rather than a circle: The awareness that we are conscious can never get off the ground, since it needs a second awareness, and the second a third, and so on.

The problem of the "transcendental turn" has several versions, each resting on slightly different assumptions. The strongest form depends on a load limit for selves of one state of consciousness per self at every moment. The simultaneous apprehension of one consciousness by another adds up to two conscious states in one self, exceeding the load limit. Yet the load limit seems implausible, especially in the light of the taxonomy in section 7.1. For example, I think about my next chapter while I am doing the dishes. I finish the chore with an idea or two for *Simple Minds* and clean dishes. Because the dish washing was a continuous activity throughout the whole time, uninterrupted (alas) by cries of "Eureka!", it seems likely that I was aware of what I was doing. But throughout that same period, I was reflecting on this book, and that too was continuous. Why not both at once? And if that is possible, why not apply one introspective consciousness to another, co-occurrent nonintrospective consciousness? Certainly something like that occurs routinely.

But it is just here that the problem of subjectivity can be merged with the problem of transcendence. We can import the Nagelian problem into the Sartrean inner realm: Looking at one state of consciousness from the perspective of another abandons the subjectivity of the first. Introspecting a state of perceptual awareness, for example, entails the disregard of the essential subjectivity of that state of awareness, replacing it with the subjectivity of the introspective state. Thus transcendence remains as an epistemic problem. We not only do not know what it is like to be a bat, we do not even have direct knowledge of what it is like to be us. (We only know what it is like to be us for us.)

The troubles with both transcendence and subjectivity are thus problems of points of view. Knowing our own consciousness involves stepping outside of it. Whether the outside is outside our skin or merely outside by virtue of introspecting from one conscious state toward another, we seem to have lost what is essential to the state of consciousness. The sum of subjectivity and transcendence is ineffability. Our best approaches add up to zero, and what we thought was the domain of most certain knowledge seems suddenly to be plunged into most certain ignorance.

7.3   Making a Virtue of Ineffability

The phenomena of consciousness thus scatter before us. What is to be done? Several writers advise us to scuttle consciousness altogether. Wilkes, for example, doubts that anything physical will ever correspond to categories in her taxonomy of consciousness (quite similar to the taxonomy in section 7.1). Dennett (1988) makes the case against sensation on conceptual grounds: The alleged immediate and certain access we have to our own sensations is short-circuited by the unresolvable fallibility and ambiguity that meets any rigorous effort to say what our sensations are. Our sensations thus have contradictory properties, good grounds for scrapping them in favor of more respectable concepts. Add to that the paradoxical ineffability developed in section 7.2, and one can well sympathize with the impulse to jettison these weird entities.

But suppose, instead, we decide to preserve our conceptual loyalties, and to hang on to something close to good old-fashioned consciousness. There is, after all, reason to want to keep consciousness. Not only has it a long and robust extratheoretical life, but concepts of consciousness, in all four guises, are woven into our ethics, our art, our conception of human nature and civilization. In the invocation to the *Odyssey*, Homer tells us what to expect of the story of Odysseus:

> Many were they whose cities he saw, whose minds he learned of, many the pains he suffered in his spirit on the wide sea.

And from that moment forward a civilization undertook a long odyssey of consciousness, not always glorious. Against the canny Odysseus, one might set the benighted figure of Adolf Eichmann. Hannah Arendt (1963:49) diagnoses his wickedness, in its terrifying banality, thus:

> The longer one listened to him, the more obvious it became that his inability to speak was closely connected with an inability to *think*, namely, to think from the standpoint of somebody else.

Of course, those who recommend the elimination of consciousness from our vocabulary are emphatically not recommending that we abandon any of the ethical or human measures framed in terms of feeling, perception, reflection, or introspection. My point here is simply that elimination of consciousness commits us to a major overhaul of much of our conceptual scheme—or to put it another way, we have prima facie reasons to seek reform before revolution, reasons linking our perplexing subject to many other arenas of life.

Thus we have robust and entrenched phenomena, the four types of awareness, hobbled with pervasive problems. What next? My suggestion is that we take the preceding, warts and all, as data; specifically, as constraints that must be met by a successful theory of consciousness. First, we seek a theory that carves its domain, naturally, in ways that respect the original taxonomy of types of awareness. The theory, in its domain, should mirror the distinctions in table 7.1 and do so cleanly. Second, the theory should explain subjectivity and transcendence. That is, it should not construe conscious agents as wiser than they are, but rather preserve and explain the limits we experience as knowers of consciousness. In this one inquiry only, ignorance is strength, in that the boundaries of our knowing, particularly our introspective knowing, reflect the boundaries of the capacity we seek to know, itself a form of knowing. This does not mean that the theory itself should be subjective or transcendent; the theory is not its target, nor does the theory appeal to introspection or other conscious phenomena in its defense. It is a product of reflection only, aided by synthetic imagination and such empirical guidance as we can muster—just like all the theorizing in this book. Thus when one looks within to explore the pros and cons, one is not introspecting but rather reflecting on the theory against the background of beliefs held to be true on other grounds.

Representation and Consciousness
Here we go. One of the central distinctions in the initial carving concerned content. Perceptual awareness, reflection, and introspection were all composed of contentful states; sensation was not. For contentful states, we write in representations. Straightforwardly, perceptual awareness, reflection, and introspective states are all representational states. Of course, so far this is trivial—what matters is the further specification. For starters, we need to reflect the fact that states of consciousness are occurrent. Thus, if they are representational states, they should not be stored or latent representations. Instead, we will specify that they are *active representations*— representations whose input channels, output channels, or both are currently transmitting information. How much more than a plain representation is a state of consciousness (or in the case of sensation, how much less)?

In answering these questions, I suggest that we remember Occam's handcuff. In the present context, that means that we should accept no gratuitous complexity, complexity for its own sake. Of course, we have wonderfully complex and subtle minds. But one theme sounded long ago in this essay now has some substance to it: Much of our complexity springs from the iteration and multiplication of much simpler representational components. We have seen that simple representations, installed in the right nexus, can have very complex content and mediate complex behavior. Now (caveat emptor) I shall attempt a similar stunt with consciousness.

Perceptual Awareness as Active Representation
Let us consider a representational system of arbitrary depth; that is, with representations whose output can comprise (but need not) input to further representations through several layers leading to ultimate behavioral output. For now, we will exclude metarepresentation— thus we are pondering a range of systems from the bargain-basement synthetic systems of chapters 3, 4, and 5. Are there grounds for considering these systems to be perceptually aware? I think the answer is yes, and I think the content of their active representations comprise the content of their perceptual awareness.

Let us consider the toad. Has the toad any awareness of its surroundings? The direct support for anuran awareness: (1) The toad is capable of complex behavior that evidences a capacity for perceptual discrimination of distal stimuli in its environment. It steers by a complex set of environmental beacons. (Dennett offers complementary arguments in 1987a:106ff.) (2) If we ask, in the spirit of (1), of what is the toad aware, we find ourselves answering (if at all) along representational lines. The toad cannot discriminate between worms and bugs or between living things and ball bearings rolled within striking distance. That is, the toad cannot represent those objects as worms, bugs, or b-b's. Similarly, one might say that the toad is not aware of those objects as worms, bugs, b-b's, or under any other human description. Of what is the toad aware? Our best approach might mention moving shapes of certain sizes and configurations—but that, of course, is just a reapplication of the content of the active representations in the toad brain. (And the discriminatory behavior alone is also insufficient—a paralyzed but awake toad would still be aware of preylike stimuli. It just would not be able to do anything about them.)

Indirect support for anuran awareness: 1. Suppose that we decide that the toad is not perceptually aware at all, that it is a little zombie. The grounds for this might be that we have found nothing for consciousness to do in the toad—neurons take care of the toad's needs, and the research reviewed in chapter 5 tells part of the story of how they serve the toad. The problem with this line of argument is that neurons take care of every need in every brain, and the denial of consciousness to the toad opens up to a slippery slope. Surely bats are open to the same counterargument, and if bats, then cats, monkeys, and, ultimately, human beings. The burden of proof is on those who would deny consciousness to the toad. It is up to them to explain what the toad lacks. And it is not open to say simply that the toad isn't complex enough.

2. We have a good concept of unconsciousness in the toad: Toads asleep or with head injuries or drugged are all unconscious. To say that awake, behaving, functional toads are also unconscious is to flex the concept of unconsciousness in an odd, even incoherent way. One would need another concept of unconsciousness to apply to the zombie toads with their zombie awarenesses and zombie pains and pleasures. Again, the burden of proof lies with those who deny awareness to the toad.

3. Awareness (unlike subjectivity) admits of degrees. Not only do we acknowledge that it is possible to be acutely aware of some things while only dimly aware of others, but we acknowledge gradations of breadth and complexity of the general capacity for awareness. For example, I happen to be nearly anosmic—lacking the sense of smell. So my awareness is narrower than that of most people, since there is a whole class of perceptual objects that they experience but I do not. Another example: Lovers of classical music can identify familiar composers even on hearing unfamiliar works by those composers. The identification is quick and involves no conscious inference. It is safe to say that they are aware of Brucknerian or Stravinskian features of musical lines, a complex awareness to be sure and one lacking in those whose tastes run exclusively to Talking Heads (the latter, on the other hand, enjoy other discriminatory abilities). Furthermore, we all know of the daily oscillations of overall awareness from the first groggy seconds of consciousness's radical confrontation with the alarm clock, through prime time, and back toward those last groggy seconds spent setting the alarm clock again. Finally, the case of somnambulism not only suggests a narrowing of perceptual awareness, but the absence of other states of consciousness, reflection and introspection. If a sleepwalker can navigate among objects and obstacles, then he must see while failing to know that he sees. Only in an extreme case, in which he is totally oblivious to all surroundings, should we say that the sleepwalker is completely unaware of his environment. (The impulse to deny that the somnambulist is conscious, accordingly, follows from the tendency to identify consciousness with introspection.)

We readily extend the ideas of gradations of perceptual awareness to animals: Dogs are aware of more than mice are aware of, and mice beat goldfish. Thus, in ascribing awareness to the toad, we are not ascribing to it a fine palate and a taste for pastoral poetry. We are ascribing a narrow portion of awareness, but something on a continuum that bottoms out with the undescribable simplicity of active representation in simple brains, and hits its pinnacle in beings like us.

Gradations of awareness again recommend the equating of awareness with active representation. How do we assign the various degrees of awareness glossed above? I suggest that we rank a system's capacity for awareness at a given time as an aspect of its capacity to actively represent at that time. The classical music lover has learned to represent certain higher order features of passages of music, but those with other tastes cannot represent those features. Thus they cannot become perceptually aware of them, either.

Reflection and Metarepresentation
The portion of perceptual awareness attributed to toads is not only modest in extent but circumscribed in type. We have emphatically not ascribed to the toad a capacity for reflection or introspection—two other crucial parts of human consciousness. (Nor have we yet reviewed sensation, coming below.) Arthur Danto (1985:342) speculates that animal consciousness is the sort of consciousness

> under which, in Nietzsche's phrase, one "exists blindly between the walls of past and future." That to which such consciousness is blind is, precisely, those walls. Hence it is blind to the fact that the present is present, and hence to the fact that one's consciousness exemplifies animal consciousness.

The toad is, again, a good exemplar, not only of the temporal blindness that Danto discusses, but of several other limitations of experience as well. Though the toad itself bears the traces of its experience—in neural circuits deflected by associative conditioning, in motivational factors that rise and fall as its belly does the opposite, and in the scars of injury—arguably the experiences of feeding and fleeing pass through its consciousness but once, no matter if it has those experiences a thousand times, and no matter if it has within itself the stored representation of a regular conjunction of certain event types. As Danto suggests, the toad's experience is permanently in the now and consists of an unending succession of particular conscious episodes oscillating among a very few themes.

Why is the toad thus blind? The answer, again, lies in what the toad can and cannot represent. Consider the representational resources required for reflection (in its ordinary instances). Near the end of *Murder on the Orient Express*, Hercule Poirot and two associates direct themselves to the facts of the case. Poirot's reflections do not appear, but Agatha Christie describes the musing of one of the weaker minds:

> He is queer, this little man. A genius? Or a crank? Will he solve this mystery? Impossible—I can see no way out of it. It is all too

confusing. . . . It would be easier to understand if he had been shot—after all, the term "gunman" must mean that they shoot with a gun. A curious country, America. I should like to go there. It is so progressive. When I get home I must get hold of Demetrius Zagone—he has been to America, he has all the modern ideas. . . . I wonder what Zia is doing at this moment. If my wife ever finds out—

But whether logical or scattered, the inner monologues are reflective. Though Christie's conception of the stream of consciousness may be idiosyncratic, it evokes the experience of reflection well enough, I hope, that we are reminded of its central features: (1) Reflection deploys active representations of specific past and future events as well as generalizations, counterfactuals, and other complex representations. (2) Reflection re-presents events in any order, but we retain an awareness of the temporal order of occurrence of those events. (3) Reflection has a structure like that of discourse. Specifically, the reflector is able to remember the path taken by reflection and thus can usually avoid inner loops and redundancy.

Unless toads possess some astonishing and undisclosed machinery, the features just mentioned seem to lie well beyond them. But what about the general capacity of natural representing systems, particularly those with combinatorial circuits? We can conceive of an inner chronicle built within such systems along the following lines: in addition to representing each event individually, the system represents pairwise temporal associations, a chain of events stretching some distance into the past. (In chapter 5, we surveyed some of the potential neural bases for these pairings in the discussion of motion detection and memory.) But merely possessing that representational chain is not sufficient for consciousness, since the representations of consciousness must be active representations. But what can activity amount to here, since reflection is paradigmatically distinct from action? The reflected representations are not guiding behavior. To be active, then, the reflected representations must themselves be inputs to further representations. It is possible, then, that these further representations metarepresent the reflected representations. Reflection could be the production of inner metaspeech along the lines discussed in the previous chapter. (Mark Rollins (1989) proposes a similar connection between reflection and metarepresentation in conjunction with mental imagery.)

The three apparent features of reflection mesh nicely with the proposal that reflection is metarepresentation. The first underlines the breadth of content available to reflection (and far exceeds that available to perceptual awareness). That content, I argued in the preceding chapter, can only be represented in a natural language. In that chapter I described how it is that natural language can be internally represented, and its content metarepresented. Now we merely narrow our focus to active metarepresentations, and we have reflective consciousness. The ability to metarepresent also seems called upon in the second and third features of reflection. Each involves keeping track of features of the reflective train of thought and the relations between those orderings and order among the events represented by the reflections. Again, it appears that some sort of metarepresentation is involved, though this time not the metarepresentation of external representations, but rather the metarepresentation of other internal representations, including other metarepresentations. Thus while reflection often involves the metarepresentation of language, it need not.

This suggests that reflection does involve the representation of states of consciousness, an apparently introspective capacity. Nonetheless, I will argue that introspection has a distinct office to fulfill. Making that case, however, involves a loop through another undiscovered country, that of sensation.

Sensation as Subrepresentation

One of the central distinctions among nervous systems separates systems (or parts of systems) using representation (a special treatment of information) from those using plain information without representation—the subrepresentational systems. Any nervous system can be made of both representational and subrepresentational parts. Spinal reflexes, for example, are presumably subrepresentational, while much of the rest of our central nervous system activity is representational. These second systems have the strange property of firing without central mediation. We are spectators of our own reflex action, suggesting, to a first approximation, that these systems are not conscious.

Yet in our first assay of their properties, sensations seemed to lack content. The suggestion to pursue, accordingly, is that the processes of sensation are extrarepresentational, beneath or beyond representation. But sensations do not seem to travel in separate subrepresentational pathways. What else in the nervous system lies outside the net of representation?

Representation is a process of informational triangulation. Its aim is the specification of distal stimuli. It achieves that aim by corralling the output of multiple information channels integrated at their point of confluence. The integration process, in short, disambiguates individual information channels via the mutual constraints each channel provides the others. The specificity won thereby falls on a continuum from the highly unspecific (simple transducers, little integrative depth) to the highly specific (subtle transducers, manifold integration). Importantly, there is no endpoint along the continuum of specificity. No matter how precisely a distal event is represented, yet more channels and transducers might be roped in to further constrain it. Putting the same point in terms of the extensional content of representations, we might say that there are always facts about the object of representation that overflow or lie beyond the representational capacity of the system.

These extrarepresentational facts fall in two classes. First, there are those beyond the sensitivity of the transducers; in ordinary life, for example, we are insensitive to neutrino flux. But we are not conscious of neutrino flux, either; thus this extrarepresentational fact has nothing to do with sensation. (We can, however, think about neutrino flux by reflecting upon it, building on the resources of metarepresentation and language.) But there is a second extrarepresentational dimension of information processing that does influence the process, but need not be represented: the transducer's share. The transducer's share is that information generated by the transducer itself and uncompensated by integration with the outputs of other transducers. For example, imagine a stripped-down representational system (call it Big Blue) equipped only with phototransducers sensitive to blue light. (Blue here refers to wavelengths between approximately 430 and 500 nm.) Such a system could represent a full range of shapes in motion and use fancy arrays and integration to achieve complex and specific representations of its visual world. But can it represent the fact that all of those visual representations are mediated by blue light? From its point of view, the transducers might really be red-sensitive and everything blue in the world switched for red. Nothing would change internally, and the system would operate with the same visual representations as in the blue world.

What information is available to the brain of Big Blue about the wavelengths of light falling on the blue-transducers? The information the transducers transduce, given their range of sensitivity, is that light of a certain wavelength is falling on them, but the representational system cannot represent this fact, because the representational system cannot represent the range of sensitivity of its own transducers. The inner representations are all ambiguous with respect to input sensitivity, or in other words, all comprise transducer-relative information. The blue system represents objects emitting light of the wavelength to which its transducers are sensitive. But what wavelength that is could be determined only if the system had independent access to either the wavelengths emitted by objects in its visual world or to the wavelengths of sensitivity of its transducers. It has independent access to neither, and the transducer's share cannot be isolated from the world's. The information about wavelength, like any information, is indefinite, neither proximal nor distal, but indeterminate.

Compare this with the information the blue system receives about the location of objects in its visual world. Any one transducer in Big Blue is indefinite about object distance, but the net effect of many transducers, each with a different receptive field, is to cross-tabulate and integrate the indefinite outputs of the separate transducers into a much more specific representation of object location in the visual field. The ambiguity about location fades. Not so with wavelength: Lots of blue-transducers afford no additional cross-check, since with respect to wavelength, all those transducers are the same.

Now suppose Big Blue is outfitted with retinas more like our own, with transducers sensitive to several distinct ranges of wavelength. Its spatial representations (of shape apart from color) remain the same, but now it has available to it several versions of its visual world, one for each wavelength of maximum sensitivity. These can be compared, giving the system the wherewithal to represent qualitative differences among the colors. But it nonetheless cannot represent the wavelengths of visual objects, for the same reason as before. The system cannot factor out the transducer's share in contriving either the monochromatic or polychromatic representations of the world. In short, the Diary of a Transducer can only be checked against the facts of the case to the extent that many other diaries are available. The fewer the cross-checks along a certain dimension (wavelength, location), the more indefinite the information (or the less representational).

Thus we find that the continuum of specificity is mirrored by an inverse continuum of ambiguity. Every representational system is using information which it does not represent, not only through side channels, but through representational channels as well. This subrepresentational information makes a difference to the system (since its transducers detect it), but representing the specific fact of the matter is beyond the system. This information, when it is active, is *sensation*. I hazard the hypothesis because of the fit between the concept of sensation and the concept of subrepresentational information. Following the discussion of subrepresentation above, we can see that the fit is detailed. Sensations are contentless but have qualitative character.

Subrepresentational information is contentless too but can be discriminated by representational systems (as being, for example, the output of transducer A rather than transducer B). The phenomenal properties that we sense have a strange indefiniteness: Blue seems to be a property of things, but on reflection we conclude that the sensation of blue is caused by properties of things other than "phenomenal blueness." Likewise with subrepresentational information: it is indefinite, neither proximal nor distal, but given that it is information, nonetheless reflects dependencies among events.

Reading the Diary of a Transducer: Introspection
Suppose one day we notice a new sensation, a peculiar tickle that seems centered about half-an-inch behind the bridge of the nose. The tickle comes and goes and invites introspection—reflection about the sensation. That introspection might lead us to dwell upon the tickle's qualitative properties, providing a log of its ticklishness, apparent location, and so forth. It might also lead us to wonder about the cause of the tickle. Suppose we notice it more in some public places—it is a faint tickle at an academic convention, but acute in motel cocktail lounges. Sometimes the presence of one friend or another will provoke the tickle, and sometimes not. Then one day we realize that the tickle seems to be correlated with what those around us are wearing. The final revelation is swift—we are gifted with an inexplicable nose for polyester. The tickle acquires a particular meaning for us, and from that moment forward when we feel the tickle, we think: polyester.

The case illuminates one of the ways in which reflection and sensation interact in introspection. Sensation is an occurrent state of consciousness, but a contentless, subrepresentational, state. Nonetheless, it is (I propose) an informational state. It never rises to the status of perceptual awareness, for want of a sufficiently rich transducer triangulation to isolate the information-generating properties of the stimulus from the transducer's share. But with the help of reflection and especially language, we have built a model of the world far exceeding in depth and complexity the immediate world of perceptual awareness. Bootstrapping from that immense articulate picture, we spin a new sort of theory, one that includes our own states of consciousness. We understand what our sensations mean by placing them within the reflective superstructure, and the occurrent states of consciousness that represent the sensation plus its worldly context are introspective states. Such states are not limited to the understanding of isolated instances of consciousness, but can also extend to complexes of conscious states, until finally we have a reflective picture of the world with us as consciousnesses within it (Churchland 1979). The final step allows us to step out of the center of that world picture, to witness a world of multiple consciousnesses and forces that act outside of all consciousness. We call that objectivity, and it is clearly a reflective achievement. But when reflection sidles into introspection, it is no less a theoretical and fallible construction. The model here thus follows the modern "Myth of Jones" told by Sellars (1956), wherein introspective consciousness begins as a reflective hypothesis about certain inner occurrences and later turns into a report. The polyester tickle undergoes a similar evolution: First, it is pure sensation, a mysterious mental episode that we do not know how to interpret. Then we form a reflective hypothesis that the tickle is a symptom of polyester, making a conscious and deliberate link between the two. Finally, the hypothesis is so familiar that it becomes a sort of reflex. The tickle is just the way polyester feels.

Introspection, in short, is a special sort of reflective intellectual achievement. As such, it is probably found in only the most sophisticated brains. But sensation is just the opposite, a basic process occurring in even the simplest representing systems. Simple brains experience sensations. But as with the other states of consciousness, the sensations of the simple are less specific than those of the sophisticated, reflecting (as always) the limits of their brains. More important, simple minds, being exempt from introspection, are unaware that they have sensations. Thus if one feels an impulse to deny sensation to the simple, I suspect it traces to the tendency to confuse having a sensation with being (introspectively) aware that one is having a sensation. The latter may be our specialty, but the former is widespread in the animal world.

In sum, we find four categories of representational phenomena answering to four categories of consciousness, summarized in table 7.2.

Preserving the Ineffability of the Ineffable
The multiple hypotheses proposed above do a fair job of preserving the taxonomy of consciousness and representing the various distinctive features of separate types of awareness. We turn next to two general features of consciousness, features that rendered it, the most intimate of states, paradoxically out of reach. I will argue that both subjectivity and transcendence appear as special properties of representational systems. When complex systems rise to the challenge of representing themselves, they hit exactly the barriers traditionally assigned to consciousness. If there is a surprise in this result, it might be due to the fact that subjectivity and transcendence turn out to be

Table 7.2
Consciousness and Representation

Type of Consciousness	Representational Correlate
Sensation	Subrepresentational information
Perceptual awareness	Active natural representation
Reflection	Active metarepresentation
Introspection	Theory-building about conscious phenomena

symptoms of a certain physical organization. Alison MacIntyre and James Deutsch have noted (in conversation) the possibility of ineffability arising from physical causes—we shall see how it is realized in practice.

Subjectivity
The first of the roots of ineffability was subjectivity, our inability to characterize what it is like to be an X without losing the essential subjective point of view of X. This appears instantly in any representational or informational theory as the perspective of the system's transducers or representing devices. Throughout this study I have stressed the limitations of perspective, that what a system's transducers tell a system is far less than what might be true of the world the transducers face. Every representation inherits some of the limitations of its sources, and though ambiguity is increasingly resolved in deeper systems, those limits are never entirely overcome. So representational systems are subjective from start to finish.

Can the subjectivity of representation be fairly captured from outside the system? I think it can be captured in exactly the sense we would like to capture it: by describing the explicit content of various representations, and in turn describing the features of an environment that are discriminable and salient from the perspective of the system. Sensory physiology is in the business of exactly this sort of description, and the marriage of physiology and representation theory gives us thorough explanations of why a system responds as it does to a stimulus—why toads respond to worms and not to antiworms, for example. This seems like an objective description of subjectivity.

Nagel's central question invites this reply: A description of the perspective of a system (a bat, for example) still does not tell us what it would be like to be a bat. He invites us to try various bat empathizing activities—hanging upside down with our arms folded behind us—and points out that this would only tell us what it would be like for us to behave like a bat. True, hanging upside down does not alter the human perspective of our representing system. Trading sensory apparatus with the bat would help, but finally to empathize with a bat completely would entail a complete brain exchange—and then we human knowers would not know what it would be like to be a bat, since we would no longer exist, having been replaced by a monstrous new type of bat (cf. Hofstadter 1981b). Nagel is right to conclude that we can never have a bat's experiences. (Note that the argument just sketched depends on experience and identity both being tied to the brain. Dualists, being exempt from the constraints of physical reality, might allow for preservation of identity despite radical changes in experience.)

But does the fact that we cannot have another species' experience entail that we can never know what it is like to be that species? Knowledge of the consciousness of others consists of a body of representations of their conscious states. When that knowledge is actively entertained, the entertainment is a reflective state of consciousness. At the reflective level, the problem of bat elusiveness does not arise, for two reasons. First, bats are probably not reflective creatures themselves. As discussed above, there is nothing that it is like to be a bat for the bat, no bat reflection or introspection on the subject of bat life and times. And so we are not missing anything on that level if we do not "share the experience" with bats.

Second, and more important: Suppose that bats were reflective creatures. Then swarming inside them would be representations of themselves, their states of consciousness, and the relations of each to their world. Can we enter into the world of bat reflection? We can; metarepresentation empowers the leap. We would need to uncover representations in the bat. Once we understood how those representations interacted, we would interpret them as a sort of inner language, bat mentalese. If we learn to manipulate tokens in our vocabulary that represent tokens in batese, we will be able to reflect on bat reflections—to metareflect. The achievement would not be one of empathy, but rather one of theory construction. It could only follow the painstaking analysis of bats as representational systems, an analysis largely beyond present neuroscience.

Transcendence
One thing no dialectical representation can represent is itself. The conditions on representation cannot be met when the content and representation are one because there is no way to conceive of an event transmitting information to itself, and there is certainly no way for an event to convey information about itself via multiple channels. So the effects of transcendence reproduce themselves among repre-

sentations just as they appeared among states of consciousness. A representation cannot catch itself in the act of representing.

But while every state of consciousness is transcendent to itself, it is an open question whether states of consciousness are available to introspection by other states of consciousness. In attempting to determine the range and effectiveness of introspection, we cannot rely on our own introspective "givens," since these are fallible. Instead, a consciousness can know itself if it is a representational system with the appropriate function and content. We suppose that we possess a complex and variegated introspective awareness, because this is our best reflective account of psychic life. But that account is as limited as any reflective account must be. It is one fallible theory among others.

The Legendary Unconscious

One consequence of the hypotheses of this chapter is that we are a lot more conscious than we thought: Every representation is a state of consciousness, and information that feeds representing devices composes sensations. This heresy contradicts one recurring assumption of the last century of psychology, namely, that there are unconscious representational states and processes. Is there any room left for the unconscious? To this question there are several replies.

First, I suspect that the intuition that there are representational states of which we are unconscious stems, once again, from the identification of consciousness with introspection. Introspection, I have suggested, is a complex reflective achievement involving sensation and a theory of one's own sensitivities to the physical world. There are innumerable states that never become subject to introspection—these states are introspectively subconscious. If consciousness is exclusively introspective, then there are many subconscious states.

I have argued, however, that introspection cannot be the whole of consciousness, suggesting that every representation, whether introspective or not, is at the same time a state of awareness. If so, then in some cases we are aware of something without being aware that we are aware. Thus if we accept that there are nonintrospective conscious states, there are no unconscious representations.

Nonetheless, there is much in the brain of which we are unconscious. First, we are no more aware of the physiological and biochemical operations of the brain than we are of those of the pancreas. Second, any information processing that does not contribute to representation processing will not fall within the circle of awareness. Third, and most important, we will not be conscious of the processes by which representations change and interact. This follows from the claim, defended in chapters 4 and 5, that significant cognition can occur without the explicit representation of rules. The alleged explicit rules that govern cognition are inaccessible to consciousness not because they are buried but because they do not exist. When cognition is rule-governed, the explicitly represented rules are also available to consciousness.

In short, it is easy to understand the appeal of the legend of the unconscious. But the legend of the unconscious has worsened the problem of consciousness by entailing that over and above representation and information there is something special, a magic quintessence, that generates consciousness. This is a legend I have sought to overthrow.

The Contingent Unity of Consciousness

If, as seems possible, at any moment a system contains a host of conscious states—active representations from the simple to the complex—then must we abandon the well-entrenched view that we occupy a single subjective point of view, that our self is unitary, and that in the auditorium of the mind, there is a single seat of consciousness? Nothing in the physiology (synthetic or real) that we have surveyed forces the unity of consciousness upon us, since representational systems could be designed to be only very weakly unified (also see P. S. Churchland 1986: chapters 5 and 9). Nonetheless, the phenomena of unity, contingent though they are, may be general features of the brains of complex animals. We will survey some of the reasons why consciousness, though lacking an assigned seat, nonetheless tends to exhibit itself as a single-minded entity.

First, the compactness and boundedness of our bodies provides a corporeal unity to everything that happens within. One's sense organs are housed at roughly the same location, so as low-level representations are integrated and their individual subjectivities fall away, eventually there emerges a single point of view which is that of the body overall—a personal point of view. Thus, highly integrated representations within a single brain will exhibit overlap in content—they will be similar representations, even if not the same.

But a stronger pull toward unity comes from deep within the sensorimotor system. Two factors conspire to bring about the de facto unity of consciousness, convergence and lateral inhibition. The net effect of these two factors is the emergence of privileged representations with maximal integrative content and maximal control at a given time (Barlow 1972). We observed convergence in the representational systems of the toad, where multiple representations could serve as inputs to further representations upstream: The retinal representations fed the tectal representations, which in turn were integrated in hypothesized motor command representations. The less peripheral representation contains the same information as the more peripheral, and it contains additional information not present in the more peripheral representation—due to the integration of information from several upstream representations (or information channels). Thus there is a hierarchy of representations from the less specific and more peripheral to the more specific and central. In terms of content, the central representations contain the peripheral. In this respect, their position is privileged.

Does this mean that all inputs lead to a master representation, a single cell or circuit meaning OM or "Here comes everybody"? Of course, such an arrangement is possible but highly unlikely in any but the simplest organisms. That is because the point of highly integrated representations is the initiation and coordination of specific complex behaviors. The outputs of a single central "Grandmother cell" could hardly determine the complex behaviors of even a toad, let alone those of overwrought creatures like ourselves. Instead, we expect a certain amount of informational squeeze between the periphery and the center, as in figure 7.1.

Thus there is a potential swarm of most central representations, and at any time several might be active. But at the same time, there is only one body available to initiate the complex behaviors each of the central representations controls. For this reason (among others), cells at all levels in the nervous system compete with others to become active. That is, an action potential in one cell not only tends to excite cells downstream, but to inhibit neighboring cells—this lateral inhibition is observed regularly among sensory and motor cells and may well be a general feature at many layers in the CNS. Lateral inhibition might also emerge as a feature among representations. If representations are identified with single cells or synapses, we might expect lateral inhibition; but even if representations are distributed over

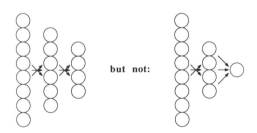

Figure 7.1
Moderate versus extreme convergence.

many cells, we may still infer that lateral inhibition occurs. We generally do better than Buridan's ass, avoiding acute indecision.

Now let us take yet another speculative step, to the level of consciousness. The organization of behavior reflects a single-mindedness of the representations that control it. That is, the activation of the most integrated representations is controlled not only by the inputs to those representations but by competition among them. The forces of lateral inhibition suppress activity in all but a few, possibly only one, of the central motor control assemblies. Thus, at the most central, most integrated level, at any one time there might be just one or a very few active representations—which is to say, from moment to moment we may be in only one or a very few highest states of consciousness.

We might paraphrase these speculations in terms of homunculi. The idea of little humanoids in a cranial control tower is anathema to serious philosophy or psychology, the primary method of passing the buck with respect to genuine explanation. Daniel Dennett (1978d) has nicely diagnosed this problem of homunculi and in so doing described an innocent homunctionalism (that word, however, is due to Lycan 1981). Homunculi are tolerable provided they can ultimately be discharged by analysis into progressively simpler subunculi, until finally each micrunculus is so stupid that we can readily see how a mere bit of biological mechanism could take over its duties. Representing devices, I suggest, are homunculi right at that edge of dismissal, and representational systems are interacting committees of homunculi, assembled into, for example, the department of retinal motion extraction of the ministry of vision (a part of the executive branch). In the corner offices (of which there are many) high in the ministry of vision sit homunculi who receive extremely sophisticated advice from their subordinates, advice that we would interpret as meaning "There's a worm," or "Time to renew those library books." But the homunculus receiving that report is far too stupid to handle it in our words. It receives, at best, the signals Yes or No from its clamoring staff. But it also receives inhibition from its peers, and this inhibition can freeze it into inaction. Thus, at any one time, only a few homunculi actually pick up their red phones to shout "Do it!" or "No way!" to the next higher ministry. Stupid though they are, we have interpreted the homunculi in the myriad executive suites as the potential most central loci of consciousness. None of them is intelligent in itself, but over time intelligence emerges in the pattern of their actions, which is to say, in the behavior that they control.

In commenting on the nervous system of toads, Dennett (1987b) has called for us to eliminate the "middletoad," an internal anuranculus into which all of the toad's mind or consciousness is miraculously packed. In the bureaucracy above, it is clear that none of the homunculi occupies the seat of consciousness, and none is the magic talent behind the intelligence of the whole. The best sense to be made of the unity of consciousness, it seems, is in terms of the rapid succession of authority among specialists of extremely limited expertise, idiot in themselves, savant in the content they oversee by virtue of their position in a vast network of similarly minded dedicated workers. The wisdom is, as Dennett puts it, in the wiring—which is to say, it is implicit everywhere, but explicit nowhere.

7.4 The Future of Consciousness

Since most of the above is speculation, we cannot see from here the future of the concept of consciousness. We can outline, however, the future of the study of consciousness. I have suggested that various features of representational systems reflect the various features of the concept of consciousness as we know it. The next step, then, is the further study of representational systems. This was on the agenda in any case since representation is itself crucial to the study of mind and behavior, but it packs a surprise when it is reconceived as the study of consciousness. The surprise: The study of consciousness need have no introspective element at all.

Discounting the authority of introspection is inevitable, however, in the context of the reflections of this chapter. We opened, first, a logical distinction between introspection and other states of consciousness and with it the logical possibility of introspective error. In other words, there are conscious episodes that happen out of sight to introspective consciousness. But the equation of consciousness with active representation opened the way for a scientific analysis of conscious states from the third person point of view. In studying representations in their complex structures, we study consciousness as well.

Thus we can expect the study of representation to inform or correct our reflective picture of ourselves and our interpretation of our own experience. Hence we can expect the study of representation to bring about a change in introspective experience. What will Golden Age introspection be like? Paul Churchland (1985) outlines one possibility:

> Consider now the possibility of learning to describe, conceive, and introspectively apprehend the teeming intricacies of our inner lives within the conceptual framework of a matured neuroscience, a neuroscience that successfully reduces, either smoothly or roughly, our common-sense folk psychology. Suppose we

trained our native mechanisms to make a new and more detailed set of discriminations, a set that corresponded not to our primitive psychological taxonomy of ordinary language, but to some more penetrating taxonomy of states drawn from a completed neuroscience. And suppose we trained ourselves to respond to that reconfigured discriminative activity with judgments that were framed, as a matter of course, in the appropriate concepts of neuroscience.

Churchland regards the realization of these possibilities as a boon for self-knowledge, but the boon he describes rests on an assumption we should question. Churchland apparently imagines an exclusive dichotomy between folk psychology and neuroscience, with the latter replacing the former (a reading supported by Churchland 1981). None of us, of course, knows what concepts will found the completed neuroscience of the future. But I hope it is clear that such a science will be the substrate and not the replacement for a science of representations (P. S. Churchland 1986:297). Churchland's speculations seem committed to representation to the extent that they preserve introspection, a faculty by which we achieve knowledge of our own brain states (and thus an introspective or representational faculty).

More importantly, one of the labors of this study has been to specify a level of description above the neural, a level of description that abstracts away from neurons to refer directly to content bearers. If the science of consciousness leaves us with anything to introspect, it will be representations, abstracted from the brain states that support them. The introspected representations will probably be quite different from the categories of folk psychology (though this is an open question; see, for example, P. S. Churchland 1986: chapter 4), but they will share with it the preservation of the common-sense foundations of mind: representation and consciousness.

Thus if the central theory mongering of this book turns out to be correct (or even close), there will be an enduring place for representation in the understanding of the brain. And if the additional speculations added in this chapter also turn out to be correct, there will be an enduring place for consciousness and an intimate link between representation and consciousness. In sum, we will have answered one central question of the book by locating the mind—the locus of representation and consciousness—in nature. We will have rooted both in brains of the sort that have evolved on this planet. Mind thus rooted can stay with us as a central, real part of our world view.

And what of the science of the mind? So far, our efforts at finding representations have all been interpretive. We have examined systems by analysis of their components, in their isolated functions and interconnections. On that basis, one might construct a predictive (rather than merely interpretive) science of the mind—but because the components, even at the representational level, are small, the predictive account of a complex mind made of hundreds of billions of basic functional parts may be too complex to be humanly graspable (Pylyshyn 1984:10). We ask, accordingly, whether there will be emergent structure in the dynamics of minds. Do states of minds, both representational and conscious, evolve over time in ways that afford predictive explanation of mental life? This shall be the final question of this study.

Chapter 8
And Then What? Cognition, Narrative, and Mind

Man . . . has no nature; what he has is history. Expressed differently: what nature is to things, history . . . is to man.
—Ortega y Gasset (1961:217)

We have looked at representation from several perspectives. First we examined it in theory, proposing that certain physical information processing systems can generate, store, and use representations. Then we examined representation in practice, using the theory of part I as an interpretive framework in empirical neuroscience and connectionism. Finally, we have examined the philosophical and speculative extensions of the theory of representation. I suggested that our heads are full of both basic representations of our past and present perceptual experience and metarepresentations of events outside of our direct experience. I further suggested that the various types of representation reflected a natural and plausible taxonomy of consciousness. The basic theory of dialectical representation meshes with the accounts of metarepresentation and consciousness. Minds, specifically human minds, are loaded with complex representational states, many of them conscious. Now we are in a position to say the same of brains and see how it might be so.

But metarepresentational and conscious states are never static. In the dynamic mind, representations continuously evolve and interact. What laws govern this dynamism? As always, we could approach the question from the bottom up, as we did in section 5.2 concerning the processes of recall. But the bottom-up approach adopted there was limited as the empirical neuroscientific evidence rapidly shaded into speculation concerning cognition in a complex brain. Lacking the hard data that grounded some earlier excursions, in an attempt to outline human "psychodynamics," we turn instead to the suggestive but sometimes indefinite results of cognitive psychology. This shift of ground has the advantage, however, of permitting us to address that most interesting animal, the human being.

In this chapter, I am interested in describing how new representations form, or old ones mutate, strictly according to the influences of other representations—call this by its familiar, if approximate, title, the theory of reasoning. Second, I am interested in describing the activation of existing representations, the conditions under which a preexisting stored representation awakens from dormancy and enters the psychodynamic fray—call this a theory of entertainment. The two together comprise an account of conscious reasoning, or reflection for short.

8.1   Rationality and "Standard Psychodynamics"

Ideal Rationality

We all know how we would like to reason; we want to be ideally rational, following a central principle like the following:

> IR: Given a specific set of representations, acquire *all* of the additional representations that logically follow from the initial set, and eliminate *all* of the representations logically inconsistent with the initial set (or some privileged subset of it). (Cherniak 1986:7)

This is the exhortation to reasoned thought—a similar maxim covers reasoned action. For present purposes, we need not say much about the governing logic as long as it guarantees that conclusions are true when premises are. Nor need we specify the membership of the initial set of premises, which could range from a set of special axioms to the set of all established representations.

Ideally rational is what we long to be, but it is another question whether ideal rationality even approximates what we are. Taken as a descriptive theory, ideal rationality conceives us as logic machines, stocked with a set of explicit rules of inference which we apply methodically to the premises afforded by the representation set. In AI, the image of this ideal rationality is the production system, in which a list of productions, generally "if-then" rules, is applied and reapplied to a data-base, to extend the data-base and determine a system's next action.

Prima facie doubts about ideal rationality as a theory of real psychodynamics are signaled immediately in the word "ideal." If the force of "ideal" in ideal rationality is normative, this fact alone suggests a distance between the theory of ideal rationality and our target, the real psychodynamics of humans. Plugging the one in for the other would be analogous to taking an ideal ethics as a theory of behavioral psychology. In this fallen world of ours, someone who bases behavioral predictions on, say, the categorical imperative may win our admiration for ethical optimism but will fall short of reliable predictions. Similarly, in theories of reasoning there will be a gap between the oughts of ideal rationality and the actuality of real psychodynamics.

But perhaps ideal rationality fits us, warts and all, in another sense. Perhaps it refers to the idealization which any theory imposes upon its unruly domain, overlooking the rough edges of reality to get off the ground. The ideal gas laws are ideal in this sense. Does rationality afford a useful abstract idealization of representational psychodynamics? The answer seems to be no. We begin with a test question for reasoners: How many hyenas are window washers? Doubtless in seeking the answer no one scrambled for the encyclopedia. You already knew everything you needed to know about both hyenas and window washers; all you needed was a quick inference between their domains. The proposition that no hyenas are window washers followed logically from your store of preexisting beliefs; yet I would guess that none of you had deduced it prior to reading the question. Your failure to make the inference before now was a departure from ideal rationality, which demands that we acquire all the beliefs and desires appropriate to our belief-desire set. Until I asked my animal question, you were not ideally rational—you missed one.[1]

The problem, of course, is that there are an unlimited number of logical inferences that follow from our belief store; not only about hyenas as window washers, but armadillos as astronauts, aphids for president, and so on. Even the single simple inference rule, P implies (P or Q), could occupy us forever. We face what Chris Cherniak calls the finitary predicament (1986): There simply is not world enough and time to compute all the consequences of our beliefs. In response to the finitary predicament, Cherniak sensibly moves to a position he calls minimal rationality (1986:9). We might similarly scale IR down to another principle:

> MR: Given a specific set of representations, acquire *some* of the additional representations that logically follow from the initial set, and eliminate *some* of the representations logically inconsistent with the initial set (or some privileged subset of it).

We might briefly elaborate minimal rationality to outline the familiar parts of what we might call *standard psychodynamics*. Standard psychodynamics has two components. First, primary psychodynamics is described by ideal rationality. The real world incarnation of this form of primary psychodynamics is found in AI, in the brute force technique of exhaustive search, which deduces every obtainable consequence of the current state of affairs. AI programs, like any actual system, shipwreck on the finitary predicament in the form of the frame problem—roughly, the problem of keeping track in real time of the relevant consequences of actions and ignoring the endless string of irrelevant deductions.

This predicament, accordingly, begets a secondary psychodynamics, piggyback on the first. Secondary psychodynamics prunes the potentially endless branching deductions, indicating which inferential paths to take first, and by computational triage leaves an unlimited number of other inferential paths untrod. Whereas logic governed the inferences undertaken within the primary level, secondary psychodynamics marches to (merely) heuristic rules, rules of thumb which cannot guarantee ultimate derivation of the best solution.

Cherniak's own hypothesis about actual human psychodynamics is a roughly standard account. The primary psychodynamic for him is rational. At the secondary level, however, rather than interpolating a further set of heuristic rules, Cherniak appeals to hardware limitations. For various good evolutionary reasons, our memories are compartmentalized or modular. This has the sometimes embarrassing side effect that we can fail to connect evidence across the modules, missing relevance. As a result, we fail to execute some of the inferences we ideally should.[2]

To Err Is Human
Regardless of the details, standard psychodynamics predicts the following outcome: The inferences that people do execute are logical. That is, given a decision task for which there is world enough and time, people should get it (logically) right. But, in a large array of apparently straightforward reasoning tasks, people fail. Their mistakes falsify the prediction, suggesting that the standard psychodynamic is false.

Herein follows a survey of some of the more striking shortfalls of reasoning routinely exhibited by folks like us. Others have surveyed these results, but since the pattern of failure will ultimately prove important here, I will tour this territory again. (See Wason and Johnson-Laird 1972; Kahneman, Slovik, and Tversky 1982. Some of these cases are also surveyed, with a different final conclusion, in Stich 1985.)

Let us begin with some instructive failures of deductive reasoning. First, the "Wason Selection Task": We are presented with a set of four cards, each of which has a letter on one side and a number on the other. We can see only one side of each card:

Concerning these cards, we are asked which cards we would need to turn over to determine the truth or falsity of the following hypothesis:

If there is an R on one side of the card, then there is a 2 on the other side of the card.

Most people immediately see that the R card will need to be turned over, to confirm the hidden 2. But very few realize that the 8 card must also be turned over to make sure that there is not an R on its reverse. In addition, a high percentage of subjects wrongly recommend flipping the 2 card—even though no matter what is hidden there, it will not disconfirm the "R–2" hypothesis. The overall success rate at variants of this task can be as low as 4% (Johnson-Laird and Wason, 1970). Even students of logic do fairly poorly.

A second group of experiments concerns the rationality of belief revision. They explore the tendency of subjects to abandon specific beliefs in the face of disconfirming evidence. For example, subjects are led to believe, through a fake aptitude test, that they are particularly good at some subtle discrimination (e.g., the ability to distinguish real from fake suicide notes) (Ross, Leper, and Hubbard 1975). Then, in a debriefing session, they are told that the aptitude test was a pure sham. Some weeks later they fill out a self-assessment form wherein they are asked to rate their ability at the subtle discrimination of the original bogus aptitude test. Subjects who were originally told that they had (or lacked) the knack predominantly continued to believe in their talent (or lack of it) despite the explicit discrediting of the evidence on which the belief rested.

What emerges from this and similar experiments is a tendency toward belief conservatism. Apparently this tendency is strong enough to withstand explicit contradiction by other, more certain evidence. Like the Wason selection task, the experiments on belief conservatism reveal instances of failure of deductive reasoning. We will return to these failures after a survey of failures of inductive reasoning.

Likely Lapses in the Estimation of Likelihood
Next we survey experiments concerning failures of probabilistic reasoning. Here there are five separate tendencies, each a departure

from correct inductive reasoning. We begin with a task posed by Tversky and Kahneman (1982): Subjects were given brief descriptions of individuals and asked to rank statements according to their relative probability. One of the capsule descriptions follows:

> Linda is 31 years old, single, outspoken, and very bright. She majored in philosophy. As a student, she was deeply concerned with issues of discrimination and social justice and also participated in anti-nuclear demonstrations.

We are asked to rank the following statements about Linda's probable occupation or activities, with 1 for the most probable and 6 for the least probable:

1. Linda manages a bookstore and takes yoga lessons.
2. Linda is active in the feminist movement.
3. Linda is a psychiatric social worker.
4. Linda is a bank teller.
5. Linda is an insurance salesperson.
6. Linda is a bank teller and is active in the feminist movement.

The crucial statements are numbers 2, 4, and 6. Subjects generally ranked 2 as fairly likely and 4 as fairly unlikely. Statement 6 generally fell in the middle of 2 and 4—its probability was apparently judged to be the average of 2 and 4. But after a moment's reflection, one can see that this judgment is a mistake. Statement 6 is the conjunction of statements 2 and 4; since both 2 and 4 need to be true in order for 6 to be true, 6 cannot be more probable than 4.

Tversky and Kahneman propose that in probability assignments like this, people rely on a "representativeness heuristic" (1982). That is, for each relevant class (e.g., feminists, bank tellers), people have a stereotype of a typical member of that class. The target individual (Linda in this case) is compared to the stereotype. Insofar as the target resembles or is representative of the stereotype, to that extent the target is judged to be a probable member of the class. Linda seemed representative of feminists more than of bank tellers, so the probability estimate of her membership in the former class was higher than in the latter. The stereotype of the intersection, the class of feminist bank tellers, is apparently a compromise of the features of the other two stereotypes, so Linda's representativeness was judged in the middle.

Tversky, Kahneman, and colleagues also flag several other heuristics which seem, in experiments, to depart from correct probabilistic reasoning. First, in estimating probability, people also seem to rely on what Tversky and Kahneman call the availability heuristic (1973): We judge the frequency of cases by how easy it is to call samples to mind. Samples may be more available to memory, more vivid, easier to imagine, or combinations of these availability enhancers. For example, are more students returning to traditional liberalism? If in the last three days you have heard a student express liberal opinions, the chances are you will judge the frequency of campus liberalism to be significantly higher than you would without the encounter with the liberal student. The proposed mechanism, the availability heuristic, suggests that you make the judgment simply by trying to call to mind instances of liberal or conservative opinions in students. The more available instances produce the higher perceived probability. In other words, the impact of the encounter on perceived frequency far outweighs the literal contribution of one case to the actual frequency.

Three other biases deserve brief mention. First, people exhibit, perhaps as a result of applying the availability heuristic, a "fundamental attribution error": In general, we discount the environmental contributions to behavior and accentuate the contributions to behavior from individual dispositions and personality. If you have ever felt generally stupid in a country whose language you have not mastered, you may have made this very error with respect to yourself. Another case: Ross and Anderson (1982) asked a group of subjects to make up and administer a difficult quiz, based on their own knowledge, for another group of subjects. Obviously, the situation favored the quiz-makers, who framed questions that displayed their expertise at the expense of the quiz-takers. A third group of subjects observed the quiz-makers and takers and were fully aware of the lopsidedness of the presentation. Nonetheless, this third group judged people in the quiz-making group to be more intelligent than those in the quiz-taking group. (Even the quiz-takers agreed with this judgment.) Apparently, they attributed the effects of the experimental design to the independent capacities of the participants.

Second, there are regular misestimations of probabilities in multistage evaluation. A multistage evaluation is a probability estimate of a complex process or event based on the probabilities of components. For example, the safety of a nuclear power plant depends on the optimal functioning of many components, the failure of any one of which might lead to catastrophe. Suppose there are ten subsystems, each with a probability of failure in the next ten years of only 5 percent— each is a lot more reliable than most familiar mechanical devices. What is the probability of failure for the whole plant? Most people are overconfident and surprised to learn that the actual probability of failure is around 40 percent. Apparently people engage in "as if" reasoning in multistage evaluation: When a component probability is high, they assume it to be certain. One feels that one can rely on a component with only a 5 percent failure rate, as if it will never fail. The optimism ramifies to other components, leading to regular over-estimation in multistage evaluation (Gettys, Kelly, and Peterson 1973).

Finally, people display a marked bias toward causal prediction over other predictors which are equally effective. For example, people are more willing to predict the height of children, given the height of parents, than they are to predict the height of parents, given the height of children. Statistically, either is as good a predictor as the other, but the direction of causality inspires more confidence (Tversky and Kahneman 1980).

Each of these failures is general. The research suggests that most of us are quite susceptible to these errors of reasoning, and we are susceptible most of the time. To complete the case, we need merely add our own private files of irregular lapses—those moments, sometimes agonizing, when we simply forget or neglect some obvious fact or consequence; reality is quick to point out our lapse. Some of these derailments of the train of rational thought can be corrected. But many escape notice, accumulate, and result in rerouting of the tracks themselves.

The research I have surveyed suggests that even if ideal rationality is ideal in the nonnormative sense, it still is far afield from real psychodynamics. We might well doubt the basic structure and assumptions of primary psychodynamics, undermining the distinction between a primary, basically rational psychodynamics, and the heuristic overlay. Instead, reasoning seems to be governed by a loose bunch of heuristics and biases. They do the work, and rationality is called into play only infrequently—to the dismay, perhaps, of those who thought we were rational animals.

The conclusion that reasoning is governed by a rather loose set of heuristics is dismaying on another front as well. The aspiration to science falters at phrases like "loose bunch of heuristics." The heuristics discussed above are each suggestive, plausible hypotheses, and each explains and predicts a gratifyingly wide range of phenomena. But we are additionally searching for the unified theory of psychodynamics which links the various heuristics together. It is hard to see those links now. Without unification under theory, however, we find ourselves facing the prospect of more heuristics, introduced to handle other reasoning situations. As the loose bunch grows, the whole sinks toward the ad hoc, a set of rules adaptable to any explanatory need. Thus the departure of standard psychodynamics leaves a void. The research is suggestive, but the big picture is wanting.

It seems that the various heuristics and biases do not collectively add up to a theory of psychodynamics. Yet the data supporting the heuristics poses explanatory tests for any candidate theory. In that sense, the undermining of standard psychodynamics can contribute to the construction of a more unified theory. Are there, one wonders, additional, positive constraints which a theory of psychodynamics must respect? The heuristic package leaves one central question dangling: How does our psychodynamic system manage as well as it does? We are, in general, truth maintenance systems (Doyle 1979; Fodor 1987:154). By and large we manage to get from truth to truth, and our reasoning, though not ideal, is good enough to get by—otherwise our kind would be extinct. Every step away from ideal rationality seems, at first glance, to undercut our truth maintenance resources. A theory of psychodynamics needs to account for this apparent empirical fact. It needs to show how we are at least rough-hewn truth maintainers.

Thus we are looking for a middle way: Ideal rationality, even in the truncated version I called standard psychodynamics, is too good to be true of us—or so the empirical evidence suggests. On the other hand, the heuristics that spring from that evidence directly are too loose to be good. We need something to bind them together, a new story of human psychodynamics.

8.2   The Nature of Narrative

Reasoning and reflection are perhaps our most constant occupation. We continually think about things and think through problems, in silence and out loud, alone and with others. It is surprising that when we examine the overall and typical patterns of reasoning, a process so familiar turns out to be hard to characterize. We would expect the basic patterns of human psychodynamics to be ubiquitous and quite obvious, once we know what to look for. They ought to be patterns that we observe in both private reflection and public discourse.

The following sections examine the hypothesis that one such public pattern of discourse does in fact reflect a basic pattern of thought. That is the pattern of *narrative*. Concerning narrative, Roland Barthes (1975) writes:

> Carried by articulated language, spoken or written, fixed or moving images, gestures, and the ordered mixture of all these substances, narrative is present in myth, legend, fable, tale,

novella, epic, history, tragedy, drama, comedy, mime, painting, stained glass windows, cinema, comics, news items, conversation. . . . Caring nothing for the division between good and bad literature, narrative is international, transhistorical, transcultural: it is simply there, like life itself.

Narrative is simply there in thought as well, in the rehearsal of memories, the formation of expectations, and in the story explanations we readily offer for events of all sorts. This engenders a hunch: Since, as Barthes suggests, narrative is so ubiquitous, and since historically narrative precedes science in humankind's efforts to render the world intelligible, could it be that the form of narrative has something psychodynamic at its roots? We will test the hunch in two stages. First I will try to clarify the nature of narrative. Then we can return to the psychology of reasoning, to inquire whether human reason follows a narrative path.

Narrative Texture: Form and Content
My aim is to provide a characterization of narrativity. The approach might be illuminated by a comparison and contrast with the task of providing a theory of meaningful sentences. Such a theory imposes constraints on the syntax and semantics of sentences; that is, it sorts word strings, first, according to whether they are grammatical and complete and, second, according to whether the words in their grammatical context are meaningful. These are two separate constraints. The word string "Samara in tonight him with appointment an had I" fails a grammatical constraint on word order. Chomsky's corker, "Colorless green ideas sleep furiously," on the other hand, is grammatically fine but semantically deviant. We rank sentences along both continua: "I had an appointment him with tonight Samara in" is not as bad as the first instance; neither is "Pale green ideas sleep fitfully." These examples both remain deviant but come closer to the intuitive standards of meaningfulness.

The domain of the theory of meaningful sentences is the set of word strings in a natural language. In contrast, the domain of a theory of narrative will be representations and their concatenations, where these include sentences and parts of sentences but are not limited to representations in language—Barthes's list indicates that any representational system can be a medium of narrative. Thus when I refer to a narrative text, it should be heard as a shorthand for the various narrative concatenations of representations.

Another contrast between meaningfulness (of sentences) and narrativity (of larger texts) is also something of a caveat. Whereas the grammar of sentences imposes fairly rigid constraints on the structure of good sentences, narrative structural constraints are looser. Narratives are supersentential and superrepresentational, binding together component sentences and representations. As we shall see, it is not always easy to hear (or see) narrativity the way one hears grammaticality. Among other things, the distinction between complete narratives and narrative fragments is not as clearly defined as the corresponding distinction with respect to sentences. As a result, we might speak of narrative texture rather than narrative structure. Coming up, then, is a theory of narrative texture. Insofar as textures are looser than structures, I will not be providing necessary and sufficient conditions for narrativity. Instead, I will be setting out some recognizable central tendencies of narrative.

Despite these differences, the theory of narrative resembles its counterpart theory of sentences: It includes an analogous pair of constraint types, roughly corresponding to the syntactic and semantic constraints. And just as the theory of sentences ideally covers all sentences, from the most prosaic to the most poetic, so the theory of narrative stretches from anecdotes in cafeteria lines to *War and Peace*. Specifically, however, it is not intended to be a theory of artistic genre. My aim here, as in other chapters, is to outline the foundations of a theory. Installing those cogs in a Mercedes is a task left for another time. (Accordingly, my thought experimental approach is less empirical than that of most literary theorists, who mount their theories on the analyses of as many instances of a narrative type (e.g., the folktale) as possible.)

Narrative textures can be delineated, I think, in terms of central tendencies in both form and content. I begin with the formal constraints, which number two. First, the representations that comprise the basic units of a narrative tend to be both singular and affirmative. It is easiest to see the force of this constraint in language: Singular statements are those whose subjects are names (Buck Mulligan) or definite or indefinite singular descriptions (the queen, a loyal knight). Statements typical of narrative are affirmative in that they ascribe positive properties to their subjects. They tend to say what is the case rather than what is not the case (though, of course, they imply what is not the case). Kafka tells us that Gregor Samsa was transformed into a giant insect, and not that he was not transformed into a water buffalo. Let us call this tendency the *affirmativity constraint*.

Even this first constraint, the tendency toward singular affirmations, goes some distance toward explaining the wonderful ubiquity of narrative, since the ability of linguistic representations to ascribe properties to particular individuals is shared by nonlinguistic media. Traditionally, pictures and other iconic representations are regarded as limited in the manner just discussed—you cannot draw (or paint or photograph) a negation or a universal generalization. Pictorial schemes that do suggest universal or negated statements, like signs in airports, usually incorporate conventional elements that are nonpictorial (e.g., the diagonal red bar meaning no or don't). The limits on pictorial representation suggest why pictures are at best an incomplete medium for argument. But pictures are nonetheless fine vehicles for narrative, since narrative tends toward the singular and affirmative, consistent with the limits of pictorial and iconic representation.

The second formal constraint on narrativity involves the connections between the representations of the narrative. It is a simple tendency: Narratives tend to give information about the temporal ordering of narrated events. We might call this condition the *temporality constraint*. The most familiar connective is "and then" and similar guideposts: meanwhile, when, until, and so forth. Note that the temporality constraint does not require that the component representations (in real time) occur in the same order as the events they represent (in story time). They can occur in any order, as long as the narrative itself includes hints toward sorting the order out.

We also note that on the other hand, the temporal order of represented events can be tacitly given. In a straightforward narrative, we can assume that the sequence of representations follows the sequence of narrated events; thus we can assume a tacit "and then" operator between each of a string of representations. The tacit "and then" operator behaves like the tacit conjunction in a proof: The premises of an argument can be lumped together as a single big conjunction. But "and" is not "and then." "P and not-P" is a contradiction, but "P and then not-P" is consistent. Contrast "It was stormy and it was not stormy" with "It was stormy and then it was not stormy."

Affirmativity and temporality exhaust the formal constraints of narrative. We turn now to the single semantic constraint, a constraint that applies to the relations among the contents of the component representations. This is also simple: Narrated events are represented as being dependent on one another. That is, (as ever) the occurrence of one event affects the probability of the occurrence of another. Call this the *dependency constraint*. The constraint has two aspects: First, it requires that (in general) the representation of one event will travel with the representation of another, dependent on the first; second, the two events are represented as dependent—the narrative states or strongly implies the dependency link. However, just as temporality can be merely tacit, so, sometimes, is dependency. Thus a bald pair of particular affirmative statements can often seem to be a narrative if we take their concatenation to be explained, in part, by the dependency of the represented events.[3]

The dependency condition has an important corollary: Each narrated event tends to have a complement (an antecedent or consequent) that is also narrated. This arises naturally in the representation of dependent events—to represent an event as dependent is to represent it as dependent on another event. To meet the dependency condition, then, narrative needs at least two mutually dependent events. We might call this the *parity constraint*. Of course, the dependencies can chain, and the consequent of one event can be the antecedent to a third. But however long the chain, the parity constraint tends to militate against the unattached, against events represented in the narrative but not dependent on other events. (In some cases, a dependent event need not be stated explicitly in the text. But it will be strongly implied.)

Of course, the first narrated event in a story is just such an event until it is tied up with another dependent event. On page 1, Colonel Mustard lies dead in the library; on the last page, we find out that it was Miss Scarlet with the lead pipe who did him in. Parity provides a good inkling toward plot closure and is one of the conditions that allow us to distinguish complete stories from narrative fragments. Perhaps intuitions about parity also motivated Aristotle as he declared in the *Poetics* that good tragedies must have a beginning, middle, and end (1450b, translated in Grube 1958):

> The beginning, while not necessarily following something else, is, by definition, followed by something else. The end, on the contrary, follows something else . . . but nothing else comes after it. The middle both itself follows something else and is followed by something else. To construct a good plot, one must neither begin nor end haphazardly but make a proper use of these three parts.

In sum, the formal conditions on narrative are two: affirmativity and temporality. Narratives are usually singular affirmative representations concatenated with "and then" or other temporal indicators. The content conditions are also two: dependency and its corollary, parity. Narrated events are represented as interdependent, which means (among other things) that each narrated event eventually picks up a dependent complement. Since dependency is symmetric, the chain of dependent events can end when the various represented events find one or more partners—thus narratives achieve closure.

Indirect Support for the Theory
Let us examine a brief illustrative example and then return to the business of defending the theory just outlined. Here is a snippet of Somerset Maugham (originally put to philosophical use by Dennett 1981):

DEATH SPEAKS
There was a merchant in Baghdad who sent his servant to market to buy provisions and in a little while the servant came back, white and trembling, and said, "Master, just now when I was in the marketplace I was jostled by a woman in the crowd and when I turned I saw it was Death that jostled me. She looked at me and made a threatening gesture; now, lend me your horse, and I will ride away from this city and avoid my fate. I will go to Samara and there Death will not find me." The merchant lent him his horse, and the servant mounted it, and he dug his spurs in its flanks and as fast as the horse could gallop he went. Then the merchant went down to the marketplace and he saw me standing in the crowd, and he came up to me and said, "Why did you make a threatening gesture to my servant when you saw him this morning?" "That was not a threatening gesture," I said, "it was only a start of surprise. I was astonished to see him in Baghdad, for I had an appointment with him tonight in Samara." (From *Sheppey* (London: Heinemann, Ltd., 1933).)

Though this is a literary text, I think it is recognizably similar to narratives we might encounter in both literary and nonliterary contexts. It also plainly exemplifies the tendencies discussed above: Most of its sentences are singular affirmations, and the temporal links among represented events are clear enough, whether explicit ("and in a little while," "just now") or implicit (as in the servant's report of his encounter with Death). One can also discern the dependency among the narrated events: Because he had been jostled by Death, the servant wanted to borrow a horse. Because the merchant wanted to know why Death had threatened his servant, he went to the marketplace. Because Death had been surprised to see the servant, she made an ambiguous gesture. The whole narrative can be broken down into an overlapping or nesting set of action-reaction pairs. Each touches off another sequence, until the first event (the servant goes to the market) meets its match in the last (Death foreshadows the appointment in Samara).

Though the Samara story and, I imagine, many others could be cited as confirming instances of this theory of narrative, a more interesting defense flows indirectly from examples that deliberately violate each of the conditions on narrative. To begin, we might rework the Samara story in various ways to violate the affirmativity condition. The easiest variants involve violations of singularity. For example, we might add some universal generalizations to the text. Imagine it interlaced with lawlike statements such as "When people perceive themselves to be threatened by death, they become frightened" and "Frightened people tend to flee the objects they fear." My intuition is that these interpolations yank the text from the realm of narrative into the realm of scientific explanation. Though still meaningful, the text is no longer purely narrative.

And yet, our favorite stories do seem to convey universal messages. How, given the affirmativity constraint, can they do so? The answer, far from undermining the theory, in fact supports it: Generally stories achieve their universality by exemplification of the universal truths; they invite us to induce from the offered instance to the general law. We may in some stories (typically comedies) recognize character types (the callous yuppie, the good-hearted cop) and extrapolate toward various generalities. Or in other stories (typically tragic) we recognize tokens of generic events or processes and pass along to universals through seeing those events as repeating, perhaps cyclically. In either case, the main point stands: The universals do not appear in the text (see Frye 1957).

We can round out the indirect defense of affirmativity by considering negations. In the Samara tale we try to translate the affirmative statements of the tale into negations: "There once was a merchant in Baghdad who did not send his servant to market to buy provisions, and in a little while the servant did not come back. . . ." This interpolation results in a scenario where, in a strange way, nothing happens. There is a text, but no story (cf. Barthelme 1976).

We can see the need for dependency by interpolating or displacing the narrated events of the story like this: "There was a merchant in Baghdad who sent his servant to market to buy provisions, and then the Red Sox lost the World Series." Probably even the most paranoid accounts of the tragedy of 1986 leave Baghdad out of it. At best, the example is some sort of chronicle—but no narrative. Similarly, we can leave narrated events uncomplemented: "There was a merchant, etc., and in a little while the servant came back, white and trembling. THE END." Here the text remains narrative, but it is at best a fragment of a whole story. Two events are narrated (merchant sends servant, servant returns, white and trembling), but both are left hanging, lacking any events to complete or explain them.

Finally, we complete our circuit of narrative with a pass along two other borders. Poetry, first, seems to me to be distinct by virtue of slipping the dependency and temporality constraints. (Writing the Samara haiku is left to the reader.) Of course, just a short step away is poetry that preserves temporality and dependency—narrative poetry.

Logical argument, on the other hand, conspicuously violates both clauses of the affirmativity constraint. Argument demands both explicit universals (the laws of logic, if nothing else) and negation, both of which are missing in typical narrative.[4]

Other Theories

The story about narrative I have been telling is both more limited and more general than those told by other writers. (Recent discussions of narrative in literary theory include Prince 1982, Martin 1986, Scholes 1974, De Lauretis 1984, Todorov 1977, Genette 1980.) It is more limited in that, unlike some narratologists, I have not undertaken a theory of narrative interpretation, a theory of reading. As with representation in general, uptake is not important for constituting the narrative. Nor have I undertaken a theory of narration—the conditions for narrativity say very little about the origin, medium, and presentation of narratives.

So tales may be told or read by an idiot. But they must signify something—since they depend on representation. And they must keep their yesterdays and tomorrows straight unto the last syllable of their recorded time—which is to say, they exhibit a characteristic structure. Thus this theory is crony to structuralism while not being itself a structural theory. Like other structuralist theories, I've specified the building blocks of narratives (representations), the minimal narrative structures (specified by the conditions on form and content), and their elaborations (again, via the conditions on form and content). Thus I share my hour upon the stage with an odd couple: literary narratologists and cognitive scientists. For example, Propp (1928), in his seminal anatomy of the Russian folk tale, delineates narrative spheres of action and functions (the basic character types) within those spheres. From the ranks of the cognitive scientists, we have Schank's theory of scripts, one for each of a medley of common situations. (See Schank and Abelson 1977, Mandler 1984, Dyer 1983, cf. Lehnert 1981.) For example, the restaurant script includes slots for ordering, eating, paying the bill. These story grammars, both literary and cognitive, share a general strategy of fixing agents, actions, and sequences involving agent-action relations.

Each of these strike me as a special case of the general theory outlined here. Each involves specifying patterns of events, grouped either by their common origin within a single character or by their relations in various specified plot units. But each of these relations is a relation of dependency; so any text satisfying a structuralist theory, I suggest, will also satisfy my more general theory.

Ideally, we would spend time on the detailed assessment of each of the theories alluded to above. But even in a book we face a finitary predicament, so I will confine myself to one comment: A reason for preferring a general theory to most of the more specific options is that narrative is nearly unlimited in its forms, including the banal, boring, and brief. For example, the theories mentioned above all begin with human agency, so they have quite a stretch to encompass natural narratives. Here is a natural narrative: "During the thaw, a sheet of ice on the roof loosened and fell. It struck a parked car, cracking the windshield." Though hardly the stuff of great novels, this nonetheless seems to be a narrative. Yet it unfolds without human agency and as a result pressures the theories glossed above with a potential counterexample. For the same reason, it may be hoping for too much to provide a generative grammar of stories, a set of rules of allowable elaborations of story kernels (as in Prince 1982). Beyond the constraints we have discussed, it seems likely that anything goes. Once again, we see texture rather than structure.

8.3 Psychonarratology, an Introduction

Narrative Reasoning

Now it is time to explore the full application of a theory of narrative: Not only might there be subliterary narratives, but there might be cognitive narratives, or in other words human psychodynamics might be a narrative psychodynamic—one might call it psychonarratology. Now that we have discussed the approximate nature of narrative, we can begin to consider the hunch concretely.

Narrative psychodynamics looks promising as the middle road between the rigors of rationality and the looseness of multiple heuristics. An important component of cognition is narration: It informs effective action by attempting to spin true or likely stories about the events represented in perception or memory. We are effective truth maintainers to the extent that the dependencies we represent the world as having are real dependencies. Thus when we pose to ourselves the urgent question "What's next?" we are asking for plot, not proof. Kahneman and Tversky (1982) refer to this tendency toward inner tale-spinning as the "simulation heuristic":

> There appear to be many situations in which questions about events are answered by an operation that resembles the running

of a simulation model. The simulation can be constrained and controlled in several ways: The starting conditions for a "run" can be left at their realistic default values or modified to assume some special contingency; the outcomes can be left unspecified, or else a target state may be set, with the task of finding a path to that state from the initial conditions. A simulation does not necessarily produce a single story, which starts at the beginning and ends with a definite outcome. Rather, we construe the output of the simulation as an assessment of the ease with which the model could produce different outcomes, given its initial conditions and operating parameters. . . . The ease with which the simulation of a system reaches a particular state is eventually used to judge the propensity of the (real) system to produce that state.

If the inner narrative is optimal, then its denouement should be the ideally rational conclusion, but the process whereby the conclusion is generated need not be rational. Specifically, insofar as it is narrative, it need not be governed by explicit rules. I am suggesting, moreover, that the tendency toward narrative psychodynamics is not merely a heuristic overlay, nor one heuristic among others, but rather reflects a basic structure of cognition.

The new story about cognition, then, might refer to various psychonarratives: As Kahneman and Tversky describe, prediction and planning might be reconceived as the construction of plausible hypothetical stories on the basis of perceived or remembered events. Explanation would involve linking explanans and explanandum in a single tale—which, by the way, is the most familiar form of explanation. We explain most of what happens around us without explicit mention of covering laws. We would not be too far off to regard narratives as scientific explanations of particular events minus the explicit covering laws.

Narratologic versus Rationality
The best ground for optimism, however, is in the potential the theory of psychonarratology has for accounting for the deflections of reasoning exhibited in section 8.1. Let us return to this data and review it in a narrative light.

The first condition, affirmativity, may underlie performance in the Wason selection task. The pattern of failure in that task involved a regular oversight: Subjects failed to search for a disconfirming instance of the R-2 rule. Success on the task required the entertainment of negations in two ways. First, one had to realize that falsification is as much a part of the task as confirmation. That is, one had to enter-tain the hypothesis "Not(if R, then 2)." Second, one had to seek the instance in which the falsifying hypothesis is confirmed, namely, "If R, then not-2." Narratives, however, are allergic to negation. Thus narrative cognition might well be expected to miss the cases required for success at the Wason task. Subjects facing the cards told the posi-tive story to themselves and overlooked the required *via negativa*. Affirmativity also predicts (qualitatively) the phenomena of belief conservatism. Evidence undermines a belief only when it is perceived to entail the negation of that belief. But, again, narrative neglects negation.

The tendency toward singular affirmative representation has fur-ther consequences. Such representation is also allergic to generaliza-tions, since generalizations are no longer the representation of individual events or objects. In other words, the pull of psychonarra-tion is always toward the concrete. That pull seems to explain several of the data of probabilistic reasoning. It suggests, in general, that humans are averse to thinking about samples of groups, and hence, about frequencies. Instead, reasoning condenses around concrete in-stances which replace representations of frequencies in a larger popu-lation. Both the representativeness and availability heuristics follow. For each, a concrete instance stands in for a group, and the properties of that instance (its resemblance to other instances, its vividness) stand in for probability reasoning. Similarly, we would expect people to be poor at multistage evaluation, where the probabilities must be multiplied. Finally, the condensation around concrete cases may play a role in the fundamental attribution error. The properties of a con-crete individual may seem more salient to a narrating cognizer than the more indefinite effects of environmental conditions.

Affirmativity signals the reluctance of cognition to generalize not only over things, but also over thoughts. We expect the inner narra-tives to unfold without the explicit invocation of rules of reason. As indeed they do: When asked to account for how they solved rea-soning tasks, subjects evidently confabulate explanations of their own reasoning (Wason and Evans 1975; Evans 1982; Marcel 1983). Introspective explanation turns out to be post hoc rationalization; apparently, most people do not know what principles they apply when they reason. Psychonarratology predicts this result, since there are no explicit principles in the inner narrative. Psychotales move from event to event without explicit covering laws. There is nothing there for us to introspect.

These predictions follow from aspects of the affirmativity con-straint. The other conditions (and their corollaries) have less work to do but nonetheless add to the account. The temporality condition, for example, has the effect of ordering events. The natural tendency of narration, of course, is to follow the order of events downstream—following the direction of causality. This anticipates the hesitancy of people to make upstream predictions and their preference for following causal paths.

We turn next to dependency. Without the dependency constraint, reasoning would be chaotic; with it, we have some hope at truth extension. But it has its bad influences as well. Through the corollary constraint of parity, dependency tells us when the story is over: A narrative can end whenever the initial events are all complemented by other events on which they depend. So, via parity, narratives achieve closure. Part of the delight of literary narratives is their artful resistance to closure, but psychonarrators may be more easily amused, or perhaps less patient. Narrative cognition rests with the first adequate denouement and only reluctantly stirs forth to examine alternative endings. Premature closure is the symptom, I would argue, of many failures of reasoning, including most of those surveyed here, and most of the unsystematic lapses that all too often afflict us all. Again, the invisible hand of narrative guides our reason to its ends, even when they are short of the rationality to which we aspire.

In sum, I propose that the primary patterns of reasoning are narrative patterns. If narrativity defines the primary psychodynamics, is there a secondary counterpart? We are, after all, able to see how our reasoning fails, so there is in us some capacity to judge our narratological leaps by some other standard. What is that standard? Logic, of course. The emerging big picture is one that stands standard psychodynamics on its head: The primary psychodynamics is narrative, and the secondary psychodynamics is rational. The role of the secondary psychodynamics, accordingly, is not to prune the burgeoning fruits of unrestrained primary psychodynamics, but rather to correct it, and in some cases, prod it into further action.

8.4 Minds and Simple Minds

With the distinction between primary and secondary psychodynamics thus refurbished, we can wax speculative and synthesize the proposals of the last few chapters. In the inquiry into the capacities of dialectical representation, we found two conspicuous limits: dialectical representational systems, built of the structures explored in chapters 1 through 5, had no obvious capacity for representing negations or universal generalizations. Yet our public language, with its convention-determined resources, could represent them. In chapter

6, accordingly, we smuggled the resources of public language inside to give thought the representational capacity of talk. Now the smuggling seems to be going the other way: the patterns of primary inner psychodynamism are being smuggled back out into the public world where they appear as spoken, written, or depicted stories. Narratives reflect exactly the limits of natural representational systems: They too avoid explicit negation and universal generalization. Furthermore, since narrative thinking falls short, in specific ways, of logical thinking, and since narrative lacks some specific representational resources of language, one suspects that logic in the brain arises primarily through the simulation of symbol manipulation, as described in the chapter on metarepresentation.

We might draw another connection as well. In chapter 4, I argued that connectionist learning networks performed their quasi-cognitive processing without the explicit representation of governing rules (exactly as most connectionists claim), and in chapter 5 the same seemed true of some vertebrate brains. We find that strand picked up again in the discussion of narrative, which also unfolds without the explicit invocation of governing rules. In short, we might hypothesize that cognition in each of us displays three overlapping aspects. Different tasks elicit different types of cognition; their disjoint features are tabulated in table 8.1.

Table 8.1
Types of Cognition

	Cognition		
	Natural Representational	Narrative Meta-representational	Rational Meta-representational
Uses dialectical representation (nonconventional) (inner origins)	yes	yes	yes
Uses languagelike metarepresentation	no	yes	yes
Uses non-languagelike metarepresentation	no	yes	no
Narrative psychodynamics	yes	yes	no
Rational psychodynamics	no	no	yes
Rule-described	yes	yes	yes
Rule-governed	no	no	yes

Each row of the table invites comment. First, the three types of cognition, being internal, depend on one form of representation, the natural or dialectical representation proposed in chapter 3. Metarepresentations, introduced in chapter 6, are natural representations that represent special objects (namely, other representations) in special ways (namely, as possessing their individuating features). Thus any form of metarepresentation is also a form of natural representation.

Second, languagelike representational powers were the product of metarepresentation, with is bootstrapping capacities for inherited content. The analysis of narrative suggested that narratives can comprise representations of all forms (including, for example, pictorial representations). But only language is capable of readily representing negation and universal generalization, both requirements for a general capacity for logical reasoning. As the second and third lines of the table reflect, rational cognition is accordingly exclusively languagelike, while narrative cognition can employ both languagelike and nonlanguagelike metarepresentations.

The distinction between narrative psychodynamics and rational psychodynamics reflects the conjecture that the latter is a heuristic overlay, constraining, correcting, and extending the basic narrative apparatus. The rational system arises through the explicit learning of rules of reasoning. Those rules govern (as well as describe) the system when it is operating as a rational system. Accordingly, if cognition is culturally relative, that relativity will be more conspicuous in styles of explicitly rational thought.

Overall, note that the distinction between these three types of cognition arises only at the representational level. The distinction does not rest on any anatomical or physiological boundaries. The same neural network, if it is sufficiently complex, could realize any of the three systems from moment to moment. The tripartite division provides a way of grouping cognitive phenomena and coordinating hypotheses about different aspects of cognition.

It also provides an aerial view of the territory of mind. The basic theory of representation led to a distinction between representation and metarepresentation, and this in turn led to four divisions of consciousness. Three of those types of consciousness then reappear in table 8.1 as different cognitive styles. But in addition to the breaks in the landscape, we have observed a great span from the simple to the complex within each category. Basic representational systems extend from the imaginary vehicles of chapter 3 to the mammalian brains of chapter 5. Among the parameters of system complexity were the sensitivity and variety of transducers and the networks which processed the transducer outputs. These varied widely in depth (the number of layers of representing devices) and breadth (the bandwidth of the system, or the number of parallel representing devices at work in each layer). In biological systems, depth seems to range from one to dozens of ply, while breadth can stretch from a few hundred devices to several million. Modules devoted to certain informational and behavioral tasks add a further dimension of complexity, allowing system behavior to be the output, in concert, of several sophisticated representational specialists. Thus there is an impressive expanse in both the content of individual representations and their interactive capacities. These complexities are, moreover, mutually reinforcing. Roughly speaking, the perceptual and behavioral sophistication of an animal varies with the product of these various qualitative measures of complexity. The whole is much greater than the sum of the complexity of its parts.

Chapter 7 suggested that the same scale of complexity applied to states of consciousness. These too ranged from the very simple to the very complex. As with representation, human awareness is much—perhaps vastly—more complex in content and interaction than the nearest animal awareness. This may boggle our efforts to disengage our own sophistication for the sake of some sort of empathy with beasts and also lead to the surmise that animal awareness is such a dim shadow of human consciousness that it should not be called consciousness at all. I have suggested that, on the contrary, our best understanding of consciousness should allow for gradations in complexity within similar types of consciousness.

The continua of representation and consciousness just surveyed both fell within the category of representation simpliciter. The category of metarepresentation emerges from that of representation but affords additional reaches of complexity. Metarepresentation, as reviewed in chapter 6, does not arise nearly as readily in animal brains. Arguably, it is a capacity exclusive to human brains. Though I have not undertaken any discussion of how a languagelike metarepresentational system could work, it seems likely that this is a human specialty, only faintly realized, if at all, in other primates. If the conjectures of chapter 7 are confirmed, then reflection and introspection are also nearly exclusive to human consciousness. The deliberate and explicit application of rules of reflection is almost certainly an exclusively human skill.

Where on this intricate landscape shall we stake out the mind? The borders between each of the systems in table 8.1 offer three options. First, following a somewhat extreme version of computationalism, one might identify the mind with the rational metarepresentational system, with its explicit rules for the rational government of languagelike representations. The evidence we have reviewed challenges both the rationality and rule-governancy planks of this extreme view, suggesting that much cognition occurs without rules. Thus the operations of the rational mind are a narrow and circumscribed aspect of cognition. Next, a more moderate view could identify mind with the narrative metarepresentational system. This seems truer to human cognition, but it excludes a lot of phenomena that clearly seem to be both contentful and conscious. The third, liberal option would admit, accordingly, the basic natural representational system and all that is built upon it.

We might make the choice according to this principle: The mind consists of entities located in the organism and appealed to in psychological explanation. This principle leads to the most liberal construal of mind, since we have seen ample application for even simple representations in the explanation of behavior. For that reason I recommend the liberal concept of mind (see also Lloyd 1986). But there is one important qualification: Just as we find continua of representational complexity along several dimensions, we should allow for a continuum of mindedness. Some minds are sophisticated and complex. But others are simple minds. Between them stretch a continuum of minds, a great chain of being with many significant distinctions from bottom to top. The various thresholds (e.g., between representation and metarepresentation) make a great difference for the cognition of animals on either side of the cut, but nowhere in the chain do we find a leap to Mind in a glorious Cartesian sense. All the representers form one astonishing continuum, simple to complex.

Simple minds have been the subject here, and now perhaps we see the benefits of thus lowering our sights. Thanks to the sustained work of philosophers, cognitive modelers, and neuroscientists, there has been progress toward the understanding of simple minds. In comparison, the provocative and exciting data on complex minds leave us sometimes at a loss. We lack the emerging big picture, so these data are hard to interpret. The contrast, I suspect, is conspicuous even within this book. To me, parts I and II are resilient and factual compared to this final section. Part III provokes that special anxiety that accompanies speculation in public. (This is a relative judgment. Only the passing years will show which of these chapters really contains any truth.) Simple minds, due to their concreteness and accessibility, are fecund minds for those who study them.

Finally, however, the question of the definition of mind is a tactical one (in the sense of tactical introduced in Dennett 1988). We may make the mind cut anywhere we please, roughly according to rhetorical and connotative convenience, because the concept of mind is no longer doing much work in our psychology. In its place, cognitive science has offered a set of technical terms that fill in for mind in scientific discourse. This book similarly deploys terms other than mind (like "representational system") to bear the weight of "mind." I have made bold to declare the systems I have discussed to be minds, with the big qualification that they are nonetheless remote from the human mind. But readers who are discontent with that equation may abandon it without touching the content of the rest of the book.

8.5   Thinking about the Mind

The final twist in the story takes us again to narrative thinking. In this chapter, we have reviewed some of the evidence suggesting that the human mind uses quick and dirty heuristics to grapple with even simple reasoning tasks. I have endorsed a unifying dynamic for the various heuristics: narrative thinking. Cognitive storytelling will not always yield all and only sound conclusions—the tales we tell fall short of ideal rationality. But all things considered, is this such a bad thing? It remains for us to consider the value of narrative thinking. There is an application, too: One of the most complex objects of our scrutiny is our own mind. Might narrative offer us a fruitful heuristic approach to understanding ourselves? To this final end, we weigh the pros and cons of inner storytelling.

Against Narrative

One might make the case against narrative thinking in these terms: Narrative is the vestige of a primitive, prelinguistic way of thought. That mode of thought was appropriate in brains lacking the capacity for language—in those brains narrative thinking was the best thinking available. It was also appropriate for life in the wild, where survival depended on acquiring skills more than on extending a body of propositional beliefs. On the savannah, it is all praxis and no theory.

After the rise of language, narrative thinking remained appropriate for small social groups with fixed structures where roles and behaviors were clear and stable, and both dangers and pleasures obvious to all. Under these circumstances, there would be a diminished need for ideal rationality, the explicit adherence to the canons of logic, and a diminished need to enter into logical discourse. People in such circumstances have little need—and little time—to talk theory. When they do talk, their most useful discourse might be narrative. Narratives can extend their group perceptions as individuals communicate their particular experiences to the group. At the same time, narrative can provide memorable examples of what to do and what not to do to survive.

All this is not too bad, but the opponent of narrative thinking will remind us that we no longer live in the world described above. Our world demands rationality and explicit reasoning; the approximations of narrative thinking land us in trouble. Now the project of survival has been transformed: Our continued well-being depends on events that happen far from us, and our actions have important distant consequences. In the global village, we rely on an elaborate theoretical understanding of agents, institutions, natural processes, and, increasingly, machines. The complexity of all of these interactions demands rigorous and explicit guarantees of truth maintenance, the guarantees of logic. Leibniz imagined a time of perfected reason when disputes would be settled by ideally rational methods, the sword obsolete: "Come, sir, let us calculate." Perhaps we should make that our ideal as well. Narrative may well flourish as art and entertainment, but it should be confined to that. The earnest business of living in a complex and interconnected world demands a higher standard.

If the higher standard is exceptionless, then our study of mind is equally subject to it. We are enjoined to aim for that distant goal of axiomatized psychology wherein all the activities of the brain are the deducible consequences of its starting state and some crucial environmental parameters. The fact that this level of scientific understanding will probably not occur in our lifetime is no deterrent.

In Defense of Narrative and the Narrative Study of Mind
Logical truth is preferred, if you can get it. But in the real world, the ideal of deductive soundness must balance with other constraints. Truth wars with time. On the basis of limited evidence, we often must leap to a conclusion long before we can finish the Leibnizian calculations. The beauty of narrative thinking is exactly the virtue of heuristics in general: They make optimal use of limited resources. As such, narrative thinking really is ideal, in the sense of representing an ideal balance of endlessly bifurcating thought and instant action (Harmon 1985). This is especially apparent in the calculation of probabilities, in which the combinatorial explosion quickly overwhelms our capacity for computing the outcome in our heads.

Thus narrative thinking has a defensible role in practical reasoning. But not every reasoning task has a deadline. Basic scientific and theoretical reasoning unfolds outside of the press of immediate consequences—at least for those with tenure. Should we not seek the rational ideal in these arenas? Specifically, should not the understanding of mind be a purely scientific understanding?

It may be, however, that time is not the obstacle to the scientific understanding of mind. The intrusion of other obstacles may make the deductive-nomological science of mind a utopian goal. Physicists face the many-body problem, the task of describing the dynamics of many simultaneously interacting particles. Psychologists face a similar problem: the many-representation problem. In several passages herein (especially in chapters 4 and 8), we have observed the unruliness of representational interaction. And the overall emphasis on representation in its simplest cases implies that the human brain contains many potential and actual interacting representations. "Many" here might be billions. Some simplification is possible, but oversimplification is an immediate danger: The brain is an immensely sensitive broad-band amplifier. Tiny energies (less than ten quanta of light, in the case of human retinal cells), occurring almost anywhere in the brain, issue in gross effects, often behavioral. Just as brains multiply energies, they multiply idiosyncrasies, and tiny differences in nature or experience between people could well issue in differing psychologies. Thus we might expect any predictive theory of the brain to be a theory of just one brain. An understanding of human psychology in general may be at best the conjunction of the separate psychologies of myriad individual humans. Finally, the whole enterprise is reflexive—the mind pondering itself. One could argue, with Douglas Hofstadter (1981), that the complex dynamics of the human brain could not be encoded by the brain itself. The complexity of the knower must exceed the complexity of what is known.

We face a prospect that has haunted us in different forms throughout: superhuman science. That is, the rigorous science of mind, achievable (if at all) with computer crutches, may be a science that no human can understand. Such a science may afford prediction and control, but it strangely defeats the central purpose of science, the comprehension of the natural and social world.

If that scenario turns out to be correct, then there may be a place for a narrative study of mind, a looser look toward the brain that remains within the human cognitive grasp. Such a study gives up the goals of prediction and deductive-nomological explanation in psychology. Instead, it aims at interpretation and description. It might be conceived as a hybrid of two disciplines already on the books: history and biology.

History is sometimes regarded as a nascent deductive science wherein historians attempt to fit past events into the frameworks of laws (this is Hempel's (1963) view, for example). But here I would like to consider the other view of history, found, for example, in Collingwood 1946, Dray 1963, and Mandelbaum 1961. This view sees history not as the subsumption of events under laws but as the rationalization of actions through interpreted narrative. A modern analogy, close to the subject at hand, is the view of rational psychology found in Davidson (1970, 1971) and Dennett (1981). Both of these authors (for different reasons) doubt whether belief will ever be captured in the net of nomological science. Psychological explanation, accordingly, is different in kind from explanation in, for example, physics.

The study of simple minds has been similar to both history and rational psychology in its appeal to interpretation. Events were considered under specialized descriptions, as representations. Thus the study of mind practiced here shares with history and rational psychology the concern with content.

But there are differences: First, the study of the representational mind is not the study of the rationalization of action. Some representations are beliefs, and some beliefs provide reasons for action, but the study of simple minds has not been the study of beliefs and reasons. These higher phenomena emerge from the interaction of representations, and I have not discussed the conditions for their emergence. Thus the psychology of simple minds looks at simple content as suits the interpretation of behavior rather than (exclusively) action. Accordingly, the anomalousness of simple minds, if they are anomalous, traces not to holism nor difficulties of individuation—problems with belief—but rather to sheer physical complexity, complexity that boggles the understanding.

Biology, like history, is variously understood as a discipline. Here I wish to stress the analogy between the study of simple minds and biology as an "irregular subject" (Scriven 1959; see also Davidson 1970, Fodor 1975: Introduction, Fodor 1987:5). The irregularity of irregular subjects refers to the extratheoretic disruptions that prevent successful prediction on the basis of the principles of the irregular subject. In other words, the phenomena the irregular science explains are causally affected not only by entities within the domain of the irregular science, but by outsiders, the referents of the *ceteris paribus* clauses that sprinkle the irregular science. Thus the laws of irregular sciences are stochastic, referring to probable outcomes but subject to exceptions.

The study of representation is an irregular subject, by Scriven's standards. There are three reasons for this: First, representation depends on information, which is itself defined by statistical or probabilistic relations between events. Second, the simplifications imposed on our models of mind in order to make them comprehensible tend to omit details which may change the behavior of whole systems. The symptom of oversimplification will be exceptions. Again, the explanatory principles will be stochastic generalizations more than rigid laws. Finally, the emergent patterns of interacting representations may be narrative patterns, patterns exhibiting the openness of texture rather than the determinateness of structure.

The difference between biology and the study of mind, however, has been an idée fixe: representation. Events interpreted as representations are the domain of the study of both simple and complex minds.

Thus the study of mind is a hybrid. On the one hand, its methods are biological, eagerly using the techniques of neuroscience to track the ins and outs of representations. On the other, its product is psychological, leaning toward models resembling history more than physics. It might be considered to be a record of our diversity rather than a prediction of our uniformity. This places the study of mind in a unique position among the traditional disciplines. It reaches from the sciences to the humanities and at the same time reaches from humans to other species. The big picture of the mind might be a true story as well as a true theory, after all.

One final comment: Part of what made narrative distinct was the absence of covering laws within a narrative text. Some of the research described suggests that the absence is not mere oversight: We cannot state the rules which describe our own reasoning. This suggests a different status for narrative: Perhaps stories are the expressions of truths which are beyond our ability to state by other means. What is it that makes *Oedipus Rex* enduringly powerful two-and-a-half millennia after its composition? Many have attempted to rewrite its message in explicit lawlike statements. Yet even if a particular theoretical statement of the theme of *Oedipus* is true, the story still seems to overflow the theory. Though the plot is perfectly, almost hermetically, complete, the understanding of the tale resists closure. The effect of the story, then, is to draw our attention to truths that remain hidden— a moral drawn forcefully by Freud. Perhaps, then, narrative is pre-science, the embodiment of wisdom and beacon toward which science sails. Thus, against the Leibnizian ideal we balance the apparent practice of Plato, whose deepest messages were veiled in myth. When the message is profound, perhaps that is the best he—or any of us—can do.

But the central characters here have been simple minds. As a result of that emphasis, many questions about human minds remain open, including questions about the nature of belief, desire, and the uniquely human capacities for reflection and introspection. With respect to these, the present study is merely preliminary.

Notes

Chapter 1

1. Philosophers also name this common feature *intentionality*, and readers who identify the intentional with the representational may substitute one for the other throughout. But not everyone makes that identification, since the intentional has lately grown to encompass the intensional, a broader category. See Dennett 1969: chapter 2; Wilkes 1978: chapter 2.
2. Ned Block (1986) has undertaken a project similar to mine in a long article, "Advertisement for a Semantics for Psychology." The article, like this book, begins with a list of features a theory of meaning and reference in psychology needs to explain. His desiderata overlap with some of the metatheory stated here. Specific overlaps include the following: "Desideratum 2: Explain what makes meaningful expressions meaningful." This is the central aim of my project. "Desideratum 3: Explain the relativity of meaning to representational system." I think this is what I call the perspective of a representation. "Desideratum 4: Explain compositionality." This is the same concern I address as "articulation." "Desideratum 5: Fit in with an account of the relation between meaning and mind/brain." This appears here as the need for a cognitive role for representation.

   Block's illuminating article appeared after my first attempts to formulate a useful metatheory (see Lloyd 1987); I was pleased with the convergence of views. I will discuss specific points in the article below, especially in chapter 2.

Chapter 2

1. If [aham] is a word, your job is one of translation but not a problem of *radical translation* (Quine 1960). Unlike Quine's famous imaginary linguist (who was confronted with a wholly new and untranslated language), you need settle the meaning of only one word, embedded in a language which in every other respect is your native tongue. Moreover, unlike Quine, we have supposed that you are denied the resources of ostension.
2. Information$_c$ lands the theory in hot water along a nearby front: skepticism. Certainty, says the skeptic, can never be achieved, and so Dretske's condition on content can never be met. In the present context, that means we not only can never know anything, but we can never represent anything either. This problem forces Dretske into modifying the concept of the information channel, bracketing and discounting the probabilistic influence of irrelevant and redundant information (1981:115). The distinctions between relevant and irrelevant, new and old (redundant) are problematic. Relevance seems partly relative to the interests of users of representations (p. 133), a relativity which cannot be used when the representations

in questions are in the brain—on pain of introducing a homunculus. And limiting content to new (changing) information is open to counterexamples: Imagine a measuring device assigned to continuously monitor an unchanging source. The innards of the device might change before the source does; the new information would be about the device. But the represented object would still be the source.

3. This chapter considered internalism and externalism as two separate proposals, each with problems. The two are not exclusive, however; why not combine them? This yields a type of theory known as the "two-factor" view. (Sympathizers include Field 1972, 1978; Devitt and Sterelny 1987; Block 1986.) Typically, the two-factor view determines the content of a representation as the combination of both an FRS factor and a causal factor. In spite of some sympathy, Fodor (1987:74ff) raises a serious question for the two-factor story, namely, what happens if the FRS component and the causal component contradict each other? (Block gives some reasons for favoring the causal component in such a case. If he is right, and the causal component can always veto the FRS component, then it may be that the resulting theory is really a one-factor (causal) theory, with an irrelevant FRS appendage.) I think, however, that the main problem with the two-factor theory is that it simply inherits the problems of both factors. Before the two factors can cooperate, the contribution of each must be worked out, and this chapter has reviewed difficulties for each component. Furthermore, any conceptual problems (such as the problem of error) afflicting either component will equally afflict the composite theory.

Chapter 3

1. This suggests a simple origin for some of the crossed connections typical of most vertebrate and some invertebrate brains. Braitenberg discusses other possible origins for crossovers, including crossing in visual systems as a means of compensating for image reversal on focal retinas. The crossing here is a compensation for a simpler adaptation. Of course, different instances of crossed connections may have different evolutionary origins.

Chapter 4

1. The terms have slightly different etymologies. "Connectionism" seems to have originated in the work of Jerome Feldman and colleagues, while "parallel distributed processing" sprang up in San Diego under the aegis of Rumelhart, McClelland, and a large group of coworkers. The two groups have similar approaches, save that Feldman is a defender of "local representation." Yet in most writing the terms are used interchangeably. Members of the San Diego diaspora, in particular, use both terms. See, for example, Paul Smolensky's "On the Proper Treatment of Connectionism" (1988). I will use the terms interchangeably here.

2. Many of the ideas basic to connectionism originated at the same time as the first digital computers, with the realization by McCullough and Pitts (1943) that neurons could compute basic logic operations, which generated a fair industry in speculation about the properties of nerve nets. This peaked in the early 1960s with Rosenblatt's "perceptrons," networks of neural units capable of learning patterns (1962). By the end of the decade, however, connectionism declined, especially following *Perceptrons*, in which Minsky and Papert (1969) proved that perceptron networks suffered certain intrinsic limitations. Connectionism retreated to the fringes but has returned with the construction of networks overcoming the obstacles of Minsky and Papert. For a more detailed history, see McClelland, Rumelhart, and Hinton 1986, and Anderson and Rosenfeld 1988.

3. This counts 309 phantom connections that implement the unit thresholds. Each threshold is implemented as a phantom input line to each unit, with a fixed input value of 1 and a starting weight of -1 (which can change). The other, real inputs must overcome this fixed inhibition to cause the unit to fire.

4. Sejnowski and Rosenberg (1987) have explored vector comparisons similar to those required for representational analysis. They averaged the activation vectors associated with all letter-phoneme combinations produced by NETtalk at its most competent and then determined the distance between the averaged vectors. Vowels and consonants occupied distinct clusters. The vowels seemed to group around input letters whereas consonant groupings seemed to be determined by both letter and sound. Their analysis is not quite a representational analysis because in some cases a particular phoneme was assigned to different vectors (according to its central input letter), suggesting that vectors were not completely organized by phonologically relevant properties of input strings.

5. The project of determining when a system is rule governed sets off Wittgenstein/ Kripke alarms (see Kripke 1982). Isn't it a fact, say the alarmed, that you can never tell what rule a system is following, and hence can never tell that a system is rule following? I would like to sidestep the issue as follows: The conclusions of the Wittgenstein arguments, recently redeployed, are skeptical. They press two difficulties: First, whether the rules in question govern or merely describe, we cannot know with certainty which rule is true of a system. Second, of any rule, we cannot know with certainty that it really does govern a given process that seems to conform to the rule. I am going to excuse myself from the first skeptical plank by assuming that a specific rule does describe the behavior of a system—the question then is whether that rule also causes the behavioral disposition of the system. I avoid the second obstacle by virtue of the fact that I am not trying to establish that a given rule does govern a process but rather that a specific rule does not govern the process. I think it is possible to establish the negative conclusion even if one can never be certain of the positive conclusion.

Chapter 5

1. The dynamism of the outer plexiform layer is unique in the nervous system in two ways: First, all the interactions are by means of graded potentials, depressions or elevations of membrane potential, rather than the all-or-none spikes typical of regular neural transmission. (This affords subtler discrimination and is apparently feasible because of the short distances signals travel in that layer.) Second, retinal rods and cones signal the presence of stimuli by hyperpolarizing, while most other neurons signal by depolarization. In other words, what photoreceptors positively signal (with elevated membrane potential) is darkness. Departures from resting darkness—light, in short—causes membrane potential to decrease or hyperpolarize. Thus when we say that receptors excite bipolar cells, we mean "excite by hyperpolarizing."

Chapter 6

1. PDP models, however, are generally only simulated (on standard digital computers). A computer running a PDP model is thus at best a simulator of a simple mind. Specifically, a serial simulation of a parallel information processor will not meet the multiple channel condition for representation (section 3.2), since in such a simulation the parallel channels will not be active simultaneously.

2. In further support of mentalese, Fodor (1978) notes that thoughts and public sentences only partially correspond. We can think thoughts we don't know how to express; these inexpressible thoughts are presumably not thoughts in English. Like the argument from nonverbal thinkers, this establishes that there must be a medium of internal representation in addition to natural language, but the argument says little about this medium. It might be a system of dialectical representations, for example. But the argument does not, by itself, support the view of representation I call the radical language of thought, as discussed just below.

3. Gilbert Harmon (1970) has introduced alleged empirical disconfirmation of the hypothesis that humans think in natural language. The evidence is this: Children apparently understand sentences (like "Mommy will be home soon.") that are more complex than the "telegraphic" sentences they utter (like "Mommy home!"), and furthermore, they understand those complex sentences better than sentences that are as simple as those they utter. According to Harmon, if language learning is the assimilation of a natural language, then language understanding and language production should match as the child learns. But this is not so, suggesting instead that the child is learning two separate skills, the translation of natural language into mentalese and the retranslation of her own thoughts in mentalese back into natural language. These separate skills might develop at different rates, just as one's ability to understand a foreign language might run ahead of one's ability to produce sentences in that language.

Yet one could keep Harmon's "dual skill" interpretation without reading it as confirming a Fodorian mentalese. In one respect, Fodor and I are in agreement: The inner language is not a natural one. Words are not simply assimilated. So there is a dual process of translation involved. The encoding process—language comprehension—is a perceptual process, by my lights issuing in natural representations with words as their objects. The production task—turning inner representations back into words—is a separate, nontrivial task.

Chapter 8

1. Dennett (1975) uses the same infinitude of undeduced deductions to motivate a distinction in functional architecture (as opposed to psychodynamics) between a set of core beliefs and a much larger set of immediate (and perhaps merely latent) consequences of the core. But from there he develops thought experiments that question the coherence of inner representation in general.

2. In the end, Cherniak's appeal to hardware may not leave him too distant from the software version of standard psychodynamics. His modules are "soft" in that information in one module is not irretrievably isolated from that in another. One can come to see the relevance of one kind of information to another and learn to make inferences between previously isolated domains. Furthermore, each module, treated independently, faces the same finitary predicament and the attendant frame problem. Each needs some heuristic push toward the relevant and away from the irrelevant. It seems likely, then, that Cherniak would ultimately end up near standard psychodynamics.

3. In the dependency condition, the theory of narrative presented here intersects with Arthur Danto's theory of narrative sentences (1985: chapter 8). Narrative sentences for Danto are statements with bifurcating reference. They directly describe one event while presupposing the occurrence of others. Thus the narrative sentence "They kissed for the first time" implies a time of subsequent kisses. The nonnarrative sentence "They kissed at 10:45 PM on October 6, 1987" presupposes no other

events beside the kiss itself. (Sartre's (1964:57) comments on narrative also highlight the implicit continuation and denouement in narrative statements.) Danto's view seems to limit narrativity somewhat too much. A narrative could be constructed entirely of nonnarrative sentences like the example above. And it is hard to know how nonlinguistic representations could meet the conditions of narrative sentences. The dependency condition, by allowing for tacit dependency, encompasses both counterexamples.

4. A discussion of narrative leads inevitably to a discussion of literary narratives. Literature affords many apparent counterexamples to the view of narrative just stated, and it will add indirect support to the theory to counter those counterexamples.

First, everyone can produce examples of regular narrative texts which seem to violate the stated conditions. A suitably gifted novelist might begin a novel with a sentence like "It is a truth universally acknowledged that a single man in possession of a good fortune must be in want of a wife." Or: "All happy families are alike; each unhappy family is unhappy in its own way." Or consider novels like Orwell's *1984*, with its long embedded discourse on totalitarianism (or any of the moralizing novels of the 19th century). And then, too, there are characters who discourse at length in abstract or general terms, like nine out of ten in Dostoevsky. Each of these seems to offer violations of the singularity plank of the affirmativity condition.

Some of these counterexamples can be dismissed: When general statements are quoted, their occurrence is a particular concrete event in the plot. The occurrences of the words themselves are singular events. Thus we might dispatch the pronouncements of Dostoevsky's Raskolnikov, or the long treatise in *1984*—its sentences denote a sequence of events in Winston Smith's story. (Indeed, the fact that Dostoevsky and Orwell resort to quotation to make their own thematic statements is one index of the force of the affirmativity constraint.) But when the narrator, not a character, contributes the universal generalization, as in Austen and Tolstoy, the stated propositions have no place among the events narrated. Yet they are certainly part of their respective novels.

One is inclined to say that such generalizations are part of the novel, yet not part of the story. I think this inkling is on the right track. It unfolds as several replies: First, we might stress that the literary genres can include many elements, and that narrative is just one among them. Our tendency to consider even heavily moralizing novels to be narrative reflects a judgment that such texts are mainly or irreducibly narrative. The test for narrative in these cases might be this: Are most of the events represented in the text not explained by the explicit covering laws stated in the text? If most of the represented events fall under explicitly stated laws, then we have a text in scientific explanation. But if events sneak by, the grounds for their dependency unstated in the text, then the text is narrative (provided of course that the other conditions on narrative are met). In general, then, we test for narrative by removing all of the nonnarrative elements of a text. If there is a large narrative residue, then the whole text is narrative. As that narrative residue shrinks, however, the tendency to call the whole a narrative shrinks likewise. Similar replies fit well with other purported counterexamples—texts involving negations or fragments.

Finally, there are those texts that deliberately violate the narrative rules—as experimental novels do. Here the very act of violation in fact confirms the violated rules (a point I owe to Helen Lang). Often, our laughter flags the violation of a narrative rule. Again, we should note the distance between the theory of literary genre and the theory of narrative as such. Any artistic genre can stretch to accommodate new possibilities—consider Arthur Danto's example of an experimental novel which happens to be indiscernible from the Manhattan phone book (as well as being indiscernible from his examples of post-modernist paper sculpture, a portfolio of prints, and the score of an oratorio in which each name is chanted) (1981:136). Concerning the objects indiscernible from the phone book, Danto writes:

As a novel . . . it has little by way of plot, far too many characters in search of whatever plot it does have, and scant suspense of the sort appropriate to the conventional novel. . . . The sole motive I could suppose the novel's reader having—if there were a reader—for cheating by looking at the last page "to see how it all comes out" would be to determine whether the novelist adhered to what his intention may be conjectured to have been by ending his epic with a ladder of Zs. . . . Whereas if we turn from novel to paper sculpture, "beginning and end" surrender to "front and back," and an entirely different set of artistic experiments becomes possible. Of course it will be acknowledged that in some sense narrative sculpture exists, and the question of what story is being told has crossgeneric application, even if rejected by the Abstract Novelist and the Abstract Sculptor alike, indignant at the stigma of narrativeness. Still, the way in which their respective works lack stories differs from the way in which the Manhattan Telephone Directory lacks one, for the novel and the sculpture are defined through the fact that each belongs to a genre within which such questions have application. . . . Thus we have abstract painting, plotless novels, unrhymed verse, atonal music, to mention some of the monuments to this mode of categorial exploration. (1981: 137–138)

Thus to be a novel is, in part, to be a text concerning which the question "Is it a narrative?" can arise. Similarly, other artistic genres (both literary and nonliterary) can be grouped by the relevant questions they provoke. Implicit in this conception of genre is the possibility that the answer to such questions is no. It follows that nonnarrative novels do not undermine a theory of narrative. Not every novel need conform.

References

Abraham, W. C., and G. V. Goddard. 1984. "Functions of afferent coactivity in long-term potentiation." In G. Lynch, J. McGauch, and N. Weinberger, eds., *Neurobiology of Learning and Memory*. New York: Guilford.

Adams, D. 1985. *Life, the Universe, and Everything*. New York: Pocket Books.

Anderson, J. A., and E. Rosenfeld. 1988. *Neurocomputing*. Cambridge, MA: MIT Press. A Bradford Book.

Arbib, M. A. 1987. "Levels of Modeling of Mechanisms of Visually Guided Behavior." *Behavioral and Brain Sciences* 10:407–435.

Arendt, H. 1963. *Eichmann in Jerusalem*. New York: Viking.

Barlow, H. B. 1972. "Single Units and Sensation: A neuron doctrine for perceptual psychology?" *Perception* 1:371–394.

Barrionuevo, G., and T. H. Brown. 1983. "Associative long-term potentiation in hippocampal slices." *Proceedings of the National Academy of Sciences, USA* 80:7347–7351.

Barthelme, D. 1976. "Nothing: A Preliminary Account." In *Guilty Pleasures*. New York: Dell.

Barthes, R. 1975. "Introduction to the Structural Analysis of Narrative." *New Literary History* 6:237–277.

Bennett, J. 1964. *Rationality*. London: Routledge and Kegan Paul.

Bennett, J. 1976. *Linguistic Behaviour*. Cambridge, Engl.: Cambridge University Press.

Black, I., J. Adler, C. Dreyfus, G. Jonakait, D. Katz, E. LaGamma, and K. Markey. 1984. "Neurotransmitter plasticity at the molecular level." *Science* 225:1266–1270.

Black, I. 1986. "Molecular Memory Mechanisms." In G. Lynch, *Synapses, Circuits, and the Beginnings of Memory*. Cambridge, MA: MIT Press. A Bradford Book.

Block, N. 1980. "Are Absent Qualia Impossible?" *Philosophical Review* 89:257–272.

Block, N. 1986. "Advertisement for a Semantics for Psychology." *Midwest Studies in Philosophy* 10:615–678.

Borchers, H.-W., H. Burghagen, and J.-P. Ewert. 1978. "Key stimuli of prey for toads (*Bufo bufo* L.): configuration and movement patterns." *Journal of Comparative Physiology* 128:189–192.

Braitenberg, V. 1984. *Vehicles*. Cambridge, MA: MIT Press. A Bradford Book.

Byrne, J. H. 1987. "Cellular analysis of associative learning." *Physiological Reviews* 67:329–439.

Campion, J., R. Latto, and Y. M. Smith. 1983. "Is blindsight an effect of scattered light, spared cortex, and near-threshold vision?" *Behavioral and Brain Sciences* 6:423–486.

Cherniak, C. 1986. *Minimal Rationality*. Cambridge, MA: MIT Press. A Bradford Book.

Churchland, P. M. 1979. *Scientific Realism and the Plasticity of Mind*. Cambridge, Engl.: Cambridge University Press.

Churchland, P. M. 1981. "Eliminative Materialism and the Propositional Attitudes." *Journal of Philosophy* 78:67–90.

Churchland, P. M. 1985. "Reduction, Qualia, and the Direct Introspection of Brain States." *Journal of Philosophy* 82:8–28.

Churchland, P. M. 1986. "Cognitive Neurobiology: A Computational Hypothesis for Laminar Cortex." *Biology and Philosophy* 1:25–51.

Churchland, P. S. 1980. "A Perspective on Mind-Brain Research." *Journal of Philosophy* 77:185–207.

Churchland, P. S. 1986. *Neurophilosophy*. Cambridge, MA: MIT Press. A Bradford Book.

Collingwood, R. G. 1946. *The Idea of History*. Oxford: Clarendon.

Crick, F., and C. Asanuma. 1986. "Certain Aspects of the Anatomy and Physiology of the Cerebral Cortex." In McClelland and Rumelhart 1986.

Cummins, R. 1983. *The Nature of Psychological Explanation*. Cambridge, MA: MIT Press. A Bradford Book.

Danto, A. C. 1981. *The Transfiguration of the Commonplace*. Cambridge, MA: Harvard University Press.

Danto, A. C. 1985. *Narration and Knowledge*. New York: Columbia University Press.

Danto, A. C. 1986. *The Philosophical Disenfranchisement of Art*. New York: Columbia University Press.

Davidson, D. 1965. "Theories of Meaning and Learnable Languages." In Y. Bar-Hillel, ed., *Proceedings of the 1964 International Congress for Logic, Methodology, and Philosophy of Science at the Hebrew University of Jerusalem*. Amsterdam: North Holland. Also in Davidson 1984.

Davidson, D. 1970. "Mental Events." In L. Foster and J. W. Swanson, eds., *Experience and Theory*. Amherst, MA: University of Massachusetts Press. Also in Davidson 1980.

Davidson, D. 1971. "Psychology as Philosophy." In S. C. Brown, ed., *Philosophy of Psychology*. New York: MacMillan. Also in Davidson 1980.

Davidson, D. 1980. *Essays on Actions and Events*. Oxford: Oxford University Press.

Davidson, D. 1984. *Inquiries into Truth and Interpretation*. Oxford University Press.

Davidson, D. 1986. "A Coherence Theory of Truth and Knowledge." In E. LePore, ed., *Truth and Interpretation: Perspectives on the Philosophy of Donald Davidson*. New York: Basil Blackwell.

De Lauretis, T. 1984. "Desire in Narrative." In *Alice Doesn't*. Bloomington: Indiana University Press.

Dehaene, S., J.-P. Changeux, and J.-P. Nadal. 1987. "Neural networks that learn temporal sequences by selection." *Proceedings of the National Academy of Science, USA* 84:2727–2731.

Dennett, D. C. 1969. *Content and Consciousness*. London: Routledge and Kegan Paul.

Dennett, D. C. 1975. "Brain Writing and Mind Reading." In K. Gunderson, ed., *Language, Mind, and Knowledge, Minnesota Studies in the Philosophy of Science VII*. Minneapolis: University of Minnesota Press. Also in Dennett 1978a.

Dennett, D. C. 1978a. *Brainstorms*. Cambridge, MA: MIT Press. A Bradford Book.

Dennett, D. C. 1978b. "Why Not the Whole Iguana?" *Behavioral and Brain Sciences* 1:103–104.

Dennett, D. C. 1978c. "Where Am I?" In Dennett 1978a.

Dennett, D. C. 1978d. "Artificial Intelligence as Philosophy and as Psychology." In M. Ringle, ed., *Philosophical Perspectives on Artificial Intelligence*. New York: Humanities Press. Also in Dennett 1978a.

Dennett, D. C. 1981. "Three Kinds of Intentional Psychology." In R. Healy, ed., *Reduction, Time, and Reality*. Cambridge, Engl.: Cambridge University Press. Also in Dennett 1987a.

Dennett, D. C. 1982a. "How to Study Consciousness Empirically: or, Nothing Comes to Mind." *Synthese* 53:349–356.

Dennett, D. C. 1982b. "Beyond Belief." In A. Woodfield, ed., *Thought and Object*. Oxford: Clarendon Press. Also in Dennett 1987a.

Dennett, D. C. 1982c. "Styles of Mental Representation." *Proceedings of the Aristotelian Society* 83. Also in Dennett 1987a.

Dennett, D. C. 1983. "Intentional Systems in Cognitive Ethology: The 'Panglossian Paradigm' Defended." *Behavioral and Brain Sciences* 6:343–390. Also in Dennett 1987a.

Dennett, D. C. 1984a. "Cognitive Wheels: The Frame Problem in AI." In C. Hookway, ed., *Minds, Machines, and Evolution*. Cambridge, Engl.: Cambridge University Press.

Dennett, D. C. 1984b. "The Logical Geography of Computational Approaches: A View from the East Pole." In R. Harnish and M. Brand, eds., *The Representation of Knowledge and Belief*. Tucson: University of Arizona Press.

Dennett, D. C. 1987a. *The Intentional Stance*. Cambridge, MA: MIT Press. A Bradford Book.

Dennett, D. C. 1987b. "Evolution, Error, and Intentionality." In Y. Wilks and D. Partridge, eds., *Source Book on the Foundations of Artificial Intelligence*. Cambridge, Engl.: Cambridge University Press. Also in Dennett 1987a.

Dennett, D. C. 1987c. "Eliminate the Middletoad!" *Behavioral and Brain Sciences* 10:372–373.

Dennett, D. C. 1988. "Quining Qualia." In A. Marcel and E. Bisiach, eds., *Consciousness in Contemporary Science*. Oxford: Oxford University Press.

Devitt, M., and K. Sterelny. 1987. *Language and Reality*. Cambridge, MA: MIT Press. A Bradford Book.

Dewdney, A. 1987. "Braitenberg Memoirs: Vehicles for Probing Behavior Roam a Dark Plane Marked by Lights." *Scientific American* 256, no. 3:16–24.

Dowling, J. E. 1987. *The Retina: An Approachable Part of the Brain*. Cambridge, MA: Harvard University Press.

Doyle, J. 1979. "A Truth Maintenance System." *Artificial Intelligence* 12:231–272.

Dray, W. 1963. "The Historical Explanation of Actions Reconsidered." In S. Hook, ed., *Philosophy and History: A Symposium*. New York: New York University Press.

Dretske, F. I. 1981. *Knowledge and the Flow of Information*. Cambridge, MA: MIT Press. A Bradford Book.

Dretske, F. I. 1983. "Why Information?" *Behavioral and Brain Sciences* 6:82–90.

Dretske, F. I. 1986. "Misrepresentation." In R. Bogdan, ed., *Belief*. Oxford: Oxford University Press.

Dretske, F. I., and B. Enc. 1984. "Causal Theories of Knowledge." *Midwest Studies in Philosophy* 9:517–528.

Dupré, J. 1984. "Probabilistic Causality Emancipated." *Midwest Studies in Philosophy* 9:169–176.

Dyer, M. G. 1983. *In-Depth Understanding*. Cambridge, MA: MIT Press.

Eccles, J. C. 1983. "Calcium in long-term potentiation as a model for memory." *Neuroscience* 10:1071–1081.

Evans, J. 1982. *The Psychology of Deductive Reasoning*. London: Routledge and Kegan Paul.

Ewert, J.-P. 1971. "Single unit response of the toad (*Bufo americanus*) caudal thalamus to visual objects." *Z. Verg. Physiol.* 74:81–102.

Ewert, J.-P. 1980. *Neuroethology: An Introduction to the Neurophysiological Fundamentals of Behavior*. New York: Springer.

Ewert, J.-P. 1984. "Tectal Mechanisms That Underlie Prey-catching and Avoidance Behaviors in Toads." In Vanegas 1984.

Ewert, J.-P. 1987. "Neuroethology of releasing mechanisms: Prey-catching in toads." *Behavioral and Brain Sciences* 10:337–368.

Ewert, J.-P., B. Arend, V. Becker, and H.-W. Borchers. 1979. "Invariants in configurational prey selection by *Bufo bufo*." *Brain, Behavior, and Evolution* 16:38–51.

Ewert, J.-P., H. Burghagen, and E. Schürg-Pfeiffer. 1983. Neuroethological analysis of the innate releasing mechanism for prey-catching behavior in toads." In Ewert, Capranica, and Ingle 1983.

Ewert, J.-P., R. Capranica, and D. Ingle, eds. 1983. *Advances in Vertebrate Neuroethology.* New York: Plenum.

Feldman, J., and D. Ballard. 1982. "Connectionist Models and Their Properties." *Cognitive Science* 6:205–254.

Field, H. 1972. "Tarski's Theory of Truth." *Journal of Philosophy* 69:347–75.

Field, H. 1978. "Mental Representation." *Erkenntnis* 13:9–61.

Fite, K. V. 1969. "Single unit analysis of binocular neurons in the frog optic tectum." *Experimental Neurology* 24:475–486.

Fodor, J. A. 1975. *The Language of Thought.* New York: Crowell.

Fodor, J. A. 1978. "Propositional Attitudes." *The Monist* 61:501–523. Also in Fodor 1981.

Fodor, J. A. 1980. "Methodological Solipsism Considered as a Research Strategy in Cognitive Psychology." *Behavioral and Brain Sciences* 3:63–110. Also in Fodor 1981.

Fodor, J. A. 1981. *Representations.* Cambridge, MA: MIT Press. A Bradford Book.

Fodor, J. A. 1983. *The Modularity of Mind.* Cambridge, MA: MIT Press. A Bradford Book.

Fodor, J. A. 1984. "Semantics, Wisconsin Style." *Synthese* 59:1–20.

Fodor, J. A. 1985. "Fodor's Guide to Mental Representation: The Intelligent Auntie's Vade-Mecum." *Mind* 94:76–100.

Fodor, J. A. 1986. "Why Paramecia Don't Have Mental Representations." *Midwest Studies in Philosophy* 10:3–24.

Fodor, J. A. 1987. *Psychosemantics.* Cambridge, MA: MIT Press. A Bradford Book.

Foley, R. 1987. "Dretske's 'Information-Theoretic' Account of Knowledge." *Synthese* 70:159–184.

Frye, N. 1957. *The Anatomy of Criticism.* Princeton, NJ: Princeton University Press.

Garfield, J. 1987. *Modularity in Knowledge Representation and Natural-Language Understanding.* Cambridge, MA: MIT Press. A Bradford Book.

Garfield, J. 1988. *Belief in Psychology: A Study in the Ontology of Mind.* Cambridge, MA: MIT Press. A Bradford Book.

Genette, G. 1980. *Narrative Discourse.* Ithaca: Cornell University Press.

Gerren, R. A., and N. Weinberger. 1983. "Long-term potentiation in the magnocellular medial geniculate nucleus of the anesthetized cat." *Brain Research* 265:138–142.

Gettys, C. F., C. Kelly, and C. Peterson. 1973. "The best-guess hypothesis in multistage inference." *Organizational Behavior and Human Performance* 10:364–373. Also in Kahneman, Slovik, and Tversky 1982.

Ginet, C. 1983. "Four Difficulties with Dretske's Theory of Knowledge." *Behavioral and Brain Sciences* 6:69–70.

Gluck, M., and G. Bower. 1986. "Conditioning and categorization: Some common effects of informational variables in animal and human learning." In *Proceedings of the Eighth Annual Conference of the Cognitive Science Society.* Hillsdale, NJ: Lawrence Erlbaum.

Goodman, N. 1968. *Languages of Art.* Indianapolis: Bobbs-Merrill.

Grube, G. 1958. *Aristotle on Poetry and Style.* Indianapolis: Bobbs-Merrill.

Grüsser, O.-J., and U. Grüsser-Cornehls. 1976. "Neurophysiology of the anuran visual system." In R. Llinas and W. Precht, eds., *Frog Neurobiology.* New York: Springer.

Grüsser-Cornehls, U. 1984. "The Neurophysiology of the Amphibian Optic Tectum." In Vanegas 1984.

Gustafsson, B., and H. Wigström. 1986. "Hippocampal long-lasting potentiation produced by pairing single volleys and brief conditioning tetani evoked in separate
afferents." *Journal of Neuroscience* 6:1575–1582.

Harmon, G. 1970. "Language Learning." *Nous* 4:33–43.

Harmon, G. 1985. *Change in View*. Cambridge, MA: MIT Press. A Bradford Book.

Haugeland, J. 1978. "The Nature and Plausibility of Cognitivism." *Behavioral and Brain
Sciences* 1:215–226.

Haugeland, J. 1985. *Artificial Intelligence: The Very Idea*. Cambridge, MA: MIT Press. A
Bradford Book.

Heil, J. 1981. "Does Cognitive Psychology Rest on a Mistake?" *Mind* 90:321–342.

Hempel, C. 1963. "Reasons and Covering Laws in Historical Explanations." In S.
Hook, ed., *Philosophy and History: A Symposium*. New York: New York University
Press.

Herrnstein, R. J. 1979. "Acquisition, generalization, and discrimination reversal of a
natural concept." *Journal of Experimental Psychology: Animal Behavior Processes* 2:285–
302.

Herrnstein, R. J., and D. H. Loveland. 1964. "Complex visual concepts in the pigeon."
Science 146:549–551.

Herrnstein, R. J., D. H. Loveland, and C. Cable. 1976. "Natural concepts in pigeons."
Journal of Experimental Psychology: Animal Behavior Processes 5:116–129.

Hinton, G. E. 1986. "Learning Distributed Representations of Concepts." In *Proceedings
of the Eighth Annual Meeting of the Cognitive Science Society*. Hillsdale, NJ: Lawrence
Erlbaum.

Hinton, G. E., and J. Anderson. 1981. *Parallel Models of Associative Memory*. Hillsdale,
NJ: Lawrence Erlbaum.

Hinton, G. E., and T. Sejnowski. 1986. "Learning and Relearning in Boltzmann Machines." In Rumelhart and McClelland 1986.

Hinton, G. E., J. McClelland, and D. Rumelhart. 1986. "Distributed Representations."
In Rumelhart and McClelland 1986.

Hofstadter, D. 1981a. "A Conversation with Einstein's Brain." In Hofstadter and Dennett 1981.

Hofstadter, D. 1981b. "Reflections on 'What is it like to be a bat?' " In Hofstadter and
Dennett 1981.

Hofstadter, D., and D. Dennett. 1981. *The Mind's I*. New York: Basic Books.

Hoyle, G. 1984. "The Scope of Neuroethology." *Behavioral and Brain Sciences* 7:367–412.

Hume, D. 1748 (1977). *An Enquiry Concerning Human Understanding*. Indianapolis:
Hackett.

Ingle, D. 1976. "Spatial Vision in Anurans." In K. V. Fite, ed., *The Amphibian Visual
System*. New York: Academic Press.

Jackson, F. 1982. "Epiphenomenal Qualia." *Philosophical Quarterly* 32, no. 127:127–136.

James, W. 1890. *Psychology (Briefer Course)*. New York: Holt.

Johnson-Laird, P., and P. Wason. 1970. "A theoretical analysis of insight into a reasoning task." *Cognitive Psychology* 1:134–148. Also in Johnson-Laird and Wason
1977.

Johnson-Laird, P., and P. Wason, eds. 1977. *Thinking: Readings in Cognitive Science*.
Cambridge, Engl.: Cambridge University Press.

Kahneman, D., P. Slovik, and A. Tversky, eds. 1982. *Judgment Under Uncertainty:
Heuristics and Biases*. Cambridge, Engl.: Cambridge University Press.

Kahneman, D., and A. Tversky. 1982. "The Simulation Heuristic." In Kahneman,
Slovik, and Tversky 1982.

Kelso, S. R., and T. H. Brown. 1986. "Differential conditioning of associative synaptic
enhancement in hippocampal brain slices." *Science* 232:85–87.

Kelso, S. R., A. Ganong, and T. Brown. 1986. "Hebbian Synapses in Hippocampus." *Proceedings of the National Academy of Science, USA* 83:5326–5330.

Kemali, M., and V. Braitenberg. 1969. *Atlas of the Frog's Brain.* New York: Springer.

Kim, J. 1969. "Events and Their Descriptions, Some Considerations." In N. Rescher, ed., *Essays in Honor of Carl G. Hempel.* Dordrecht, Holland: D. Reidel.

Kim, J. 1973. "Causation, Nomic Subsumption, and the Concept of Event." *Journal of Philosophy* 70(8):217–236.

Kosslyn, S. M. 1980. *Image and Mind.* Cambridge, MA: Harvard University Press.

Kripke, S. 1982. *Wittgenstein on Rules and Private Language.* Cambridge, MA: Harvard University Press.

Lee, K. S. 1982. "Sustained enhancement of evoked potentials following brief, high-frequency stimulation of the cerebral cortex in vitro." *Brain Research* 239:617–623.

Lee, K. S. 1983. "Cooperativity among afferents for the induction of long-term potentiation in the CA1 region of the hippocampus." *Journal of Neuroscience* 3:1369–1372.

Lehnert, W. 1981. "Plots Units and Narrative Summarization." *Cognitive Science* 5:293–331.

Leibniz, G. W. F. 1677 (1951). "Dialogue on the Connection Between Things and Words." In P. Weiner, ed., *Leibniz Selections.* New York: Scribner's.

Lettvin, J. Y., H. R. Maturana, W. S. McCulloch, and W. H. Pitts. 1959. "What the Frog's Eye Tells the Frog's Brain." *Proceedings of the Institute of Radio Engineers* 47:1940–1951.

Levy, W. B., and O. Steward. 1979. "Synapses as associative memory elements in the hippocampal formation." *Brain Research* 175:233–245.

Lloyd, D. E. 1982. *Picturing.* Ph.D. Thesis, Department of Philosophy, Columbia University.

Lloyd, D. E. 1986. "The Limits of Cognitive Liberalism." *Behaviorism* 14:1–14.

Lloyd, D. E. 1987. "Mental Representation from the Bottom Up." *Synthese* 70:23–78.

Lloyd, D. E. 1989. "Extending the 'New Hegemony' of Classical Conditioning." (Commentary on J. Turkkan, "Classical Conditioning: The New Hegemony.") *Behavioral and Brain Sciences* (in press).

Lockery, S. 1989a. *Parallel Processing of Sensory Information in the Medicinal Leech.* Ph.D. Thesis, Department of Biology, University of California, San Diego.

Lockery, S. 1989b. "Representation, Functionalism, and Simple Living Systems." In A. Montefiore and D. Noble, eds., *Goals, No Goals, and Own Goals.* London: Hutchins Press.

Loewer, B. 1987. "From Information to Intentionality." *Synthese* 70:287–317.

Lycan, W. 1981. "Form, Function, and Feel." *Journal of Philosophy* 78:24–49.

Lynch, G. 1986. *Synapses, Circuits, and the Beginnings of Memory.* Cambridge, MA: MIT Press. A Bradford Book.

Lynch, G., and M. Baudry. 1984. "The biochemistry of memory: a new and specific hypothesis." *Science* 224:1057–1063.

Lyons, W. 1986. *The Disappearance of Introspection.* Cambridge, MA: MIT Press. A Bradford Book.

McClelland, J., and D. Rumelhart. 1986. *Parallel Distributed Processing: Explorations in the Microstructure of Cognition. Volume Two: Psychological and Biological Models.* Cambridge, MA: MIT Press. A Bradford Book.

McClelland, J., D. Rumelhart, and G. Hinton. 1986. "The Appeal of Parallel Distributed Processing." In Rumelhart and McClelland 1986.

McCulloch, W., and W. Pitts. 1943. "A logical calculus of ideas immanent in nervous activity." *Bulletin of Mathematical Biophysics* 5:115–133.

McDermott, D. 1976. "Artificial Intelligence Meets Natural Stupidity." *SIGART Newsletter* no. 57. Also in Haugeland 1981.

McNaughton, B. L., R. M. Douglas and G. V. Goddard. 1978. "Synaptic enhancement in fascia dentata: cooperativity among coactive afferents." *Brain Research* 157:277–293.

Mandelbaum, M. 1961. "Historical Explanation: The Problem of 'Covering Laws'." *History and Theory* 1:229–242.

Mandler, J. 1984. *Stories, Scripts, and Scenes.* Hillsdale, NJ: Lawrence Erlbaum.

Marcel, A. J. 1983. "Conscious and Unconscious Perception: An Approach to the Relations Between Phenomenal Experience and Perceptual Processes." *Cognitive Psychology* 15:238–300.

Martin, W. 1986. *Recent Theories of Narrative.* Ithaca, NY: Cornell University Press.

Masland, R. H. 1986. "The Functional Architecture of the Retina." *Scientific American* 255, no. 6:102–111.

Mauk, M., J. Steinmetz, and R. Thomson. 1986. "Classical Conditioning Using Stimulation of the Inferior Olive as the Unconditioned Stimulus." *Proceedings of the National Academy of Science, USA* 83:5349–5353.

Miller, G. A. 1984. "Informavores." In F. Machlup and U. Mansfield, eds., *The Study of Information: Interdisciplinary Messages.* New York: Wiley.

Millikan, R. G. 1984. *Language, Thought, and Other Biological Categories.* Cambridge, MA: MIT Press. A Bradford Book.

Millikan, R. G. 1986. "Thoughts Without Laws: Cognitive Science Without Content." *Philosophical Review* 95:47–80.

Minsky, M., and S. Papert. 1969. *Perceptrons.* Cambridge, MA: MIT Press.

Moynihan, M. 1985. *Communication and Noncommunication by Cephalopods.* Bloomington: Indiana University Press.

Nagel, T. 1974. "What Is It Like to Be a Bat?" *Philosophical Review* 83:435–450.

Newell, A. 1987. *Unified Theories of Cognition.* The William James Lectures, Harvard University, Cambridge, MA.

Ortega y Gasset, J. 1961. *History as a System.* New York: Norton.

Poggio, T., and C. Koch. 1987. "Synapses That Compute Motion." *Scientific American* 256(5):46–72.

Prince, G. 1982. *Narratology.* New York: Mouton.

Propp, V. 1928 (1984). *Theory and History of Folklore.* Minneapolis: University of Minnesota Press.

Putnam, H. 1975. "The Meaning of 'Meaning'." In K. Gunderson, ed., *Language, Mind, and Knowledge. Vol. 7, Minnesota Studies in the Philosophy of Science.* Minneapolis: University of Minnesota Press.

Putnam, H. 1981. *Reason, Truth, and History.* Cambridge University Press.

Putnam, H. 1986. *The Many Faces of Realism: The Paul Carus Lectures.* LaSalle, Ill.: Open Court.

Pylyshyn, Z. 1984. *Computation and Cognition.* Cambridge, MA: MIT Press. A Bradford Book.

Quine, W. V. O. 1960. *Word and Object.* Cambridge, MA: MIT Press.

Racine, R. J., N. Milgram, and S. Hafner. 1983. "Long-term potentiation in the rat limbic forebrain." *Brain Research* 260:217–231.

Reichardt, W. E., and T. Poggio, eds. 1980. *Theoretical Approaches to Neurobiology.* Cambridge, MA: MIT Press.

Robinson, G. B., and R. J. Racine. 1982. "Heterosynaptic interactions between septal and entorhinal inputs to the dentate gyrus: long-term potentiation effects." *Brain Research* 249:162–166.

Roitblat, H. L. 1982. "The Meaning of Representation in Animal Memory." *Behavioral and Brain Sciences* 5:352–406.

Rollins, M. 1989. *Mental Imagery: On the Limits of Cognitive Science*. New Haven: Yale University Press.

Rosenberg, C., and T. Sejnowski. 1986. "The Spacing Effect in NETtalk, a Massively-Parallel Network." In *Proceedings of the Eighth Annual Conference of the Cognitive Science Society*. Hillsdale, NJ: Lawrence Erlbaum.

Rosenblatt, F. 1962. *Principles of Neurodynamics*. New York: Spartan.

Rosenbloom, P., and A. Newell. 1986. "The chunking of goal hierarchies: A generalized model of practice." In R. S. Michalski, J. G. Carbonell, and T. M. Mitchell, eds., *Machine Learning: An Artificial Intelligence Approach, Vol. II*. Los Altos, CA: Morgan Kauffman.

Ross, L., and C. Anderson. 1982. "Shortcomings in the Attribution Process: On the Origins and Maintenance of Erroneous Social Assessments." In Kahneman, Slovik, and Tversky 1982.

Ross, L., M. Lepper, and M. Hubbard. 1975. "Perseverance in self perception and social perception: Biased attributional processes in the debriefing paradigm." *Journal of Personality and Social Psychology* 32:880–892.

Roth, G., and K. Nishikawa. 1987. "Worm detector replaced by network model—but still a bit worm-infested." *Behavioral and Brain Sciences* 10:385–386.

Rumelhart, D., and J. McClelland. 1986. *Parallel Distributed Processing: Explorations in the Microstructure of Cognition. Volume One: Foundations*. Cambridge, MA: MIT Press. A Bradford Book.

Rumelhart, D., and D. Zipser. 1986. "Feature Discovery by Competitive Learning." In Rumelhart and McClelland 1986.

Rumelhart, D., G. Hinton, and J. McClelland. 1986. "A General Framework for Parallel Distributed Processing." In Rumelhart and McClelland 1986.

Rumelhart, D., G. Hinton, and R. Williams. 1986. "Learning Internal Representations by Error Propagation." In Rumelhart and McClelland 1986.

Rumelhart, D., P. Smolensky, J. McClelland, and G. Hinton. 1986. "Schemata and Sequential Thought Processes in PDP Models." In McClelland and Rumelhart 1986.

Sartre, J.-P. 1937 (1957). *The Transcendence of the Ego*. New York: Farrar, Straus, and Giroux.

Sartre, J.-P. 1953 (1966). *Being and Nothingness*. New York: Washington Square Park.

Sartre, J.-P. 1949 (1964). *Nausea*. New York: New Directions.

Schank, R. C., and R. Abelson. 1977. *Scripts, Plans, Goals, and Understanding*. Hillsdale, NJ: Lawrence Erlbaum.

Schier, F. 1986. *Deeper into Pictures*. Cambridge, Engl.: Cambridge University Press.

Scholes, R. 1974. *Structuralism in Literature*. New Haven: Yale.

Scriven, M. 1959. "Explanation and Prediction in Evolutionary Theory." *Science* 130:477–482.

Searle, J. 1980. "Minds, Brains, and Programs." *Behavioral and Brain Sciences* 3:417–458.

Sejnowski, T., and C. Rosenberg. 1986. "NETtalk: A Parallel Network that Learns to Read Aloud." Johns Hopkins University Electrical Engineering and Computer Science Technical Report JHU/EECS-86/01.

Sejnowski, T., and C. Rosenberg. 1987. "Parallel Networks that Learn to Pronounce English Text." *Complex Systems* 1:145–168.

Sellars, W. 1956. "Empiricism and the Philosophy of Mind." In W. Sellars. 1963. *Science, Perception, and Reality*. London: Routledge and Kegan Paul.

Shannon, C., and W. Weaver. 1949. *The Mathematical Theory of Communication*. Urbana: University of Illinois Press.

Shepard, R., and L. Cooper. 1982. *Mental Images and Their Transformations*. Cambridge, MA: MIT Press. A Bradford Book.

Shoemaker, S. 1975. "Functionalism and Qualia." *Philosophical Studies* 27:291–315.

Shoemaker, S. 1981. "Absent Qualia Are Impossible—A Reply to Block." *Philosophical Review* 90:581–599.

Shoemaker, S. 1982. "The Inverted Spectrum." *Journal of Philosophy* 79:357–381.

Smolensky, P. 1986. "Neural and Conceptual Interpretation of PDP Models." In McClelland and Rumelhart 1986.

Smolensky, P. 1988. "On the Proper Treatment of Connectionism." *Behavioral and Brain Sciences* 11:1–23.

Stabler, E. 1983. "How Are Grammars Represented?" *Behavioral and Brain Sciences* 6:391–422.

Stampe, D. 1979. "Toward a Causal Theory of Linguistic Representation." *Midwest Studies in Philosophy* 2:42.

Stich, S. 1983. *From Folk Psychology to Cognitive Science: The Case Against Belief.* Cambridge, MA: MIT Press. A Bradford Book.

Stich, S. 1985. "Could Man Be an Irrational Animal? Some Notes on the Epistemology of Rationality." In H. Kornblith, ed., *Naturalizing Epistemology.* Cambridge, MA: MIT Press. A Bradford Book.

Stripling, J. S., D. K. Patneau, and C. A. Gramlich. 1984. "Long-term changes in the pyriform cortex evoked potential produced by stimulation of the olfactory bulb." *Society for Neuroscience Abstracts* 10:76.

Suppes, P. 1984. "Conflicting Intuitions about Causality." *Midwest Studies in Philosophy* 9:151–168.

Todorov, T. 1977. *The Poetics of Prose.* New York: Basil Blackwell.

Torre, V., and T. Poggio. 1978. "A Synaptic Mechanism Possibly Underlying Directional Selectivity to Motion." *Proceedings of the Royal Society of London: B* 202, no. 1148:409–416.

Tversky, A., and D. Kahneman. 1973. "Availability: A heuristic for judging frequency and probability." *Cognitive Psychology* 4:207–232. Also in Kahneman, Slovik, and Tversky 1982.

Tversky, A., and D. Kahneman. 1980. "Causal schemas in judgments under uncertainty." In M. Fishbein, ed., *Progress in Social Psychology.* Hillsdale, NJ: Lawrence Erlbaum. Also in Kahneman, Slovik, and Tversky 1982.

Tversky, A., and D. Kahneman. 1982. "Judgments of and by representativeness." In Kahneman, Slovik, and Tversky 1982.

Vanegas, H., ed. 1984. *Comparative Neurology of the Optic Tectum.* New York: Plenum.

Veronin, L. L. 1983. "Long-term potentiation in the hippocampus." *Neuroscience* 10:1051–1069.

Vygotsky, L. S. 1930. "Tool and Symbol in Children's Development." In L. S. Vygotsky. 1978. *Mind in Society.* Cambridge, MA: Harvard University Press.

Wason, P. C., and J. Evans. 1975. "Dual Processes in Reasoning?" *Cognition* 3:141–154.

Wason, P. C., and P. N. Johnson-Laird. 1972. *Psychology of Reasoning.* Cambridge, MA: Harvard University Press.

Wiener, P. 1951. *Leibniz Selections.* New York: Scribner's.

Wilkes, K. 1978. *Physicalism.* Atlantic Highlands, NJ: Humanities Press.

Wilkes, K. 1984. "Is Consciousness Important?" *British Journal of the Philosophy of Science* 35:223–243.

Winograd, T. 1972. *Understanding Natural Language.* New York: Academic Press.

Wittgenstein, L. 1921 (1961). *Tractatus Logico-Philosophicus.* London: Routledge and Kegan Paul.

Wittgenstein, L. 1953. *Philosophical Investigations.* Trans. G. E. M. Anscombe. Oxford: Basil Blackwell.

Index